David Nosworthy (Ed.)

# Seen, but not Heard: Placing Children and Youth on the Security Governance Agenda

Geneva Centre for the
Democratic Control of Armed Forces
(DCAF)

LIT

# Seen, but not Heard: Placing Children and Youth on the Security Governance Agenda

edited by

David Nosworthy

LIT

∞

Gedruckt auf alterungsbeständigem Werkdruckpapier entsprechend
ANSI Z3948 DIN ISO 9706

**Bibliographic information published by the Deutsche Nationalbibliothek**
The Deutsche Nationalbibliothek lists this publication in the Deutsche Nationalbibliografie; detailed bibliographic data are available in the Internet at http://dnb.d-nb.de.

ISBN 978-3-03735-252-6 (Switzerland)
ISBN 978-3-8258-1398-7 (Germany)

**A catalogue record for this book is available from the British Library**


Dufourstr. 31
CH-8008 Zürich
Tel. +41 (0) 44-251 75 05
Fax +41 (0) 44-251 75 06
e-Mail: zuerich@lit-verlag.ch
http://www.lit-verlag.ch

LIT VERLAG Dr. W. Hopf
Berlin 2009
Contact:
Fresnostr. 2
D-48159 Münster
Tel. +49 (0) 2 51-620 32 22
Fax +49 (0) 2 51-922 60 99
e-Mail: lit@lit-verlag.de
http://www.lit-verlag.de

**Distribution:**

In Germany and Switzerland: LIT Verlag Fresnostr. 2, D-48159 Münster
Tel. +49 (0) 2 51-620 32 22, Fax +49 (0) 2 51-922 60 99, e-Mail: vertrieb@lit-verlag.de

In Austria: Medienlogistik Pichler-ÖBZ GmbH & Co KG
IZ-NÖ, Süd, Straße 1, Objekt 34, A-2355 Wiener Neudorf
Tel. +43 (0) 22 36-63 53 52 90, Fax +43 (0) 22 36-63 53 52 43, e-Mail mlo@medien-logistik.at

Distributed in the UK by: Global Book Marketing, 99B Wallis Rd, London, E9 5LN
Phone: +44 (0) 20 8533 5800 – Fax: +44 (0) 1600 775 663
http://www.centralbooks.co.uk/html

Distributed in North America by:

Transaction Publishers
New Brunswick (U.S.A.) and London (U.K.)

Transaction Publishers
Rutgers University
35 Berrue Circle
Piscataway, NJ 08854

Phone: +1 (732) 445 - 2280
Fax: + 1 (732) 445 - 3138
for orders (U. S. only):
toll free (888) 999 - 6778
e-mail: orders@transactionpub.com

# Contents

# Foreword

*Graça Machel*

Children in every country, and in every culture, occupy a central place in society. They are a symbol of innocence, and they represent the continuity of life. However, the translation of this centrality into the building of a protective environment for them has failed almost universally.

The extent to which children's security, in its broader sense, has been compromised has only been acknowledged relatively recently with recognition that children have rights, globally institutionalised through the adoption of the Convention on the Rights of the Child. Continuing concerns that the provisions of the Convention were not sufficient in protecting children from additional threats, led to the introduction of two protocols. These instruments together provide a comprehensive framework of rights for increasing the protection of children and ensuring a climate that enhances their security and well-being.

However, I remain gravely concerned by the exploitation of children during wars and conflicts, and have participated in relentless efforts to bring these horrendous crimes to the attention of the wider public. I have urged condemnation and elimination of such practices – and while the plight of children affected by armed conflicts has been brought to the attention of the world, it is nevertheless far from being consigned to history – and continues to be a real and menacing issue today.

Neither poverty, nor trafficking, nor the health conditions of children have been adequately addressed, and these conditions individually and collectively continue to account for the precarious situation that children find themselves enduring.

The following figures speak for themselves! An estimated 20 million children have been forced to flee their homes and live as refugees or displaced persons. More than 2 million have died as a direct result of conflict in the last 10 years, and at least 6 million children have been permanently disabled or seriously injured. Behind each statistic is a child, a dramatic story that is unfolding in front of our eyes, and that we all should be doing something about.

It is in effect an admission of our collective inability to protect children today that we do not recognise sufficiently, or have the imagination and commitment to carve through, the obstacles that continue to threaten them. This is despite the advances that have been made in the effective and up-to-date machinery of politics and the media. However, progress has also meant that the same communication and information technologies that have taken us forward have also been turned upon children by those who would exploit them.

The role of society at large, including communities and families, cannot be underscored enough. But, above all is the challenge that the security sector, in particular parliament, faces in ensuring that children are an integral consideration within their responsibility for the protection of their peoples and their society, and to recognise themselves as prime duty-bearers in protecting children's rights.

For all those who read the pages of this important study, they will undoubtedly appreciate the important responsibility the security sector has towards children.

It will enable them to think through how child protection strategies can become an integral part of efforts to create a more secure and better world.

What is particularly impressive is that the reflection and arguments presented here bring together and combine a common vision of the priorities that influence the security sector and civil society, and this fact alone is full of promise for it envisages investments in children today that will benefit the young people who will become the leaders of tomorrow.

# Foreword

*Theodor H. Winkler*

Why should children's security matter? The reality is that children, their families, and their communities are first to be impacted by a lack of security. Children and youth may be seen everywhere, but they remain largely invisible on the security agenda. And although the children and youth of today are tomorrow's leaders, their voices are generally not heard.

What role model do we show them in not taking their concerns into account? How can children and youth be encouraged to play an active role in their societies to ensure their long-term positive contribution to social development? And how can we adapt security provision if we do not acknowledge children and youth as crucial stakeholders in security?

Developing a better understanding of how security impacts on children and youth means listening to their views and opinions, and considering them when defining security policy. This may be challenging in environments where security structures and institutions have been weakened or destroyed, but is particularly relevant to the establishment of reform processes that address the root causes of conflict and aim to break cycles of violence.

Graça Machel's groundbreaking report of 1996 highlighted the impact of armed conflict on children, and in her report a reoccurring theme at the centre of the protection of children was the peace and security agenda. However, there still appears to be a gap between the security sector and those working to promote the well-being of children. This publication aims to initiate a discussion that will lead to a closing of this divide.

The security sector is a key duty-bearer in relation to respect for human rights, and to ensuring freedom from fear. States are required to ensure that appropriate legal and political measures are taken in order to realise their obligations in this area. Security sector actors, including armed forces, peacekeepers, police, border guards, other law enforcement agencies and the judiciary, but also parliaments, all have a vital role to play.

Through this study a first step has been taken in a process that should bring a better understanding of the dynamic between children and security. In exploring the role and responsibilities of the security sector in guaranteeing children's rights, recommendations will be elaborated aimed at integrating child rights principles into the process of security sector reform.

It is hoped that this discussion will assist practitioners and policy-makers in exploring gaps in the implementation of national legislation and procedures, and the obstacles and barriers that exist to effective child protection. The primary target of the publication is a broad spectrum of security sector actors, including security providers, government agencies, democratic institutions and civil society organisations whether engaged in the protection of children or security issues. Governments and donors should benefit from the publication as a resource for guiding the development of policies and approaches towards security sector reform.

To inform and enrich the publication a series of 'expert papers' have been commissioned on selected topics with the aim of eliciting the experiences of practitioners working on specific child protection issues, and these form the basis of a number of the chapters.

Focussing on the governance agenda, the importance to democratic institutions and civil society in the protection of children is highlighted, as is the importance of developing strategies that enable the voices of children and youth to inform policy-makers on the security issues that affect them.

# About This Publication

The aim of this publication is to explore some of the linkages between children, youth and security, and to highlight that a security governance approach needs to be central to the reform of the security sector.

Part One introduces the notion of security as a public good, the provision of which should be guided by principles of good security governance, including accountability and civilian participation. This requires that all stakeholders, including young people, are engaged in assessing and defining priorities in a context of rule of law and respect for human rights. While illustrative examples are drawn throughout the publication from developing as well as industrialised countries, ultimately the largest window of opportunity for reform comes in those countries emerging from political transition or conflict. For this reason, Part Four will focus specifically on the impact of conflict on children and on the post-conflict peacebuilding activities aimed at creating lasting and sustainable peace. However, children's security affects all societies everywhere, whether experiencing conflict or not, and the security sector has a responsibility to continually evaluate its performance and to enact reforms where necessary to improve service delivery to children and youth.

Part Two develops the context of this discussion illustrating how security, or lack thereof, impacts on children's health and well-being, while also reminding the reader of the child's inherent resilience. Understanding the nature of children's development helps in better defining the approaches to assist them. Child resilience theory, in conjunction with the established international child rights standards, provides a valuable framework for informing policy-makers on security provision that reflects and responds to the security needs of children. The section concludes by looking at existing approaches and a range of international legal instruments that provide the basis for promoting children's security and healthy development.

Part Three develops the focus towards some of those institutions and actors that need to be engaged in ensuring children's security. A central argument of this publication is that an informed civil society is vital to representing and addressing the security concerns of children in security policy. An area where the link between children and security is most evident concerns children in conflict with the law. International norms and standards promote a restorative approach to juvenile justice that places emphasis on diverting children away from the formal justice system requiring that children be considered separately from adult offenders, with obvious policy implications. With the role that the security sector has as a key duty-bearer towards children, independent oversight mechanisms are vital to ensuring that security sector actors respect their responsibilities to promote and protect child rights, and that they are held accountable for violations.

Part Four focuses on children and youth affected by armed conflict from the perspective of security governance in post-conflict peacebuilding. Specific challenges are considered, such as the establishment of effective disarmament, demobilisation and reintegration (DDR) programmes for children. Good security governance requires multiple actors working together at multiple levels, and here specific reference is made to the role of regional actors and the importance of engaging non-state actors where appropriate. It concludes by affirming the positive role that children and youth are able to play in post-conflict peacebuilding initiatives and how participatory approaches with young people can assist them in assessing and expressing their views and perspectives on security.

The publication concludes by reflecting on some of the policy implications involved in improving the approach to addressing the security needs of children and youth, offering a series of recommendations for consideration by civil society, security providers, democratic institutions and the international community.

# Acknowledgments

Several people have been instrumental in helping to realise this project. Special thanks go to Anja Ebnöther, DCAF Assistant Director, and Head of Special Programmes, for her support, encouragement and patience throughout the process of developing this publication, as well as in reviewing all of the content. The vision of Ambassador Dr. Theodor H. Winkler, DCAF Director, is recognised in identifying the critical link between security and the protection of children, and establishing and supporting the children's programme in the first place.

I would like to warmly thank Eden Cole for voluntarily taking on the role of internal reviewer. His comments and feedback have been hugely important in shaping the discussion and argument for addressing the security needs of children as a governance issue.

Over the past 18 months various DCAF colleagues have willingly provided their time and encouragement for free and open discussion, and been valuable sounding boards for exploring what are in effect some unconventional ideas. In particular thanks go to: Hans Born, Alan Bryden, Alison Buchanan, Anne-Marie Buzatu, Marina Caparini, Adedeji Ebo, Teodora Fuior, Heiner Hänggi, Guy de Haynin, Arnold Luethold, Ivana Schellongova, Albrecht Schnabel and Anca Sterie.

And finally, very special thanks go to the external reviewers Rebecca Symington (UNICEF), Anne Grandjean (UNICEF) and Paul Jackson (GFN-SSR Network, University of Birmingham, UK) who subjected the text to their rigorous scrutiny and provided valuable feedback that has allowed us to tighten up the final text.

David Nosworthy

# Glossary

**Accession** is the act whereby a state that has not signed a treaty expresses its consent to become a party by depositing an instrument of accession. Accession has the same legal effect as ratification, acceptance or approval.

**Adolescence** is the period of life in which the biological and psychosocial transition from childhood to adulthood occurs. The World Health Organization defines adolescence as the period of life between 10 and 19 years of age.

**Child labour** refers to work that is mentally, physically, socially or morally dangerous and harmful to children, and interferes with their schooling by depriving them of the opportunity to attend school.

**Child protection** refers to prevention and response to violence, exploitation and abuse against children – including commercial sexual exploitation, trafficking, child labour and harmful traditional practices, such as female genital mutilation/cutting and child marriage.

**Child associated with armed forces or armed groups** (or the term child soldier) refers to any person below 18 years of age who is or who has been recruited or used by an armed force or armed group in any capacity, including but not limited to children (boys and girls) used as fighters, cooks, porters, messengers, spies or for sexual purposes. It does not only refer to a child who is taking or has taken a direct part in hostilities.[1]

**Children in conflict with the law** refers to anyone under 18 who comes into contact with the justice system as a result of being suspected or accused of committing an offence.

**Civil society** constitutes a third sector, existing alongside and interacting with the state and profit-seeking firms, of which non-governmental organisations (NGOs) are an important part.[2]

**Democratic institutions**, in the constitutional sense, comprise the executive, the legislature and the judiciary, but in broader terms also encompass the contributions of civil society organisations, political parties, independent oversight bodies and the independent media.

**Disarmament, demobilisation and reintegration** (DDR) is a process that contributes to security and stability in a post-conflict recovery context by removing weapons from the hands of combatants, taking the combatants out of military structures and helping them to integrate socially and economically into society by finding civilian livelihoods.[3]

**Duty-bearer** is any agency or individual with a role to play in promoting and protecting the rights of the child.

**Juvenile** is a child or young person who, under the respective legal systems, may be dealt with for an offence in a manner which is different from an adult.

**Offence** refers to any behaviour (act or omission) that is punishable by law under the respective legal systems.

**Ratification** is the act whereby a state establishes its consent to be bound by a treaty. If the treaty has entered into force, the treaty thereafter becomes legally binding to parties that have ratified the treaty.

**Security sector governance** (SSG) refers to a multilayered system of control that fully incorporates civil society, provides for the foundation of a transparent, accountable, responsive, efficient, participatory, and inclusive political system and which delivers security according to people's needs on the basis of a comprehensive legal framework.[4]

**Security sector reform** (SSR) is a term used to describe the transformation of the security system – which includes all the actors, their roles, responsibilities and actions – working together to manage and operate the system in a manner that is more consistent with democratic norms and sound principles of good governance and this contributes to a well-functioning security framework.[5]

**State Party** is a state or other entity with treaty-making capacity that has either ratified or acceded to a particular treaty, thereby becoming bound by its provisions under international law.

**Transitional justice** refers to the short-term and often temporary judicial and non-judicial mechanisms and processes that address the legacy of human rights abuses and violence during a society's transition away from conflict or authoritarian rule.[6]

**Treaty** is an agreement entered into by two or more states, which creates binding rights and obligations in international law. A treaty may go by many different names, such as convention, covenant or protocol.

**Youth gang** is any durable, street-oriented youth group whose own identity includes involvement in illegal activity.[7] Youth gangs typically engage in delinquent, criminal, and violent activities, often for financial gain.

## Endnotes

1 French Ministry of Foreign Affairs (MFA) and UNICEF, *The Paris Principles: Principles and Guidelines on Children Associated with Armed Forces or Armed Groups* (MFA, UNICEF, February 2007), http://www.diplomatie.gouv.fr/en/IMG/pdf/Paris_Conference_Principles_English_31_January.pdf (accessed October 2008).

2 United Nations Development Programme (UNDP), *UNDP and Civil Society Organisations: A Practice Note on Engagement* (UNDP, 2001).

3 United Nations Inter-agency Working Group on DDR, 'Integrated Disarmament, Demobilisation and Reintegration Standards (IDDRS), Module 1.20, Glossary: Terms and Definitions' (UN, 2006), http://www.unddr.org/iddrs/framework.php (accessed October 2008).

4 Hans Born and Vincenza Scherrer, *Democratic Oversight and Accountability of the Security System: Challenges and Lessons Learned* (Geneva: DCAF, forthcoming 2009).

5 Organisation for Economic Co-operation and Development - Development Assistance Committee (OECD DAC), *DAC Guidelines and Reference Series: Security System Reform and Governance* (OECD Publishing, 2005), http://www.oecd.org/dac/conflict/ssr (accessed October 2008).

6 Sanam Naraghi Anderlini, Camille Pampell Conaway and Lisa Kays, *Transitional Justice and Reconciliation, Inclusive Security, Sustainable Peace: A Toolkit for Advocacy and Action* (London, Washington: Hunt Alternatives Fund & International Alert, 2004).

7 Frank M. Weerman and Scott H. Decker, *European street gangs and troublesome youth groups: Findings from the Eurogang research program* (California: AltaMira Press, 2005).

# Acronyms

| | |
|---|---|
| CAAFG | Children Associated with Armed Forces and Groups |
| CPA | Child Protection Advisor |
| CPU | Child Protection Unit |
| CSOs | Civil Society Organisations |
| CZOP | Children as Zones of Peace |
| DCAF | Geneva Centre for the Democratic Control of Armed Forces |
| DDR | Disarmament, Demobilisation and Reintegration |
| ECOWAS | Economic Community of West African States |
| ELN | Ejército de Liberación Nacional/National Liberation Army |
| ICC | International Criminal Court |
| ICCPR | International Covenant on Civil and Political Rights |
| IDDRS | Integrated Disarmament, Demobilisation and Reintegration Standards |
| IDPs | Internally Displaced Persons |
| IHL | International Humanitarian Law |
| ILO | International Labour Organization |
| MBT | Mine Ban Treaty |
| MDGs | Millennium Development Goals |
| MILF | Moro Islamic Liberation Front |
| MINUSTAH | United Nations Stabilization Mission in Haiti |
| MONUC | United Nations Mission in the Democratic Republic of Congo |
| NGO | Non-governmental Organisation |
| NSA | Non-state Actor |
| OECD | Organisation for Economic Co-operation and Development (DAC - Development Assistance Committee) |
| ONUB | United Nations Operation in Burundi |
| ONUCI | United Nations Operation in Côte d'Ivoire |
| SRSG | United Nations Special Representative of the Secretary-General for Children and Armed Conflict |
| SSR | Security Sector Reform |
| UN | United Nations |
| UNAMSIL | United Nations Mission in Sierra Leone |
| UNMA | United Nations Mission in Angola |
| UNMIS | United Nations Mission In Sudan |

| | |
|---|---|
| UNMIL | United Nations Mission in Liberia |
| UNICEF | United Nations Children's Fund |
| UPDF | Uganda People's Defence Force |
| UXO | Unexploded Ordnance |
| WHO | World Health Organization |

# List of Tables, Diagrams and Boxes

# Part I

# Introduction

## Chapter 1

# Placing Children and Youth on the Security Governance Agenda

*David Nosworthy*

The provision of security as a public good should be considered achievable in much the same way as democratic institutions deliver other public services. However, tensions over issues such as secrecy have often inhibited – or deliberately been used to inhibit – such an approach, freezing out large elements of the population from security discussions – including many of those most in need. Recently though, inclusive approaches to security have increasingly been promoted based on principles of good security governance, including civilian participation and accountability. The appearance of the human security concept, highlighting the security of the individual from pervasive threats to their 'rights, safety or lives' and in particular from the threat of violence, has been reflective of this shift.[1] Security requires that all stakeholders are involved and engaged in assessing and defining priorities, as well as overseeing their implementation. Those with the ultimate stake in good security are the population at large and as such security provision should be defined based on ensuring that they participate and contribute to the process. All perspectives need to be heard, weighed and balanced, and without an adequate understanding of the needs, expectations and aspirations of young people it is unlikely that their security needs will be adequately catered for. Ultimately though, the insecurities that young people face today are likely to become the insecurities that societies experience tomorrow.

Recognising security beyond the traditional notion of state security requires policy approaches that respond to the security concerns of communities and individuals, and require governance mechanisms capable of managing very different, and at times conflicting, objectives. Delivering effective security to the population requires multiple actors working together at multiple levels. And while at state level this calls for a cross-government approach, it also requires acknowledgement that state as well as non-state actors will need to be engaged.

Realising such a vision of security will require respect for human rights and the rule of law, and an acknowledgement and strengthening of the role of civil society in governance and oversight. Building local capacity to achieve this aim is of primary importance in regard to the protection of children and youth as it is at the local level, within families and communities, that their security and safety are realised, or abused.

However, in seeking to shape the security sector agenda to be more inclusive of children it is important to avoid the risk of securitising young people in general. Equally, in recognising them as key stakeholders in security provision, it is important to acknowledge that they interact with the security sector in different ways, from being victims, to being offenders or perpetrators, and witnesses. In regard to their role as offenders a series of tensions are evident in the approach to be taken. An area where this is perhaps most pronounced is in relation to former child combatants in transitional justice processes in the context of post-conflict peacebuilding.

Security is something that each and everyone should be entitled to and, in much the same way as human rights, the enjoyment of this public good also infers obligations on the individual to respect the security of others. The imperative of dealing with children and youth who negatively impact on security raises questions that go to the core of the security governance agenda, questions that are often overlooked or subsumed by political debate. The approach promoted by a range of international legal instruments focuses on diverting those involved in criminal or violent activity to more constructive roles and a meaningful place in society. This also involves promoting preventive strategies that avoid individuals coming into conflict with the law in the first place. Translating such standards into practice is however not without its challenges.

Developing a better understanding of how security impacts on the lives of young people is essential in helping to better inform policy-makers. One particularly important consideration in this regard is recognition of children's evolving capacities. They are not part of an inert or static 'vulnerable group', but rather developing individuals with constructive and valuable contributions to make to society and, above all, they are tomorrow's decision-makers. Nowhere does the link between human rights, development and security come into clearer relief than in relation to the challenges that young people face in transiting from childhood to adulthood.

## Seen, but not Heard

In a world increasingly influenced by mass media, images of children have come to symbolise the suffering of armed conflict and natural disasters. Their faces are transmitted around the world in real time with the aim, on one level, of drawing public attention to the plight of others but, perhaps more cynically, of providing the 'shock' content that draws viewers, generates sales and as such attracts advertising revenue.

While their images may be seen everywhere, their voices are rarely heard. They appear on our televisions, in our newspapers and in the publicity material of humanitarian organisations. But in terms of defining the policies that govern the response to such emergencies, and in finding solutions that can address or alleviate the impact of these events, the perspectives of children and youth, their experiences, concerns, priorities and expectations, are seldom sought.

Children are not simply the passive, vulnerable victims often portrayed. From their very arrival in the world they interact with the people and events around them. They impact on their surroundings as individuals in their own right, and by the age of ten their cumulative experiences have largely forged their personality and defined their future direction.

While the vast majority of children are in need of the protection that the security sector ostensibly provides, as they begin the transition to adulthood they increasingly come into contact with different parts of the sector and, for some, find themselves in conflict with it. How children and youth experience these first contacts – good, bad or indifferent – will have an important effect on their future perceptions of security and as such carry significant policy implications. These implications stretch across all segments of the formal security apparatus including justice, law enforcement, intelligence, oversight, as well as military.

The security sector has obligations to protect children and youth as victims, but also has obligations to the children and youth that it encounters as offenders or perpetrators, whether involved in criminal activity, violence or radicalisation.

While youth may on the face of things have a more obvious impact on the security agenda, their life choices were generally mapped out for them as children. Negative circumstances or surroundings, whether associated with family, school or other experiences, are more likely to lead to negative outcomes. However, it is important to remember that not all children resort to crime or violent action, even in the face of the most extreme adversity, but a small number do – a minority who can have a devastatingly negative impact on the lives of other people around them.

Despite the developments in international norm setting in recent years, children remain largely invisible on the security agenda. The emergence of the human security concept does however provide a vehicle that enables a refocussing of the security debate that encompasses not only state security but also the obligation to provide for the security of each and every individual within a country. While there may be debate about the 'reach' of human security, what has been recognised is the link between security, development and human rights, which should logically include the protection of children's rights.

In conflict and post-conflict situations the need to recognise these links is perhaps at its most acute. Guaranteeing the security of the civilian population in these situations is paramount and, ensuring the durable and sustainable transition to peace, a complex and politically charged process. A key post-conflict peacebuilding activity that is receiving increased attention within the international community, particularly in relation to assisting fragile states achieve stability, is security sector reform. This publication examines the interaction between the security sector and children, and argues strongly for a broader rights-based approach to security governance that clearly responds to the security needs of children and youth in both policy and practice. It is suggested that such an approach provides for a win-win scenario in that respecting and responding to the views of young people in security discussion represents a preventive component of longer-term strategies to address security concerns.

As already mentioned, in trying to take forward discussion of children and youth in terms of the security agenda, it is important to avoid the risk of 'securitising' them as some sort of thematic group. Children and youth are not a security problem awaiting a security solution, but rather individual and active members of society who should be encouraged to engage in developing a secure environment. While they may be politically invisible, they still have the right to have their security needs addressed. It is argued here that better recognition and therefore increased focus on the specific security issues affecting children can best be achieved through strengthening, rather than altering, the existing security governance framework in particular through reinforcing the human rights perspective of security.

The crucial interface between families and communities is vital for ensuring the protection of children. One of the features, indeed guiding principles, of security sector reform is the emphasis that is placed on local ownership in order to achieve effective and sustainable implementation. In relation to children, this means going beyond the reform of national institutions to focus on the community level dynamics of security provision. This will require processes that are driven by an informed parliamentary system that engages with all levels of government including local authorities in establishing and overseeing family and child-friendly policies. Consideration for children's security needs to be a key component of this collaboration, and addressing children's security from this perspective ultimately contributes to the wider community's longer-term security.

In the media, children tend to be characterised as either vulnerable, helpless victims of circumstance, or delinquent troublemakers who pose a threat to security. Neither perspective is representative of the vast majority of children, or helpful for a better understanding of children's own security needs and concerns. Restricting one's perspective on children risks undermining their own ability to contribute to their healthy development, and ignores the fact that they share a set of universal human rights with all other persons as well as certain additional rights that recognise their particular dependence, development and protection needs.

What is certain is that considering them as victims undervalues their potential to be active agents with a contribution to make to society, and casting them as offenders or perpetrators misses the point that many of these children and young people are themselves coming from backgrounds associated with abuse and neglect, making them vulnerable to selecting negative coping strategies (such as drugs, violence or crime) that result in negative security outcomes.

## Moving Forward

In order to respond to the protection needs of children it is clear that a range of actors and agencies need to be engaged. This has significant policy implications, in particular in ensuring effective communication between all of those involved. It is suggested here that by using a human rights framework to define and analyse the roles and responsibilities of relevant actors, it is possible to inform the process of security sector reform in such a way as to develop and strengthen child protection systems.

Responsibility for ensuring children's survival and well-being lies in the first instance with parents, family and community, while national and local authorities are the primary duty-bearers for ensuring that children's rights are respected. A key relationship will be the one between local authorities and the local community. From a security perspective this directly implicates the police and, more broadly in protection terms, this will require the involvement of a range of civil society groupings working in tandem with local authority agencies such as social and welfare services, education, health and local development authorities.

A key premise of this publication is that security governance considerations provide the necessary framework to assist the security sector in developing a better understanding of the nature of the insecurities experienced by children and youth, and the ways in which to respond to these insecurities. Within this analysis is the acknowledgement that children and youth, their families, and their communities are all security providers in their own right and that the importance of their engagement needs to be at the heart of security policy development. Children and youth represent an enormous resource for communities and, as such, it is communities that have the greatest vested interest in promoting and ensuring the security and protection of children. In particular, children and youth can be, and indeed are, active agents in their own security and there is therefore a need for them to be recognised as partners, and efforts made to ensure and promote their active participation in security matters.

Communities are the first to experience the effects of security or insecurity and the ones who live with the day to day consequences, and as such it is they who are best placed to describe their security realities and define their most pressing issues and concerns. In addition, it is communities who, according to social dynamics such as cohesion and inclusion, will determine the security environment, and be best placed to provide appropriate front-line service delivery. By working through civil society bodies the security sector has the potential to identify and develop creative and sustainable approaches to 'preventive security'.

The family is particularly important as it provides the primary source of care and protection for children, and the best environment for the child to develop to her/his full potential. Adolescence is a key stage at which a supportive family has a major role to play in guiding and assisting the young individual in making appropriate life choices. The United Nations Convention on the Rights of the Children (the 'Convention') acknowledges the primacy of this relationship, and calls on states to give assistance to parents and guardians to support their child-rearing. The Doha Declaration of 2004 reaffirmed that the family is the natural and fundamental unit of society and is 'entitled to the widest possible protection and assistance by society and the State'.[2]

Supporting families relies heavily on the partnership between local authorities and civil society organisations in order to ensure that not only are quality services available to those who require them, but that those in need are adequately informed of how to access these services. The capacity of local authorities and communities to monitor the progress of children is vital to effective preventive strategies and interventions to help families in need of special assistance.

This publication looks at the child's protective environment and security concerns in day to day life, drawing on principles relevant to understanding the effects of the deprivation brought on by armed conflict. It uses this analysis to reflect on the implications for security sector reform. The post-conflict peacebuilding context provides one of the most important theatres for reform not only because of the urgent need to put in place new structures but also the imperative of avoiding a slide back towards conflict. The centrality of security sector reform to the post-conflict peacebuilding process is now widely recognised and acknowledged, but what is less well understood is the importance of getting it right for children and youth, and the potentially negative ramifications of not doing so.

The relationship between children and youth and security needs to be considered from two different and contrasting perspectives. Not only do children need to be considered as victims or survivors of insecurity and provided with a secure environment as part of an overall protection regime, but it must also be acknowledged that children and youth have the potential to be perpetrators of crime and violence and that this can pose a considerable challenge to security institutions used to dealing with adult offenders.

There is a growing realisation that special consideration needs to be given to dealing with children who come into contact with the law. The effectiveness and efficiency of traditional draconian measures are increasingly being called into question as an appropriate way to deal with young offenders. Diverting children from the legal system avoids embroiling them in institutions populated by criminals, and provides the space to promote their rehabilitation by reinforcing social values and responsibilities, or even re-socialising them.

Such approaches are already established within international human rights and humanitarian law. Whether talking of security or protection, the performance standards represented by international law provide a framework of accountability to guide actions in the area of security provision. In ratifying an international treaty, states have assumed an obligation to promote and protect human rights, which directly implicates the statutory organs of security provision, making them key duty-bearers.

This publication aims to encourage reflection on the part of the security sector to develop context-specific approaches to reform, which are appropriate to the specific circumstances. Each context has its own realities, and responses need to be tailored as such. Examples will be drawn throughout the book from experiences in both industrialised as well as developing countries. What is most important is the acknowledgement and recognition that each setting has its own peculiarities in terms of issues, dynamics and actors, be that at national, provincial, local or community level, and as such will require robust assessment of priorities and flexible solutions appropriate to the situation and challenges to be addressed.

## Children, or Youth in Waiting

Throughout this publication reference is made to both 'children' and 'youth'. Although the two terms actually overlap in regard to the age categories that they define, and while some of the issues dealt with here are age specific, the terms are used together at times to stress that child rights and children's security do not relate simply to dependent, defenceless and vulnerable individuals, but that they also refer to, for example, 15-, 16- or 17-year-olds who are active participants in society, many of whom are already working and have families of their own. Indeed, from a strictly security perspective children will begin to appear on crime statistics even from under the age of 10 years. In conflict situations, children will likely be associated or even actively involved with fighting forces.

Using the two terms also aims to convey the message that policy and decision-making processes for these two groups have to be dynamic and flexible to reflect the very different realities of the individuals concerned. The transition between these two life stages marks an important change that takes place in everyone's lives, and ensuring that this experience is as positive as possible is key to shaping the type of citizen that individuals become, and as such to their interaction with their surroundings.

This has implications for defining and developing policies that not only fulfil the legal obligations to protect victims, but also to prevent future delinquency and recidivism. As a key duty-bearer, the security sector has a clear obligation to protect and promote the rights of children, and not abuse them. Both of these aspects require consideration in relation to children and youth not just as victims but also as offenders, and imply a need for developing and promoting educational, preventive approaches.

## *Defining the Child*

The reference point for the term 'child' is straightforward. The Convention defines the child as a holder of rights, specifying that for the purposes of the Convention this means 'every human being below the age of 18 years unless under the law applicable to the child, majority is attained earlier'. It is legally binding on every government which is a party to it and applies to all children within the jurisdiction of each state, not only to those who are nationals of that state.

The reference to 'law applicable' is a recognition that majority may actually be obtained at an earlier age in certain jurisdictions (although in some American states majority is not attained until 21 years). However, the scheme of the Convention means that this exception should be interpreted as an empowering one – in other words, someone attaining majority before 18 years can claim the benefits of adulthood as granted by national law, while still being able to claim the protection of the Convention.

However, use of the term 'childhood' may be interpreted differently to the strict definition of child used for the Convention. It is important to separate our understanding of childhood from the legal definition of child. A challenge often raised in discussion of legal responsibility and security is that different cultures perceive childhood differently and as such the interpretation of when and how a child becomes an adult varies significantly. But, as mentioned above, this does not change the entitlement of the individual concerned to claim the benefits of the Convention.

A legal term that is also used to define young people is minor. 'Minor' quite simply refers to someone who has not attained the age of majority – the age specified in law at which an individual assumes full responsibility for their own decisions and actions (up to that point parents will have also exercised control in decisions affecting the individual). Another term used in relation to the justice system is juvenile justice, a 'juvenile' being someone at or below the age of juvenile court jurisdiction, which generally, but not necessarily, refers to anyone under the age of majority.

From approximately the age of ten years children begin to enter into adolescence.[3] During this period they begin to establish their own identities and establish their independence. They mature sexually, and develop the capacity to reason in more abstract ways, to explore the concepts of right and wrong, and to think about the future. However, this group is consistently overlooked by decision-makers, perhaps because they do not quite conform to the behaviour that is expected of children and do not exhibit the maturity expected of adults. Especially in insecure environments where they lack safety and structure, adolescents may be left to make difficult choices for themselves. While most will find positive channels to express themselves and contribute positively to society, some will make choices that will lead them towards lives of crime and violence.

In health terms, as many as 70 percent of all preventable deaths among adults, such as coronary heart disease, lung cancer and AIDS, result from health-related patterns and behaviours that began during adolescence. Adolescents are making decisions that have lifelong consequences, often without adult guidance and support, and without the knowledge and skills to protect themselves.[4]

> My dear young people, I see the light in your eyes, the energy of your bodies and the hope that is in your spirit. I know that it is you, not I, who will make the future. It is you, not I, who will fix our wrongs and carry forward all that is right in the world.
> (Nelson Mandela).[5]

*Girls and Boys*

Both girls and boys are vulnerable to violence and abuse not only from adults but also from their peers. Much of this violence and abuse is gendered, with implications both for the type of response and support required by the children affected, and for the implementation of longer-term solutions to address the root causes of such violence.

Gender plays a significant role in defining the insecurities that girls and boys experience. Girls are likely to be disproportionately affected by physical and sexual abuse, while boys are more likely to be at risk through involvement in crime, violence and substance abuse.[6] The World Health Organization (WHO) estimates that 150 million girls and 73 million boys under the age of 18 experienced forced sexual intercourse or other forms of sexual violence during 2002, and between 100 and 140 million girls and women in the world have undergone some form of female genital mutilation/cutting.[7]

In some cultures gender-based discrimination appears in a preference for sons over daughters, even resulting in foeticide and infanticide. In India, for example, there are 933 Indian women for every 1,000 men, resulting in 40 million ‘missing’ women.[8] Research recently conducted by Action Aid and the International Development Research Centre in northern India found that at three of five sites surveyed this ratio was below 800, representing even a decline from 2001 figures.[9]

Violence by young people is one of the most visible forms of violence in society. Again, there is a distinct gender component that defines male adolescents and young adults as both the main victims and the main perpetrators. Most of the countries with youth homicide rates above 10.0 per 100,000 are either developing countries or those experiencing rapid social and economic changes.[10] Among the countries for which WHO data are available, the rates are highest in Latin America (for example, 84.4 per 100,000 in Colombia and 50.2 per 100,000 in El Salvador). Almost everywhere, youth homicide rates are substantially lower among females than among males, suggesting that being a male is a strong demographic risk factor. The ratio of the male youth homicide rate to the female rate tends to be higher in those countries with high male rates. For example, the ratio is 13.1 to 1 in Colombia and 14.6 to 1 in El Salvador. Where male rates are lower, the ratio also tends to be lower.[11]

Gender-based violence needs to be assessed and understood within the wider context of the causes of violence, including individual risk factors and the influence of family and peers, as well as political, institutional, economic and cultural factors. Involvement with drugs and petty crime, access to small arms as well as poverty are important risk factors contributing to violence, while protective factors include positive relationships at school, access to livelihoods, and close connections to family and/or community organisations.[12]

Gender is a social construct that, while varying across cultural groups, too often thwarts the potential of girls. Discrimination robs girls of the power to make decisions, leaves them with limited opportunities in education and work, and even deprives them of legal protection. Gender equality means girls and boys having equal opportunities to access resources such as education and health, but in cultures where girls are deprived of information this can have devastating consequences on their ability to protect themselves. For instance, surveys indicate that compared to women who have some post-primary schooling, women with no education are five times more likely to lack basic information about HIV/AIDS.[13]

Eliminating gender disparity in primary and secondary education is a key target of the Millennium Development Goals (MDGs) and essential to ensuring that girls and boys are able to realise their full potential. And while it is important that girls can access schooling, attention also needs to be paid to the learning needs of both girls and boys – boys, for example, finding it harder to learn to read – and to preventing 'drop-out'. Girls, boys and women are generally less often heard and as such their needs and aspirations are not addressed in policy and decision-making. A gender analysis helps to provide a level playing field by considering that girls and boys have differential access to resources and that they have different needs and interests that need to be addressed within what may be unequal power relations.[14]

### *Defining Youth*

Broadly speaking the term 'youth' refers to a young person (especially a young man or boy) and to a time of life between childhood and adulthood. However, the use of the term 'youth' is far from precise, both in terms of the age ranges that it is used to portray, and the very different connotations that the term conjures up when used in different settings and locations. This interpretation of what youth means can vary from the negative portrayal of street violence and crime, through to the positive sense of freshness, resourcefulness and vitality characteristic of a young person.

In terms of age setting, since the International Year of Youth in 1995 the United Nations has defined a youth as being anyone from the age of 15 to 24 years. However, many other interpretations of this age range can be found. For the purposes of the World report on violence and health, WHO defined youth as persons between the ages of 10 and 29 years. When the Sierra Leone government referred to youth in the co-operation framework adopted with the UN Peacebuilding Commission, the government was defining youth as persons between the ages of 15 and 35.[15] In its crime definitions the Bureau of Statistics for the Northwest Territories in Canada refer to youth as individuals aged 12 to 17 years of age.[16] The US Department of Transportation, National Highway Traffic Safety Administration define a youth (or young driver) as a person (or driver) under 21 years of age.[17]

One thing for sure is that youth impact directly on opportunities for social development, and their influence can be for the positive or negative, which will have direct implications for security policy. Acknowledging and understanding the dynamics of youth is required to guide effective policy-making, not only in terms of social policy but also security policy. This recognition also has implications in relation to children, as it will be their experiences during their formative years that will guide how they assume the responsibilities associated with making that transition to adulthood. Informed efforts to support this important transitional stage, which each and every individual has to go through after all, should be aimed at harnessing the positive energy of growth for the development and the good of society.

> Each nation has different obstacles and different goals, shaped by the vagaries of history and of experience. Yet as I talk to young people around the world I am impressed not by the diversity but by the closeness of their goals, their desires, and their concerns and their hope for the future. (Robert F. Kennedy, 1966).[18]

Approximately one person in five worldwide is between the age of 15 and 24 years, but although their numbers are increasing in absolute terms, the proportion of the population between these ages has in fact been falling for some time and is expected to continue to fall.

**Table 1.1 How Many Youth Are There in the World?**

| Year | Youth Population | Percentage of Total Global Population |
|---|---|---|
| **1985** | 941 million | 19.4% |
| **1995** | 1.019 billion | 18.0% |
| **2025** | 1.222 billion | 15.4% |

Source: Youth at the United Nations – Frequently Asked Questions.[19]

The co-operation framework adopted between the government of Sierra Leone and the UN Peacebuilding Commission is worthy of special note as, in outlining some of the key challenges and threats facing Sierra Leone following its brutal civil war, tackling massive youth unemployment was identified as a priority area along with good governance, security and justice sector reform, energy sector development and capacity-building.[20]

> Youth unemployment was identified by the Truth and Reconciliation Commission as one of the root causes of the civil war and is widely considered to be a threat to Sierra Leone's continued stability. (UN Peacebuilding Commission).[21]

## Security Obligations and Imperatives

There are both obligations and imperatives that make children and youth of special importance to the security sector and deserving of increased attention. And, while a more effective and functional security sector provides direct benefits to the population as a whole, there are specific and special protection issues associated with children that need to be recognised and integrated into reform processes and policy development. A number of these imperatives are addressed in the state's obligations under international human rights law, which establish children as a group of particular importance to the security sector.

*Child Rights and Preventing Wrongs*

International human rights law addresses the protection of individuals from violations by governments of their fundamental rights and freedoms. The state is responsible for guaranteeing these human rights for each and every person, and is required to make provision for their realisation, in particular in relation to:

- Respecting the rights of individuals, i.e. ensuring that 'wrongs' are not committed against them
- Protecting individuals from violations of their rights by others

All state institutions share responsibility for implementing these obligations, with the state's formal security apparatus being a key duty-bearer. Effective application of human rights principles requires awareness and understanding on the part of government institutions and related bodies at all levels.

While parents, families and communities are responsible for ensuring the immediate well-being of children, the state in the form of its national and local authorities is responsible for ensuring that children's rights are respected. Ensuring a co-ordinated response at these different levels requires that the security perspectives of children and youth are integrated into security policy and decision-making. In practical terms, where this process is most crucial is at the level of local authorities and communities, but long-term success will be dependent on the commitment and support of central government.

Of the eight international human rights treaties the most widely ratified is the Convention, giving it almost universal application (only Somalia and the United States of America have not ratified). The Convention is a comprehensive code of rights for children, offering the highest standards of protection and assistance for children under any international instrument. The protection standards go beyond the usual guarantees of health, education and welfare, and include guarantees relating to civil and political rights including freedom of expression, religion, association, assembly and privacy.

In addition to listening to children's broader opinions and concerns regarding security, the right to 'be heard in any judicial and administrative proceedings affecting the child' is specifically referenced in the Convention.[22] It should also be noted that in the exercise of their rights, children have the same obligations as adults do to obey the law, to respect the rights and reputations of others, and not to jeopardise national security, public order, public health and morals.

However, it must also be remembered that the supposed defenders of human rights and child rights are at times the abusers. The security forces themselves are too often responsible for committing violations of international human rights law, often acting with impunity and beyond the reach of any control or oversight. Such violations have been well documented across the world and, to name just a few, include extra-judicial killings, enforced disappearances, unlawful and secret detentions, torture, rape, theft and extortion. The use of excessive force by officers of the law leading to unlawful killing is the subject of UN Principles on the Use of Force and Firearms by Law Enforcement Officials. In addition, the use of force, along with other responsibilities, is referred to in the UN Code of Conduct for Law Enforcement Officials and states that they 'shall respect and protect human dignity and maintain and uphold the human rights of all persons'.

### *Protecting Social Capital*

The wide-spread adoption of notions of societal security and human security mean communities and individuals respectively are entitled to be the focus of security provision, in contrast to the traditional state-centred perspective. 'Human security' is concerned with a wide range of threats to individuals from anti-personnel landmines, small arms and light weapons, to violations of human rights and international humanitarian law, recruitment of children and their use in armed conflict, and in its broader sense to promoting human development including economic, food, health and environmental security.[23]

Increasing attention has been paid to the threat that fragile states pose to security and in particular into trying to identify the characteristics that make them fragile. Not only do they present a risk to their own citizens, but they represent a potential threat to their neighbours and even to regional stability. One of their defining features is that they tend to be performing least well in achieving the objectives of the MDGs.

In their report, *Why We Need To Work More Effectively In Fragile States*, the United Kingdom Department for International Development links human development and security, highlighting that 'the most important function of the state for poverty reduction are territorial control, safety and security, capacity to manage public resources, delivery of basic services, and the ability to protect and support the ways in which the poorest people sustain themselves'.[24]

Fragile states tend to be failing on a range of human development indicators that impact heavily on children. The poor performance of fragile states towards achieving the MDGs, a number of which relate directly to children, becomes another indicator of the inability or unwillingness of the state and/or its institutions to provide basic protection to its citizens.

### *Demographics*

A high proportion of young people in the population is a typical characteristic of developing countries. However, data shows that development brings a reduction in fertility rates, improved health resulting in reduced mortality rates, and longer life expectancy. The combined effect is to reduce the proportion that children and youth constitute of the overall population.

This results in significant variations between industrialised countries where the percentage of children in the population is as low as 25 percent, to developing countries where as much as 50 percent of the population are under the age of 18 years. In a number of refugee and internally displaced populations, particularly in sub-Saharan Africa, the proportion of the population under the age of 18 can increase to over 60 percent.

An often cited reason for instability and conflict is the so-called youth bulge theory (see Box 1.2). However, it should also be remembered that not all developing countries, even with the same demographic profiles, descend into conflict, indicating that violence and conflict scenarios require a far more complex set of social and political conditions to come together before they can be played out. Development appears to support, even encourage, positive decision-making options and in the process reduces the opportunities for peace-spoilers to profit.

Encouraging policy-makers to recognise this dynamic is vital to understanding and engaging the positive energies that young people have to offer. Along with this recognition is the need to acknowledge the potential that an active and engaged youth have for contributing to development and economic growth – a notion often referred to as the demographic dividend.[25]

**Box 1.2 Youth Bulge Theory in Perspective**

Mirroring the language that casts children and young people as 'the problem', there has been an increasing amount of discussion around the so-called Youth Bulge Theory. In a box entitled 'Do large youth cohorts cause violence? Maybe if economic growth rates are low', the World Bank's World Development Report (2007) considers the risk that youth pose, the discussion tempered only by a reference to Urdal's (2004) observation that, 'It seems that a large youth cohort can aggravate tensions caused by growth but does not by itself lead to conflict'.

In launching the report in September 2006, François Bourguignon, the World Bank's Chief Economist and Senior Vice President for Development Economics, focussed on stressing the positive contribution that youth can make, adding 'But, these young people must be well-prepared in order to create and find good jobs'. The conclusion drawn from the report is that developing countries that invest in better education, healthcare, and job training could produce surging economic growth and sharply reduced poverty.

### *Crime and Violence*

As already mentioned, the transition from childhood to adulthood is full of challenges for the evolving individual, this period of adolescence being one of change often associated with personal turmoil. It also tends to be characterised by risk taking and actions often aimed at testing the limits of acceptable social behaviour. While some young people will transgress the law as they go through this transition, the offences they commit tend to be low-level criminal or petty offences. The propensity to offend within this age group is graphically illustrated by crime statistics for England and Wales that show the prime age for offending as 18 years for males and 15 years for females, although the latter with substantially lower offending rates.

As young people begin to establish their own identity, their role models change and they become increasingly reliant on and influenced by peer relations (sibling relations in particular have been identified as having a significant effect).[26] One of the quite normal manifestations of this, particularly in urban settings, is that young people form into groups. However, at times these groups can become associated with delinquency – the behaviour of the individual in the group often being very different to the behaviour the same individual would exhibit when alone.[27]

This dynamic can become further charged where disaffected youth are exposed to destabilising factors such as social exclusion, restricted access to education, long-term unemployment, poverty or political strife.

**Graph 1.3 Offenders Found Guilty or Cautioned for Indictable Offences, 2002, England & Wales**[28]

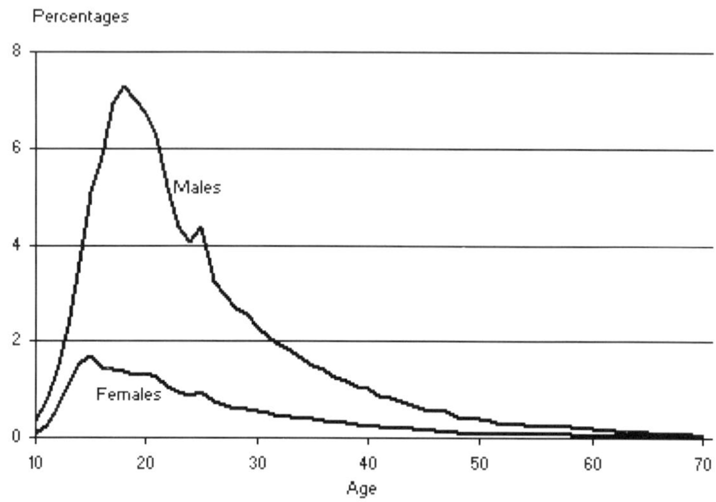


In addition, urbanisation is consistently linked to delinquency, with urban populations tending to have higher registered crime rates than rural areas. It is not simple coincidence that urbanisation is also associated with growing numbers of people living in slums – current figures indicating roughly one billion people, or one in six of the global population.[29] Target 11 of MDG 7, to ensure environmental sustainability, aims to achieve a 'significant improvement' in the lives of at least 100 million slum dwellers by 2020, or 10 percent of the world's slum population.

The extreme of delinquent behaviour is perhaps most clearly evidenced in the gang culture associated with inner-cities across the world. At this point however, it is important to draw a distinction between the petty crimes associated with group offending and the serious offences perpetrated by gangs. A recent study in the UK called for the development of strategies that aim to break the cycle that can lead from group offending in adolescence to involvement in gangs.[30]

One of the consistently quoted reasons for why young people join gangs is protection, indicating a failure of security services to provide a basic level of protection to this segment of the population. Equally, violence tends to be a defining characteristic of these gangs' social interaction. Left unchecked this dynamic often forms into an escalating rivalry between gangs fighting over territory or trade. A reoccurring theme is the close link between gangs, armed violence and the drug trade. Gang violence threatens the daily security of communities, but is a global phenomenon whose violence permeates rich and poor countries alike. One of the most notorious gangs in the United States of America, the Crips, was founded by a teenager.

> Stanley Tookie Williams was co-founder of the Crips when he was only 17 years old, and given the death penalty in San Quentin State Prison (USA) on December 13, 2005.
> (Insideprison.com).[31]

The scale of the problem should not be under-estimated. A comparison of firearm-related mortalities in Rio de Janeiro city between 1978 and 2000 showed approximately 40,000 deaths, compared with 50,000 battle-related fatalities in Colombia for the same period, while that country was experiencing civil conflict.[32] As witnessed across Central America, another concerning development has been the growing transnational nature of some of the criminal gangs, including links to organised criminal elements in North America (for example, Mara Salvatrucha, or MS-13). Equally worrying is the widespread commentary reporting the increasingly young age at which children are targeted for recruitment into gangs.

Armed conflict, though, does provide a cocktail of factors that impact directly on children and youth. Instability, uncertainty over the future, limited or no access to services, availability of small arms and breakdown in rule of law could all be factors that push young people towards negative choices such as violence, crime, joining armed groups or extremism.

Cité-Soleil in Haiti has proven to be quite a particular case. While not defined as a conflict situation, UN Peacekeepers have been deployed in Haiti since 2004 and have been repeatedly involved in launching operations in Cité-Soleil targeting gang activity. This point is noteworthy in that many of the factors driving children and youth to gangs are similar to those that result in their enrolment in armed political groups, or involvement in radicalisation.

## Security and Human Rights

Human security is often considered in terms of 'freedom from want' and 'freedom from fear'. This notion was elaborated in the 2005 report of the UN Secretary-General, *In Larger Freedom*, where the clear links between human security, human rights and human development are also established.[33]

Within such a framework the primary role of the security sector can be seen as providing for freedom from fear – the platform from which human development should bring freedom from want. Analysis of the security sector, and in particular freedom from fear, should be informed by human rights.

Human rights constitute the framework for guiding the actions of the security sector, as well as the bar against which to judge their successes and failures. When it comes to security provision, statutory security bodies have primary responsibility for implementing the state's obligations under international law. As a set of performance standards, human rights provide goals and targets by which to plan and evaluate actions.[34]

However, this apparently obvious linkage is not without its tensions, even to the extent of security sector actors at times portraying human rights as a potential obstacle to security. Such sentiments have perhaps been most evident around the debate associated with the 'war on terror', where the security sector has at times presented human rights as playing a subordinate role to its own duties, actions and jurisdiction. However, just as the actions of terrorists are aimed at undermining the human rights and fundamental freedoms associated with democratic governance, it is imperative that states do not themselves infringe upon these very same rights in the pursuit of their counter-terrorist policies. Policy cannot be seen to be above the law without immediately conceding moral ground and legitimacy. Children have not been exempt from these discussions, with perhaps one of the most high profile examples being the detentions at Guantanamo Bay. More than 60 of the detainees of the US camp were under 18 at the time of their capture, some as young as 14, with some continuing to be held despite international pressure for their release.[35]

Human rights are at times presented almost as an obstacle to security, rather than a basic component in its realisation. Instead of reinforcing collaborative efforts to promote rule of law and democracy, such language drives a wedge between what should be mutually coherent and supportive agendas. The very fact that a debate exists around a supposed tension or compromise between security and human rights demonstrates the deep complexities that many of these issues raise. That human rights could be viewed as subordinate to security does however underline the importance of robust civilian oversight and accountability mechanisms.

By presenting the relationship between human rights and security as a kind of balancing act, the two constructs somehow appear separate, with the implication that realising one would require a trade-off against the other. Such an approach rather misses the point and comes at the issue from the wrong angle. Fundamentally, human rights provide the very framework that is needed to effectively guide the actions of a credible, transparent and democratically controlled security sector.

It is for the purpose of guaranteeing the rights of all individuals to live in dignity, security and freedom that the international community has invested so heavily in establishing a legal framework and common code of rights. It could be argued that it is the combined contribution of these advances in developing common standards, along with efforts towards increased dialogue around the issue of peace and security on the part of the international community, that account for the improvements in global security that have been witnessed since the end of the Cold War.

Human rights and security are interdependent. Where this synergy is perhaps most evident is when considering the notion of 'rule of law'. Rule of law is by definition guided by human rights but, equally, security and respect for rule of law reinforce belief and trust in human rights. In other words there should be no question of compromise between the two. Quite clearly without rule of law democratic institutions cannot function.

To deal with security spoilers, security efforts must be firmly rooted in the reinforcement of democratic institutions and values, including pluralism, dialogue and respect for civil, political, economic, social and cultural rights. This involves an obligation to ensure that today's children and youth are informed, educated and given every opportunity to engage and participate in civic life.

Acknowledging that the promotion and protection of human rights are the basis of establishing security, governments need to establish a framework of democratic accountability in order to enhance the credibility and effectiveness of security policies and practice. Ensuring that the opinions and voices of children and youth are accounted for in these measures will require special consideration. In particular, an empowered and informed civil society will be central to an oversight strategy that acknowledges the importance of protecting children's rights.

### *The Convention on the Rights of the Child*

Built on varied legal systems and cultural traditions, the Convention is a universally agreed set of non-negotiable standards and obligations. These standards represent minimum entitlements for children that should be respected by governments. They are based on respect for the dignity and worth of each and every individual, regardless of race, colour, gender, age, religion, political or other opinion, origin, disability, birth or other status.

But equally, with these rights comes an obligation not to infringe upon the rights of others.

The Convention, along with its two Optional Protocols, sets out the basic human rights of children everywhere: the right to survival; to develop to the fullest; to protection from harmful influences, abuse and exploitation; and to participate fully in family, cultural and social life. It offers a vision of the child as an individual and as a member of a family and the community, with rights and responsibilities appropriate to his or her age and stage of development. Underlining children's status as individuals with fundamental human rights, and with views and opinions of their own, it affirms their right to participation, freedom of expression, freedom of thought, conscience and religion, freedom of association, protection of privacy and access to appropriate information.

**Box 1.4 Guiding Principles of the Convention**

**1. Non-discrimination, Article 2.1**

States Parties shall respect and ensure the rights set forth in the present Convention to each child within their jurisdiction without discrimination of any kind, irrespective of the child's or his or her parent's or legal guardian's race, colour, sex, language, religion, political or other opinion, national, ethnic or social origin, property, disability, birth or other status.

**2. Best interests of the child, Article 3.1**

In all actions concerning children, whether undertaken by public or private social welfare institutions, courts of law, administrative authorities or legislative bodies, the best interests of the child shall be a primary consideration.

**3. Right to life, survival and development, Article 6**

States Parties recognise that every child has the inherent right to life, and, shall ensure to the maximum extent possible the survival and development of the child.

**4. Participation, Article 12.1**

States Parties shall assure to the child who is capable of forming his or her own views the right to express those views freely in all matters affecting the child, the views of the child being given due weight in accordance with the age and maturity of the child.

By adopting the Convention (through ratification or accession), national governments have committed themselves to protecting and ensuring children's rights, and they have agreed to hold themselves accountable to this commitment before the international community.

All levels of government need to be involved in ensuring that legislation is fully compatible with the Convention. Awareness raising, to disseminate information and understanding of the rights and responsibilities contained in the Convention, also needs to be pro-actively pursued, targeting civil society in particular, and including training for personnel involved in government policy-making. An imperative for decision-makers is to ensure that adequate disaggregated data on children and their protection concerns is collected and applied to improving the situation of all children within their jurisdiction.

Local authorities have a pivotal role to play in providing and supporting service delivery to children, including regulation, enforcement and monitoring. However, decentralisation can create vacuums in social provision, and in many cases municipal authorities and local branches of national agencies become the primary actors in providing basic services for children. Whether receiving assistance from higher levels of government or not, they remain legally responsible for protecting and realising the rights contained in the Convention.

An overall protection framework must guide all actions on behalf of children. The concept of 'protection' refers to all activities aimed at ensuring full respect for the rights of the individual – in this case a child – as set out in the relevant human rights instruments and international humanitarian law. There are essentially three complementary types of action that will define a comprehensive approach:[36]

- Responsive action aimed at preventing, stopping, and/or alleviating the immediate effects of a specific pattern of abuse
- Remedial action aimed at restoring dignified living conditions through rehabilitation, restitution and reparation
- Environment-building aimed at creating and/or consolidating an environment (political, institutional, legal, social, cultural and economic) conducive to full respect for the rights of the individual

## The Security Sector Actors as Duty-bearers

A key feature of the comprehensive approach is the notion of the 'duty-bearer' – the person or persons identified as being responsible for ensuring that a given right is not violated. If children and young people are the holders of rights and have a legal entitlement to their rights being secured, then it is essential that those responsible for delivering on these rights are identified and made accountable and responsive to any failings.

This directly implicates a whole range of institutions and structures, including in particular the state's formal security apparatus, and extends far beyond to include the judiciary, law enforcement agencies, oversight bodies, non-statutory security forces and civil society groups.

Identifying those with a duty to prevent violations is often complex for a number of reasons.[37]

- A hierarchy of duty-bearers will exist that needs to be understood in order to distinguish these most important actors at various levels.
- The tasks and obligations of security sector actors need to be clearly defined and institutional checks and balances established.
- Duties are often shared among different agencies and departments, often with grey areas where responsibilities are not clearly designated.
- The notion of duty-bearer is closely bound up with the notion of public accountability – this is not always part of public sector culture in many countries.
- In some countries the government's capacity to actually put policy into practice is extremely limited and it may simply not be able to secure the basic rights of children.

## Defining the Security Sector

A broad definition of a country's security community goes beyond the traditional concept of considering only armed forces and their oversight bodies to include a much more diverse range of actors:

- *Bodies authorised to use force:* armed forces; police; paramilitary forces; gendarmeries; intelligence services (including both military and civilian agencies); secret services; coast guards; border guards; customs authorities; reserve or local security units (national guards, presidential guards, militias, etc.).
- *Civil management and oversight bodies:* the president/prime minister; national security advisory bodies; legislature and legislative select committees; ministries of defence, internal affairs, foreign affairs; customary and traditional authorities; financial management bodies (finance ministries, budget offices, financial audit and planning units);

and statutory civil society organisations (civilian review boards and public complaints commissions).

- *Judicial and public security bodies:* judiciary; justice ministries; defence attorneys; prisons; criminal investigation and prosecution services; human rights commissions and ombudsmen; correctional services; customary and traditional justice systems.
- *Non-state security force institutions:* liberation armies; guerrilla armies; traditional militias; political party militias; private security companies; civil defence forces.
- *Non-statutory civil society bodies:* professional organisations, including trade unions; research/policy analysis organisations; advocacy organisations; the media; religious organisations; non-governmental organisations; concerned public.

The above categorisation includes 'non-statutory civil society groups', who have a key role to play in safe-guarding children's security and safety.[38] Not only are they closest to the issues of concern affecting the community, in particular children, they are often themselves service providers within the community, and have a vital role to play in monitoring and reporting abuses affecting children. The Organisation for Economic Co-operation and Development – Development Assistance Committee (OECD DAC) Guidelines and Reference Series: Security System Reform and Governance (2005)[39] and, more recently, the OECD DAC Handbook on Security System Reform (2007),[40] which probably represent the state-of-the-art thinking in terms of the security reform process, focus on the more formal security agencies or providers and as such propose a security sector covering the first four categories. In policy terms there may be an argument that this will focus analysis of respective roles and responsibilities, but the omission of the eventual beneficiaries and their role in the process should be viewed as restrictive.

Both the guidelines and the handbook stress the important role that civil society has to play in establishing local ownership of any reform process, not only in designing and implementing reform, but in its oversight as well. As the handbook observes in relation to police reform, 'It is important to engage civil society organisations, women's organisations, youth groups and the media from the start as partners in change' and, in lessons learned, 'By making the community the entry point, beneficiary and driver of the project, genuine ownership and commitment to agreed 'community safety plans' were ensured from the beginning'.

Quite clearly civil society is a major stakeholder in the provision of effective security services. Not only is it interested in terms of being a recipient of security, it has a vital role to play in terms of intelligence and oversight, as well as at times being the ultimate service provider, particularly in relation to local preventive actions.

Open discussion on child rights and children's security should involve a range of actors with key roles to play as interlocutors with security providers including local authorities, state agencies, professional associations, children's rights groups and other relevant civil society bodies including children's forums.[41]

## Conclusion

While the term Security Sector Reform may be relatively new compared to the freedom from fear concept, it provides a vehicle by which change can be brought to systems and procedures that will directly influence the protection of children. For a clearer appreciation of the significance of security sector reform and how its approach can enable a protective environment for children, it is interesting to consider the working principles that the Organisation for Economic Co-operation and Development (OECD) governments have defined as central to security sector reform:[42]

- People-centred, locally-owned and based on democratic norms and human rights principles and the rule of law, seeking to provide freedom from fear and measurable reductions in armed violence and crime.
- Seen as a framework to structure thinking about how to address diverse security challenges facing states and their populations through more integrated development and security policies and through greater civilian involvement and oversight.
- Founded on activities with multi-sectoral strategies, based on a broad assessment of the range of security needs of the people and the state.
- Developed adhering to basic principles underlying public sector reform such as transparency and accountability.
- Implemented through clear processes and policies that aim to enhance the institutional and human capacity needed for security policy to function effectively and for justice to be delivered equitably.

Quite clearly the goals of security sector reform are in themselves focussed on creating an environment conducive to human security. They therefore provide an entry point for discussion with security sector actors of the specific opportunities and constraints associated with building a protective environment for children.

The security of children and youth cannot be overlooked, and engaging them in identifying, prioritising and addressing their security concerns and expectations is a vital contribution to development and longer-term stability.

## Endnotes

1 Canadian Department of Foreign Affairs and International Trade, 'Freedom from Fear: Canada's foreign policy for human security' (Ottawa: DFAIT, 2000).

2 United Nations General Assembly, The Doha Declaration (from the Doha International Conference for the Family), UN Doc. A/59/592 (New York: November 2004).

3 The World Health Organisation (WHO) defines adolescence as the period of life between 10 and 19 years of age.

4 UNICEF, Adolescence, *A Time that Matters* (New York: UNICEF, 2002).

5 Nelson Mandela quoted on the 'The President's Award for Youth Empowerment' website, http://www.presidentsaward.co.za/new/index.php?p=70 (accessed October 2008).

6 UNICEF, *Literature Review of the Situation of Adolescents in Eight Countries in Latin America and the Caribbean: Trends and Recommendations* (Balboa: UNICEF, 2005).

7 UN General Assembly, *Report of the independent expert for the United Nations Study on Violence Against Children*, UN Doc. A/61/299 (New York: October 2006).

8 UNICEF, 'The situation of women and girls: facts and figures', http://www.unicef.org/gender/ index_ factsandfigures.html (accessed July 2008).

9 ActionAid and International Development Research Centre, *Disappearing Daughters* (London: Action Aid, 2008).

10 Etienne G. Krug et al., *World report on violence and health* (Geneva: WHO, 2002).

11 Ibid.

12 *Report of the independent expert for the United Nations Study on Violence Against Children*, 'Fact Sheet on Violence Against Children in the Caribbean'.

13 UNICEF, 'The situation of women and girls: facts and figures'.

14 Save the Children Sweden, *Children and Gender-based Violence: An overview of existing conceptual frameworks* (Kathmandu: Format Printing Press, 2003).

15 UN Peacebuilding Commission, Sierra Leone Peacebuilding Cooperation Framework, UN doc. PBC/2/SLE/1 (New York: December 2007).

16 Canada Northwest Territories, Bureau of Statistics, 'Notes, Definitions and Symbols', http://www.stats.gov.nt.ca/Statinfo/Justice/Police_Reported_Crime/Crime_Definitions.html (accessed October 2008).

17 US Department of Transportation National Highway Traffic Safety Administration, 'Technical Summary', http://www.nhtsa.dot.gov/people/injury/research/FewerYoungDrivers/tech_summary.htm (accessed October 2008).

18 'Robert F. Kennedy Memorial - Day of Affirmation' (University of Cape town: June 6, 1966), http://www.rfkmemorial.org/lifevision/dayofaffirmation (accessed October 2008).
19 UN, 'Youth and the United Nations', http://www.un.org/esa/socdev/unyin (accessed October 2008).
20 UN News Centre, 'Sierra Leone, UN Peacebuilding Commission agree on Co-operation framework' (New York: December 2007).
21 UN Peacebuilding Commission, Conference Room Paper for the Country Specific Meeting on Sierra Leone, UN doc. PBC/2/SIL/CRP.1 (New York: 10 October 2006).
22 UN Convention on the Rights of the Child, Article 12.2 (November 1989).
23 Heiner Hänggi, 'Conceptualising Security Sector Reform and Reconstruction' in *Reform and Reconstruction of the Security Sector*, eds. Alan Bryden and Heiner Hänggi (Berlin: LIT, 2004).
24 UK Department for International Development (DFID), *Why we need to work more effectively in fragile states* (London: DFID, January 2005).
25 Ronald Lee and Andrew Mason, 'What is the Demographic Dividend? International Monetary Fund' *Finance and Development* 43, No. 3 (September 2006).
26 Sir Ian Blair in an article in the *Guardian* newspaper suggested that the children of gang member families should be placed on the child protection register for children of violent or abusive parents (May 2007), http://www.guardian.co.uk/uk/2007/may/03/ukcrime.ukguns (accessed October 2008).
27 UN Department of Economic and Social Affairs, *World Youth Report 2005. Young people today, and in 2015* (New York: 2005), http://www.un.org/esa/socdev/unyin/wyr05.htm (accessed October 2008).
28 UK National Statistics Online, 'Crime. 4 in 5 offenders are male', http://www.statistics.gov.uk/cci/nugget.asp?id=1661 (accessed October 2008).
29 Canadian Department of Foreign Affairs, 'Freedom from Fear in Urban Spaces', Human Security Research and Outreach Program, Discussion Paper (2006), http://www.humansecurity-cities.org (accessed October 2008).
30 Youth Justice Board, 'Groups, Gangs and Weapons' (2007), http://www.yjb.gov.uk (accessed October 2008).
31 InsidePrison.com is an independent research site on criminal justice issues. As of 2005, 30,000 Crips street members were operating in 221 cities, some as young as 9 years old, http://www.insideprison.com/prison_gang_profile_CR.asp (accessed October 2008).
32 Luke Dowdney, *Children of the Drug Trade: A Case Study of Children in Organised Armed Violence in Rio de Janeiro* (Rio de Janeiro: Viveiros de Castro Editora Ltda, 2003).
33 UN General Assembly, *In larger freedom: towards development, security and human rights for all*, Report of the UN Secretary-General, UN Doc. A/59/2005 (New York: 2005).
34 Office of the High Commissioner for Human Rights, *Frequently Asked Questions on a Human Rights-Based Approach to Development Co-operation* (Geneva: UN, 2006), http://www.hurilink.org/tools/FAQon_HRBA_to_Development--OHCHR.pdf (accessed October 2008).
35 Severin Carrell, 'The children of Guantanamo Bay', *The Independent*, 28 May 2006, http://www.independent.co.uk/news/world/americas/the-children-of-guantanamo-bay-480059. html (accessed October 2008).

36 International Committee of the Red Cross, *Inter-Agency Guiding Principles on Unaccompanied and Separated Children* (Geneva: ICRC, 2004), http://www.icrc.org/Web/ Eng/siteeng0.nsf/html/p1101 (accessed October 2008).

37 International Save the Children Alliance, 'Child Rights Programming - How to Apply Rights-Based Approaches' in *Programming, A Handbook for International Save the Children Alliance Members* (Sweden: Tryckoffse, First Edition, 2002).

38 Nicole Ball, 'Reforming Security Sector Governance' in *Security and Development. Investing in Peace and Prosperity*, eds. Robert Picciotto and Rachel Weaving (New York: Routledge, 2006).

39 Organisation for Economic Co-operation and Development-Development Assistance Committee (OECD DAC), *DAC Guidelines and Reference Series: Security System Reform and Governance* (OECD Publishing, 2005), http://www.oecd.org/dac/conflict/ssr (accessed October 2008).

40 OECD DAC, *Handbook on Security System Reform. Supporting Security and Justice* (Paris: OECD, 2007), http://www.oecd.org/dac/conflict/if-ssr (accessed October 2008).

41 Adapted from Save the Children Sweden and UNICEF, *Children's Rights: Turning Principles into Practice* (Stockholm: UNICEF, 2001).

42 OECD DAC, *Handbook.*

# Part II

# Children, Youth and Security

Chapter 2

# Health Indicators and the Impact of Insecurities on Children

*Aleya El Bindari Hammad*

> ... if children live with tolerance, they learn to be patient; if children live with encouragement they learn to have confidence ... if children live with fairness they learn justice; if children live with security they learn to have faith ... if children live with acceptance and friendship, they learn to find love in the world. (Author unknown).

## Introduction[1]

In recent years, security and protection systems have gained in importance as the need to guard people against a broad range of hazards – crime, accidents, disasters, sabotage, subversion, civil disturbances, bombings (actual and threats), hijackings and criminal networks engaged in trafficking of arms, people and drugs – has become the hideous truth of our present landscape. Most of the time, the security sector has focussed its efforts on national security issues such as conflict and post-conflict areas and the threat of terrorism, sometimes at the expense of ensuring security in the lives of people as they go about their daily activities.

Of particular concern has been the protection of children, which has been seriously compromised and inadequate. Children are victims of unbelievably horrific atrocities and injustices. While the consequences of insecurity affect people of all ages, they have dramatic impact on children. Every 20 minutes a child under five years old dies, leading to over a million deaths a year. This is not to mention the many more who suffer the consequences of injury and trauma throughout their lives. The majority of these deaths and the suffering are preventable.[2]

The succeeding paragraphs will illustrate the impact of insecurity on children and their healthy development. As early as 1986, The World Health

Organization (WHO) in its General Assembly adopted Resolution WHA 39.22 calling on member states to use health status indicators within the population and in particular their changes over time among disadvantaged groups as an indicator for assessing the quality of development and its impact on the environment.[3]

## Health – an Indicator of Insecurity

Children's vulnerability stems from the fact that they must rely on others for meeting their physical needs for survival, including their daily requirements for food, water, personal hygiene and shelter. In this sense a child or an infant cannot survive and develop on its own – somebody needs to take care of them. Regardless of where children live, or cultural differences in care practices, all infants require warm, responsive, linguistically rich and protective relationships in which they can grow. The quality of the relationship between the caregivers and small children no doubt affects the development of the child's brain, the psychological capabilities and social adjustments.[4] The literature contains ample information and data on the basic requirement for children's normal growth during the various phases of their development, starting from *in utero* to infancy childhood to adulthood. Whereas there are many factors affecting the normal growth and development of children that do not fall within the scope of this chapter, it should be mentioned that insecure environments tend to accentuate and aggravate an already precarious environment affecting disadvantaged population groups, especially women and children. It is these women and children who are disconnected from mainstream development, facing the brutal realities of their daily lives that are further affected by divisive forces, social exclusion and insecurity enlarging the hard core of vulnerability.[5]

The WHO taskforce on health and development recognised the need to give the right to health more substance and operational content by introducing the concept of health security that 'is needed throughout the entire life span of human beings and encompasses all aspects of the right of every individual to the highest attainable standard of physical and mental health, including the right to food in sufficient quantity and of good quality, the right to decent housing, the right to live and work in an environment where known risks are minimised, and the right of access to education and information on health'.[6]

In many parts of the world, living conditions are deteriorating due to the persistence of chronic and worsening situations of abject poverty as well as communities fraught with violence, instability and insecurity. This state of affairs compels thousands of people to flee their homes each year in search for food, water, safety and a better life. The image of countless women collecting their few belongings in a bundle and, carrying their children on their backs, fleeing hostile environments is an all too familiar one.

The impact of these conditions affecting homeless children and those exposed to violent conditions such as wars and conflicts can be seen in different ways and at different levels of severity, namely morbidity and mortality rates. While no indicator can tell us all we need to know about children's health, nor can we develop indicators for everything, global estimates of the burden of disease that are derived from national statistics can be monitored for trends. These provide us with the major causes of death and illness.

One of the defining features of fragile states is that they are performing least well in achieving the objectives of the Millennium Development Goals (MDGs).[7] MDG 4 aims to reduce the global under-five mortality rate by two thirds by 2015. In 2006, the most recent year for which firm estimates are available, close to 9.7 million children died before their fifth birthday. Meeting MDG 4 implies that during the next seven years the number of child deaths must be cut in half – to fewer than 5 million per year. The number of deaths per 1,000 live births in 2006 was six in industrialised countries compared to 79 in developing countries.[8]

Child survival and primary health care for mothers, newborns and children lie at the heart of human progress, serving as sensitive barometers of a country's development and well-being, and providing telling evidence of its priorities and values.[9] Investing in the health of children is not only a human rights imperative, it is also a sound economic decision and one of the surest ways for a country to set its course towards a better future.

Some of the main categories of disease are: *perinatal illnesses,* including low birth weight and congenital malformations and birth defects[10]; *respiratory diseases,* such as pneumonia, tuberculosis and asthma; *diarrhea diseases,* including E-coli infections and cholera; *insect-borne diseases,* especially malaria; *physical injuries,* including impairments due to cluster munitions and landmines[11], burns etc.; *mental/emotional trauma,* such as post-traumatic stress disorders; and *sexually transmitted diseases,* such as HIV/AIDS. Together, these kill some 8.5 million children below the age of 15 every year, of which about 90 percent are under the age of five and account for the major causes of morbidity in children.

## Table 2.1 Health and the MDGs

| Goal | Health Targets | Health Indicators |
|---|---|---|
| **Goal 1**<br>**Eradicate extreme poverty and hunger** | **Target 2**<br>Halve, between 1990 and 2015, the proportion of people who suffer from hunger | Prevalence of underweight children under five |
| **Goal 4**<br>**Reduce child mortality** | **Target 5**<br>Reduce by two thirds, between 1990 and 2015, the under-five mortality rate | Under-five mortality rate<br>Infant mortality rate<br>Proportion of one-year-olds immunised against measles |
| **Goal 5**<br>**Improve maternal health** | **Target 6**<br>Reduce by three quarters, between 1990 and 2015, the maternal mortality ratio | Maternal mortality ratio<br>Proportions of births attended by skilled health personnel |
| **Goal 6**<br>**Combat HIV and AIDS, malaria and other diseases** | **Target 7**<br>Halt and begin to reverse, by 2015, the spread of HIV and AIDS<br>**Target 8**<br>Halt and begin to reverse, by 2015, the incidence of malaria and other major diseases | HIV prevalence among pregnant women 15-24<br>Ratio of school attendance of orphans to school attendance of non-orphans aged 10-14<br>Prevalence and death rates associated with malaria<br>Prevalence and death rates associated with tuberculosis |
| **Goal 7**<br>**Ensure environmental sustainability** | **Target 10**<br>Halve, by 2015, the proportion of people without sustainable access to safe drinking water and basic sanitation<br>**Target 10**<br>By 2020, achieve a significant improvement in the lives of at least 100 million slum dwellers | Proportion of population using an improved water source, urban and rural<br>Proportion of population using improved sanitation, urban and rural |
| **Goal 8**<br>**Develop a global partnership for development** | **Target 17**<br>In co-operation with pharmaceutical companies, provide access to affordable essential drugs in developing countries | Proportion of population with access to affordable essential drugs on a sustainable basis |

Source: Adapted from WHO, Health and the Millennium Developmental Goals, Geneva, 2005.

Evidence now shows that the seeds of ill health in adulthood and old age are sewn during infancy, childhood and adolescence.[12] This constitutes a human tragedy whose effects can endure for generations.

The proceeding paragraphs will focus on events that lead to large scale death or lessening of life chances undermining international security. Among these are economic and social threats, including poverty, that compel people to migrate, legally or illegally, and enable transnational organised crime to thrive. As stated by Kofi Annan, 'Development and security are inextricably linked … extreme poverty and disease provide a fertile breeding ground for other threats including civil conflict'.[13]

## Populations on the Move

Land and poverty pressures, political instability and natural disasters are combining to displace millions of people every year. In both developed and developing countries, internal and cross-border movement has become a key factor in changing the demographic and socio-cultural profile of countries and regions.

There are more than ten million refugees in the world today, up from 8.4 million in 2006. For example, Chad, Sudan and the Central African Republic have been plagued by decades of political instability and armed conflict. Today, a transnational exodus of civilians and combatants in all directions is destabilising the region, leaving vulnerable populations without the most basic resources. Collectively, Chad, Sudan and the Central African Republic are bound together in an interlocking calamity that constitutes one of the world's single largest concentrations of displaced people.[14]

In all three states combined, more than 2 million people are now displaced – more than 200,000 Sudanese have fled into neighbouring Chad, escaping the ongoing violence in Darfur. In Chad, over 50,000 routinely flee increasing attacks in the east, some crossing back and forth into the Central African Republic. From there tens of thousands have escaped into Sudan and Chad amidst growing insecurity and chronic poverty. Many end up in crowded camps, living in tents with little food, water, health care and often lacking protection.

It is not uncommon to find that those entrusted with their security are often the first to aggress especially women and children. Children have witnessed their mothers being repeatedly raped; others have themselves become victims of sexual or physical abuse. Some may have experienced the loss of a mother, which has dramatic consequences on a child. It has been shown that when a mother dies it doubles the death rate of her surviving sons and quadruples that of her daughters. In high-mortality settings such as in refugee camps and conflict zones there may be thousands of motherless children.[15] What is disturbing is the failure to provide them with their basic needs for food, water and health care, and the inability to protect them against violence that threaten them even in exile.

Similar to refugees, internally displaced persons (IDPs) are forced to leave their homes because of persecution, seeking sanctuary in more secure parts of their own countries. Many of the IDPs suffer from extreme poverty, brutal suppression and growing insecurity. Because they have not crossed international frontiers, they are not considered refugees protected by international refugee law and often cannot access international humanitarian assistance.

Refugees and IDPs are not only perceived as an economic burden, competing for scarce resources and services with the local population, they are even at times treated as a security threat.[16]

*Migrant Children: Targets of Violence*

Child migration has a long and chequered history surrounded by controversy and scandal. This remains true today, and although many children may seemingly be travelling as dependents with their family, along legal and secure routes, the reality behind may be less clear. Many children are victims of migration for reasons of trafficking through criminal networks, or as pawns used by their families to gain leverage and asylum, the so-called ‘Anchor Children’, voluntarily abandoned in airports or international transit zones for their parents to have a link with developed countries.

More recently, due to an increase in South-North migration and the growing trend of women migrating as household providers, an increasing number of children are being left behind, some for years before they get the chance to reunite with their parents. The social impact of this phenomenon is still under survey but there are links to school drop-out and increases in child and teenage delinquency, drug abuse and general vulnerability linked to the absence of traditional role models.

Just recently an article highlighted the violence perpetrated against young children trafficked within and outside of their continent. In Mali a house was discovered with a number of young Ivorian boys, held there until they could be sold in Europe, lured by promises of high-paying contracts in athletics.[17] More common are cases of internal trafficking for labour purposes; Ghana comes to mind immediately with the traffic in the fishing ‘industry’ around Lake Volta.[18] Young girls are often sold as household slaves or for child prostitution and thus at high risk of physical and psychological abuse.[19]

The numbers of cases are difficult to assess, but they are consequential. Particularly in the case of labour-induced trafficking, the criminal networks rely on local traditions to encourage the parents into giving their children into 'foster' care as they would traditionally with their family members.

For all three of the aforementioned cases there are bodies of international law that prohibit such abuses or abandonment, but not all have been ratified, and fewer still integrated into national legislation.[20] There is an urgent need for action (judicial, educative/preventative, curative) at the local level to raise awareness among the people and communities involved who, for reasons of either poverty or lack of education, do not understand the implications of their actions.

## Turning a Blind Eye to Forced Labour

A recent report by the International Labour Organization has shown that the normal dependence of young children on adults is dramatically increased when they move away from their home environment, across a social or national frontier, making them even more susceptible to coercion at work. In many parts of Africa, there is a strong tradition of children moving away from home. Current evidence suggests that children may represent a higher proportion of forced labourers in Africa than in other regions of the world.[21]

International law strictly prohibits forced and exploitative labour of children.[22] Moreover, in most countries laws have been enacted that specify the specific minimum age at which children can start work, the appropriate hours that they can work, and their rights to rest and medical examinations. Some countries have gone a step further by specifying the industries that are considered hazardous and in which children are strictly prohibited to work. However, there is a big gap between these policies and their translation into action and the enforcement of child labour laws that protect children and their total needs. In some cases children are preferred to adult workers because they are more docile, do not grumble and revolt, are agile, and can be paid less than adults (and at times are not paid at all on the pretext of training). For families, income from child labour can play an important role in augmenting the overall family income, and some children may have been forced to join the labour force at the insistence of their parents. In addition, it is sometimes difficult to penetrate home industries that escape formal supervision. At the same time, the law enforcement sector turns a blind eye to home-based industries that are encouraged to flourish as an important means of generating income and reducing poverty.

Children are usually employed in industries such as match-making, diamond polishing, fish scaling, glass works, plantations, brick works and handloom textiles. Common characteristics of their working conditions include exposure to toxic powders, metal dust, paint or paint thinner, noxious fumes which burn the eyes, late-night work, exposure to high temperatures and deafening noise and industrial accidents. While hard data is scarce, nevertheless there are known potential effects on children. For example, accidents in the lock industry with bodily injury, such as loss of fingertips, occur as a result of exhaustion and carelessness when carrying out the tasks of polishing, electroplating, spray painting and working on hard presses.

Due to exposure to toxic chemicals, children suffer from asthma and other chest diseases, accidental poisoning and mental disorders. In pencil factories, the incidence of silicosis in children has been reported, and in the agate industry, pneumoconiosis has been recognised as prevalent, and directly related to the duration of exposure. Children handling microscopically fine wire develop marked visual impairments within five to eight years. Children using hand tools designed for adults face higher risk of fatigue and injury, while children using seats and workbenches designed for adults have more problems in the musculoskeletal systems.[23]

The purpose of citing these health consequences is not to consider the technical responses required, but rather to provide powerful pointers as to where development has or is going wrong.

### *Child Labour to Order*

Failure of macro-economic policy and the free market system to ensure equitable distribution of wealth has led to a process of poverty 'creation' that has swelled in urban areas. Rapid urban growth has produced pockets of deprivation and subhuman living conditions that are at times more severe than in rural areas. And at the same time, the poor have been portrayed as a net burden on the process of growth. Not only have poor people remained poor but so have large numbers of poor nations.

In addition, the measurement of success in materialistic terms and lack of human solidarity are often seen as prevailing characteristics in many regions of the world. The pursuit of materialism at the cost of more traditional values of caring and sharing is having a marked impact on human behaviour. The institution of the family is undergoing unprecedented change.

The multigenerational family of traditional societies is giving way to the nuclear family which in turn is increasingly giving way to the single-parent family and to the no-parent families of street children. Armed conflict and natural disasters result in tens of thousands of unaccompanied refugee children who are often permanently separated from their families.

In this climate the pursuit of high levels of profit is permeating nearly all institutions of society. The need to ensure, for instance, essential foreign currency has led some governments to turn a blind eye to illegal business activities and the risk and harmful effects they may have on the lives of people such as young girls and children. Trafficking in human beings, especially women and children, has led to the amassing of quick fortunes and in some cases to the corruption of social institutions such as the judiciary and security sector.[24]

Illicit trade permeates all societies and has evolved into a new form of commerce that is sprouting everywhere. Modern forms of slavery are thriving in the context of coerced sex, domestic work, farm labour and construction work, often performed by illegal migrants forced to work off never-ending debts levied by their traffickers. Many of the victims will have been chosen from among the poor and the destitute who cannot fend for themselves – street children, orphans, homeless children and young girls. Some are coerced and others are just abducted to be shipped across borders.

This billion dollar illicit industry has opened up new trade routes, with a chain of suppliers that includes recruiters, extortionists, hired muscle, transporters, safe 'houses' and online dispatchers that can procure a child, girl or boy, responding to any specification desired – colour, age, nationality, physical characteristics. These are 'delivered' just as you would a parcel across continents in as little as 48 hours![25] Once delivered these victims are subjected to merciless violence, beatings, rape, sadistic treatment, working long hours deprived of seeing the light of day. Some succeed in escaping, others prefer to end their lives, and still others, who end up by contracting sexually transmitted diseases such as HIV/AIDS, are sometimes put back onto the market and resold at a cheaper cost. The health consequences are horrendous, and many can never recover from the trauma endured. Their lives are shattered and their dreams blown away.

This illicit trade is profit driven and could not thrive without the involvement of corrupt officials and the growing demand of a market to draw from. Like drugs and arms dealers, these networks make full use of the most up-to-date technologies, and features of globalisation such as porous borders. As with those who smuggle illegal migrants in response to demands for cheap labour, the traffickers of women and children cannot be tackled by simply taking the moral high ground. And although there is no doubt that those involved are criminals, what drives them to engage in this despicable business is purely the profits that they will derive.[26] The strategy to be adopted must be one that reduces their incentives, such as diminished demand, lower margins of profit, much higher stakes and risks, and laws that regard this trade as a grave criminal activity that carries with it the harshest and most severe penalties for the suppliers, but also some form of punishment for the consumers.

## Implications for the Security Sector

Child victims of abuse are not new. What is new however is that today we are learning more about the magnitude of child abuse. Our access to new information technologies has led to more transparency with, day by day, new facts and figures emerging. Child abuse can take place in the home just as it does outside it. When it does happen in the home, it usually is at the hands of parents or caregivers or relatives. Information is still difficult to obtain because of many societies' view on the sanctity of the family and the reluctance to intrude into this private domain.

However, both in traditional and non-traditional societies, child abuse and sexual exploitation are a common occurrence, just as physical assault and violence on women by their partners continue to take the heaviest of tolls. Today, somehow, the facts available constitute the tip of the iceberg – much more needs to be uncovered. This will shed light on the magnitude and depth of the scars marking children who may themselves become abusers later in life and exhibit violent behaviour towards others as adults.[27] Unfortunately, as facts are uncovered, we realise that it is society that will have to pay the ultimate price and bear the eventual burden!

### *Where Have We Gone Wrong?*

Child abuse follows closely that of women. Even in the light of heightened awareness of gender issues it is a disturbing reality that the gender gap has not been eliminated, primarily because it is a grinding process that challenges one of the most entrenched of all human attitudes, namely changing people's mindsets. It requires far more effort than just changes in law or stated policy. Succeeding will entail changing practices in the home, community and in the decision-making environment. At present, just as rape and sexual assault on women have gone unpunished in many parts of the world, so too has sexual slavery gone unpunished for very young girls. Women's particular vulnerability to violence is perhaps the most obvious aspect of reduced physical security and integrity of the person and is carried on to the offspring – *in utero* and when the child is born. In many countries, even those where there has been marked progress in the enactment of violence-related laws that protect women and children, there have been reports of spotty persecutions, vague statistics, old-fashioned judges and unresponsive governments.

The complexity of the social and cultural issues, combined with the stigma and fear of disclosure, lead to a situation where only a small proportion of crimes of sexual assault and other forms of child abuse get reported. It is not uncommon for women and girls to be blamed for provoking the violence perpetuated against them by men, with tacit approval of the judiciary and of the police. These victims become stigmatised and isolated from their own societies, and in some countries are sent into 'camp' so as not to contaminate innocent children. Still others, especially in the Middle East, are forced into marriage with their violators, with little or no control over their person. Cases have been reported of rapes committed by elderly guards of orphanages (as old as 70 years), where the guard ends up by marrying their 15-year-old victim! Each year, young girls who have no control over their bodies are subjected to female genital mutilation in spite of it being regarded as a criminal offence!

Recently, facts are emerging that have brought to light the extent to which social and cultural settings are conducive to the perpetuation of what others would consider as abusive behaviour. In some regions, such as West and Central Africa, it has been reported that poor parents may sell their children for money having been assured that they will be treated well. Others have accepted to give up their children for a specified period of time in return for a token sum or gifts. So-called bonded placement of children is the reimbursement for debts the parents have accrued.[28] In the minds of many parents, placing children does not constitute an act of selling.

The purpose of bringing up the above examples is to underscore the importance of understanding the contexts, patterns and backgrounds of families and communities that have, so to speak, facilitated migration and trafficking (both of which intersect at a given point). These fall into the following categories:

- Social cultural factors, such as the social acceptability of putting children to work, traditions of migration, educational levels and preparation for marriage.

- Economic factors, such as inequities between population groups and desire to escape poverty.
- Juridical and political factors, such as absence of legislation, mistrust of the laws, ignorance of parents as to their rights under the law, corrupt officials and porous borders.

In response to the above, it is important to raise awareness among families (with full appreciation of intra-household decision-making processes), communities, chief religious leaders, ministers and law enforcement officials.

## What Can Be Done?

Throughout this chapter it has been argued that the process of globalisation, which has brought about liberalisation of economies, facilitating the mobility of capital, goods and services, has not been matched by social protection measures, particularly for disadvantaged segments of society, especially women and children. Globalisation has given rise to conflicting rules covering the legal migration of individuals, many composed of highly skilled professionals. Those denied freedom of movement include the masses of unskilled or semi-skilled persons who are trapped in poverty, but this can also impact on those fleeing political persecution or conflict zones. This situation has contributed to the creation of networks facilitating clandestine movements by opening corridors for the illegal transport of people as one of the most lucrative ways of acquiring huge profits made from human helplessness. It has also been argued that health indicators are the most powerful indicators for illustrating the price these people pay, by analysing mortality and morbidity rates. For while health is not everything, without it there is little left!

There are specific actions that can be done by institutions entrusted with security and intelligence services and ensuring democratic accountability. Ideally they should be protected from political abuse, but at the same time should not be separated from executive governance.[29] It is important to stress that the effectiveness of all relevant institutions involved (the executive, the legislature, civil society groups, parliament, etc.) will be influenced to a great extent by a political culture that ensures transparency, responsibility, accountability, participation and responsiveness to the people. This presupposes that there exists a code of behaviour that goes beyond that of laws and regulations. Unfortunately, in many countries, democratic regimes are still in their infancy. They have a long way to go in ensuring a culture of openness, respect for human rights and the dignity of their people.

Due to the complexity of the problems facing children exposed to insecurities, three regulatory regimes need to be ensured as a whole, namely human rights protection, crime control and economic efficiency. This will require dealing with several perspectives simultaneously:

- Ensuring legislative reforms
- Policing and penalising violators
- Improved border controls that ensure authenticity of identification papers and passports
- Strengthening public order through awareness campaigns, with the involvement of the media
- Changing cultural practices
- Better sensitisation of the general public of the risks involved

Also, it means adherence to international labour standards and working conditions, and their effective monitoring. It requires above all strict adherence to the abolishment of child labour.

The above necessitates each country to identify the different forms of abuse faced by women and children. It requires the creation and/or strengthening of institutions, including civil society organisations, to effectively track down any deviations from policy directives and, if necessary, to devise specific policy instruments to counteract problems identified. Because there are several actors and institutions involved (the military, the police, border guards, etc.) it is important to establish new forms of co-operation between different agencies involved in the security of people, and children in particular. Finally, perpetrators or complicit agents must be located and receive the harshest punishment – impunity must not be tolerated. All these measures require training for border patrols, police and social workers, and direct support to victims, which includes interception, rescue, socio-economic reintegration, health care (both physical and emotional), and reintegration into education.

Improper handling of cases involving abused children (girls and boys alike) that are driven by traditional social and cultural values that carry stigmatising effects must be dealt with as a matter of urgency. One of the important means of improving the efficacy of those entrusted with security functions is to ensure that a gender perspective is introduced, allowing for competent men and women to enter this field and receive effective training and orientation, required to ensure a more humane, just and victim-friendly approach.

*Raising Awareness and Combating Impunity*

The role of parliaments cannot be underscored enough. Many are not aware of their pivotal role in curbing these abhorrent practices of child abuse, and their capacity to foster a secure environment for children. In this context, institutions whose mandate is strengthening the security sector among countries, whether nationally, regionally or internationally, should consider collaborating with parliaments in order to empower them to deal with this important issue. Special programmes should be devised similar to the ones undertaken by institutions such as DCAF, broadening their perspective to include the security of children.

A few promising developments have occurred in some countries and selected examples are worth mentioning. In Africa, Niger introduced a law in 2003 amending the Penal Code that specifically addresses the predicament of persons whose ancestors were enslaved and who are described as still being of 'servile status'. The amended law also dealt with the issue of debt bondage, imposing severe penalties in the form of lengthy prison sentences and heavy fines.[30]

Under its 2001 Penal Code, Mali provides severe penalties for child trafficking. In India, its Bonded Labour System Abolition Act of 1976 provides for imprisonment and fines for those who compel others to render bonded labour and, in August 2004, the Government of India reported 4,859 prosecutions for forced labour offences.[31]

In Egypt, in 2006 a strategy for eliminating child labour was elaborated that rested on three pillars, namely identifying the children and channelling them to continue their schooling; compensating the families' income loss; and bringing to justice those responsible for the employment of children in their enterprises. In addition, SOS help-lines have been established throughout the country that operate on a 24-hour basis and provide immediate assistance for any child requiring protection or emergency assistance.[32]

In Bahrain, a law was enacted in 2007 declaring human trafficking a criminal offence, and a strategy for combating this scourge was elaborated by a special task force that reported to parliament.

In Brazil, the government of President Lula Da Silva has introduced stronger measures to combat forced labour and impunity. A Special Mobile Inspection Group has been strengthened and inspectors assigned to priority areas. In the United Kingdom a new immigration offence of trafficking in prostitution was created in 2002, followed in July 2004 by a second new offence of trafficking people for exploitation. Both carry a maximum penalty of 14 years of imprisonment – equal to the penalty for drug trafficking.

Other European countries, especially the Nordic countries, spear-headed by Sweden, have been at the forefront of qualifying child abuse as a crime and have introduced major laws protecting women and children – laws that have subsequently been used by a number of countries as exemplary. The role of civil society in these countries has been a major force to reckon with, along with the involvement of the private sector.

There are many more initiatives within and between countries that are working to curb various forms of abuse. International institutions, such as the Organization for Security and Co-operation in Europe, Europol, Interpol and others are playing a vital role. Resources in support of such institutions are essential, but also commitment by countries themselves in dealing with these issues, especially those affecting children, is of paramount importance. And while important headway has been made, enforcement of laws is still very weak. In spite of some successful investigations, such as discovering and dismantling paedophile networks, prosecution rates remain low, victim protection mechanisms are not available, and lack of harmonisation between law enforcement authorities and the judiciary is a major flaw. Corruption also remains a major impediment.

New approaches may be needed to deal with new challenges. One example is the involvement of the private sector in areas that have been traditionally considered public domains. The fight against human trafficking is a case in point. Human trafficking represents an illicit form of business negatively impacting the functioning of legitimate business and thus putting the development of sound economic systems into danger. Therefore, there is a lot at stake for legitimate business if human trafficking continues to flourish. Most anti-trafficking initiatives have been undertaken by governments and non-governmental organisations, but very few programmes have so far engaged the business sector and harnessed their global reach and connections. Examples of programmes aimed at responsible business conduct upholding human rights include the Global Compact launched by the United Nations Secretary-General in 1999, the Anti-Trafficking Programme on Public-Private Co-operation initiated by the Organization for Security and Co-operation in Europe, and most recently the End Human Trafficking Now! Campaign launched by the business community in 2006.[33] It remains to be seen what difference can be made by such new approaches, but it has been increasingly recognised that it is more likely that a complex scourge such as human trafficking can only be diminished by the combined efforts of all players concerned.

Governments must assume their share of responsibility. They must not only enact laws, they must ensure their enforcement by exerting their legal authority and coercive powers. The security sector – police, legal experts, cross-border intelligence, etc. – must be strengthened and appropriately trained to be alert to many of the tactics used, and all must work in concert to give priority to this scourge and provide the necessary support to children victims of abuse. Child psychologists, medical experts and others must be brought in to support children who have endured abuse and suffering. To date it is mostly civil society that has come forward and filled this void.

Reduction of poverty and dealing with inequities within the countries themselves is a political commitment all countries must make. For it is when these are solved within countries, when disadvantaged groups are pulled out of their predicament, and when adequate services are provided that enable all to be self-reliant, that we will see a net improvement in the quality of life of people, with fewer choosing to flee or to migrate, legally or illegally, and fewer children being continuously plunged into and exposed to precarious and risky conditions that jeopardise their lives.

While acknowledging the importance of protecting our borders, by and large, too much emphasis has been given to catching illegal migrants rather than the traffickers and smugglers who exploit them. For many of those who violate immigration laws, their main crime has been to trust those offering them the chance of a lifetime – the promise of a better job in a far-away land – and it is they that have ended up in brothels, as domestic workers, or as illegal workers in sweat shops.

Given its complex and holistic approach the United Nations Convention on the Rights of the Child, with its Optional Protocols, offers an excellent tool in identifying the present loopholes in the system.[34] These must be rectified through better co-operation with civil society and institutions, both within and among countries and through expanding the traditional role that the security sector has had. Positive experiences need to be generated, which provide examples of the ways and means of meeting the needs of children.

## Conclusion

Children throughout the ages have always occupied a central place in society's value systems. Politicians regularly use children to convince their constituencies that their foremost commitment is ensuring the youngest of their societies a happy and secure future. Yet, paradoxically, they are the largest group that suffers the consequences of inaction, neglect, abuse, exploitation and greed. As an indicator, children's health status provides us with a staggering set of statistics that catalogue preventable death, disability and suffering. These are the results of our collective failure to commit ourselves to doing what should and could be done. Most of the failures are fundamentally political ones, not technical ones. Whether looking at conflict and wars, migration, refugees or any other serious issue that is being faced today, it is basically about access to and distribution of power and resources, within and among countries. These failures are also due to the structure of global governance, but can be found in actions and inactions of individuals, families and communities.

Until the challenges of anchoring the protection of children, and people in general, are faced up to, we will not be able to seriously resolve the many issues affecting them. Foremost among these is providing security for all those in need – within daily life, in situations of crisis and disaster, and during conflict and war. And while the obstacles loom large, it is not an option to continue 'business as usual' – ways of working differently need to be identified.

It is hoped that by documenting these issues and committing to change within these pages, that space can be found to forge a pathway for all committed persons to join, and contribute to, the kind of world where our children and future generations have a chance to feel protected, where their rights and dignity are respected, and where they are offered every opportunity to live in a healthy and peaceful environment. It is those who hold power, and the people who demand their accountability, who must take the first steps.

## Endnotes

1 This Article was prepared with the assistance of Ms. Eva Lutara, Communication and Research Officer of the Suzanne Mubarak Women's International Peace Movement (SMWIPM), Geneva.

2 World Health Organisation (WHO), 'Child and Adolescent Health and Development', http://www.who.int/child-adolescent-health/over.htm (accessed October 2008).

3 WHO, Intersectoral Action for Health (Geneva: WHO, 1986).

4 WHO, Department of Child and Adolescent Health and Development, The Importance of Care-Giving Child Interactions for Survival and Healthy Development of Young Children: A Review (Geneva: WHO, 2004).

5 Ibid.

6 World Health Assembly (WHA), Resolution 39.22 adopted by the Thirty-ninth WHA (May 1986).
7. UK Department for International Development, 'Why we need to work more effectively in fragile states' (2005), http://www.dfid.gov.uk/pubs/files/fragilestates-paper.pdf (accessed October 2008).
8 UNICEF, *The State of the World's Children 2008: Child Survival* (New York: UNICEF, December 2007).
9 Ibid.
10 It is believed that depleted uranium was one of the contributing causes to the rise in children's cancer rates in Iraq that spiralled 300 to 400 percent following the Gulf war in 1991. Leukemia incidents began rising dramatically around 1994 and 40 percent of cancer victims below the age of 15 years have leukemia, more than double the figure for lymphoma the second most common pediatric cancer. According to a survey by UNICEF, the death rate of children in Iraq rose to 130 persons per 1,000 during the 1990's after the gulf war. In addition to depleted uranium and other environmental factors, such high death rates must be also attributed to the economic sanctions. See: Uranium Medical Research Centre (2002).
11 As for accidents, among the most lethal are those resulting from the use of cluster bombs during wars and conflicts. For example, in the last war in Lebanon, 359 separate cluster-bombed locations were contaminated with as many as 100,000 unexploded bomblets. Bomblets come in interesting shapes that attract children's curiosity: some cluster munitions look like tiny bottles with short ribbons; some are yellow with tissue parachutes; some look like little grey tennis balls; some are small canisters with a white ribbon attached. All are deadly for children. A report by the non-profit organisation Handicap International, which studied the effects of cluster bombs in 24 countries and regions, found that 27 percent of casualties were children.
12 Debra L. Blackwell, Mark D. Hayward and Eileen M. Crimmins, 'Does childhood health affect chronic morbidity in later life?' *Social Science and Medicine* 52 (2001): 1269-1284.
13 Kofi Annan, *A more secure world: our shared responsibility*, Report of the High-level Panel on Threats, Challenges and Change (New York: 2004).
14 Ben Hemingway, 'Making a difference in the Triangle of Violence and displacement' (2007), http://www.imcworldwide.org/content/article/detail/1196 (accessed October 2008).
15 WHO, *Women's health: towards a better world*, Report on the first meeting of the Global Commission on Women's Health (Geneva: WHO, 1994).
16 Hemingway, 'Making a difference'.
17 'Teens abandoned in Mali', *Associated Press*, 27 March 2007.
18 Sharon La Franciere, 'Africa's world of forced labour, in a 6 year-old's eyes', *The New York Times*, 28 October 2006.
19 Human trafficking should be distinguished from human smuggling. Human smugglers facilitate the illegal entry of an individual into a country for a fee. Traffickers however use physical force, fraud or deception to obtain and transport people, and often use legal migration procedures to realise their exploitative aims. See H. Montgomery, Z. De Sas Kropiwnicki and R. Evans, *Trafficking Women and Children: Overcoming Illegal Sex Trade* (Oxford: Refugee Studies Centre, 2005).
20 United Nations Convention on the Rights of the Child (1989); Protocol against the Smuggling of Migrants by Land, Sea and Air, supplementing the UN Convention against Transnational and Organised Crime (2000); Protocol to Prevent, Suppress and Punish

Trafficking in Persons, Especially Women and Children, supplementing the UN Convention against Transnational and Organised Crime (2000).

21 International Labour Organisation (ILO), *A global alliance against forced labour*, Global Report under the Follow-up to the ILO Declaration on Fundamental Principles and Rights at Work (Geneva: ILO, 2005).

22 UN Convention on the Rights of the Child; ILO Convention No. 128 concerning the Prohibition and Immediate Action for the Elimination of the Worst Forms of Child Labour (1999); ILO Convention No. 138 concerning Minimum Age for Admission to Employment (1973).

23 WHO, *The Implications of Public Policy on Health Status and Quality of Life*, Report of a meeting in Bangalore, India, October 1989, WHO Regional Office for South-East Asia. Also Cooper D.E. Weil et al., *The Impact of Development Policies on Health* (Geneva: WHO, 1990).

24 WHO, 'Health in Social Development' WHO Position Paper, prepared for the World Summit for Social Development, Copenhagen, March 1995.

25 Moises Naim, Illicit: How Smugglers, Traffickers and Copycats are Hijacking the Global Economy (New York: Doubleday, 2005), 14.

26 Ibid., 257.

27 See for example, John F. Hough, Understanding and Preventing Family Violence: Background Briefing Report with Seminar Presentations (Sacramento: California State Library Foundation, 1996).

28 Thanh Dam Truong, Poverty Gender and Human Trafficking. Rethinking Human trafficking in Sub Sahara Africa (Paris: UNESCO, 2006), 62.

29 Hans Born and Ian Leigh, Making Intelligence Accountable: Legal Standards and Best Practice for Oversight of Intelligence Agencies (Oslo: DCAF, 2005).

30 ILO, A Global Alliance against Forced Labour.

31 Ibid.

32 *SOS Helpline*, unpublished report, on file with author.

33 See for example, http://www.endhumantraffickingnow.com (accessed October 2008).

34 Optional Protocol to the Convention on the Rights of the Child on the sale of children, child prostitution and child pornography, UN Doc. A/RES/54/263 (New York: 2000). Optional Protocol to the Convention on the Rights of the Child on the involvement of children in armed conflict, UN Doc. A/RES/54/263 (New York: 2000).

## Chapter 3

# Child Development and Resilience

*Margaret McCallin*

### Introduction

The concept of 'security' can be understood to include the ability or inability of state institutions to ensure the protection of all citizens.[1] By rights, this therefore includes children, while at the same time, implicit in any discussion of how children develop is the need for a secure environment to enable them to grow well and develop their capacities to the fullest possible extent.

As has already been elaborated in the previous chapters, the threats to children's healthy development are many and pervasive. This chapter will look at approaches that can help to strengthen children's capacities to deal with and overcome adversity.

It begins by considering psychosocial approaches that have increasingly become part of programme responses in situations of armed conflict and insecurity. The paper then briefly considers what is understood by the term childhood, before introducing two complementary constructs, namely child development and resilience, which have important implications for programme planning and design. These sections show how child development can be affected by armed conflict and insecurity, and demonstrate how an understanding of these notions can better inform approaches to reducing the impact of insecurities on children's lives. The aim of such approaches should be to limit risk factors to children's healthy development, while at the same time identifying and strengthening protective factors that exist in their surroundings.

Guided throughout by reference to the United Nations Convention on the Rights of the Child (the 'Convention'), the paper concludes by outlining a framework for action based on the inter-connectedness of resilience and children's rights.

## Psychosocial Approaches

Many programmes of intervention in situations of social instability and insecurity are implemented using a psychosocial approach. Considerable attention has been given to the psychosocial effects of conflict and complex emergencies, and the term, as a description of a form of intervention, has been used to cover a wide variety of programmes, including efforts to promote human rights, community-based projects and interventions to address mental health problems.[2]

The term 'psychosocial' emphasises 'the close connection between psychological aspects of our experience (our thoughts, emotions and behaviour) and our wider social experience (our relationships, traditions and culture). These two aspects are so closely inter-twined in the context of complex emergencies that the concept of 'psychosocial well-being' is probably more useful for humanitarian agencies than narrower concepts such as 'mental health'. Interventions focussing narrowly on mental health concepts such as psychological trauma run the risk of ignoring aspects of the social context that are vital to well-being. The psychosocial emphasis on social as well as psychological aspects of well-being also ensures that the family and community are fully brought into the picture in assessing needs.'[3]

The Psychosocial Working Group defines the psychosocial well-being of an individual with respect to three inter-related core domains:

1) Human capacity is fundamentally constituted by the health (physical and mental), knowledge and skills of an individual. In these terms, improving physical and mental health, or education and training in support of increased knowledge, enhances human capacity and thus psychosocial well-being.
2) Social ecology refers to the social connections and support that people share and that form an important part of psychosocial well-being.
3) Culture and values point to the specific context and culture of communities that influence how people experience, understand and respond to events.

Thus, psychosocial programmes complement other activities such as health, education and income-generation, and programmes implemented to address children's psychosocial needs are not always child-centred. Although their aim is to address the children's situation and to prevent risk to their development, it is considered that this can be achieved through a range of strategies. Some programmes may entail working more closely with adults in a community, building on their resources and capacities, so that children's needs are addressed in a manner appropriate to a community's situation and experiences.

This approach is in contrast to programmes that may be implemented using a 'psychological' model, where the focus is on emotional or behavioural consequences of the child's experience of traumatic events. Such programmes frequently involve the use of western, therapeutic models of intervention including 'trauma counselling', and forms of 'talk' therapy, which may not only be inappropriate to the context and circumstances, but can be prohibitive in terms of human and financial resources, generally requiring expert, expatriate intervention, and ignoring the capacities present in the local community.

Such interventions are generally conceptualised within a medical or sickness model, aimed at the 'rehabilitation' or 'recovery' of children. They do not necessarily take into account social or cultural understanding of the effects of the events the children have experienced, nor do they incorporate strategies for addressing long-term issues such as social and economic integration.[4] Terms such as 'trauma' are also frequently ill-defined, or unknown within particular populations. People's unfamiliarity with the term can lead to children being labelled as 'different', and they may find themselves stigmatised as a result. An alternative can involve training community members to hold what are termed 'supportive conversations' in order that the children feel their concerns are accepted, and that someone is available to listen and to help them resolve their problems.

Enabling children to reflect on their experiences and their implications is important. This is best conducted, however, with some practical goal in mind. For example, a child may have a particular problem controlling aggression, or difficulties concentrating in class. Practical strategies can be discussed, setting particular goals, perhaps on a daily or weekly basis. The idea is to help the child to gain gradual control of the problem, to accept personal responsibility and ultimately to experience a sense of achievement that they have mastered a problem through their own efforts. Children can assist each other in achieving these goals, and their participation in this process should be encouraged.[5]

## Definitions and Understanding of Childhood

Although the Convention defines a child universally as a person under 18, chronological age may not be a sufficient criterion for defining who is a child. Communities may use quite different criteria to denote who is a child and when children become adults. The issue of definition becomes particularly difficult when adolescents are considered. Whilst 'adolescence' may not be a term that easily translates to other cultures, it nonetheless reflects a period of significant development between childhood and adulthood. Rituals and traditions can mark points of transition, and assign children social roles and responsibilities in recognition of their maturity and capabilities, bringing them into the adult world, and conferring adult rights and responsibilities.

Modern 'western' society tends to consider the ideal model for child rearing as the nuclear family. In other cultures, child rearing may be shared by a wider range of adults and older siblings, and each may have a defined social role in contributing to the child's development. When considering child development, particularly where it may be influenced by situations of insecurity, it is important to remember that people have different understandings about who is a child, and what the term 'childhood' may mean in different social and cultural contexts. This will include 'local ideas about the roles, capacities, entitlements and obligations of the young. Furthermore, enquiry into local ideas increasingly proceeds on the assumption that, even within a single location, 'childhood' itself will not be understood in only one way. Gender, race/ethnicity, class/caste, (dis)ability, amongst other factors, are likely to influence the ways in which members of any society, including the young themselves, imagine and experience 'childhood'.'[6] Social roles and responsibilities can change, for example, as a result of conflict and displacement. Factors such as the loss of adult family members, material deprivation and social or ethnic marginalisation can mean that young people are obliged to assume roles that were formerly reserved for adults. For adolescent males in particular, this can include protection of their families. Young people are also obliged to contribute to the family economy – another form of protection. These responsibilities confer a de facto status of 'adulthood', and adolescents in unstable and insecure environments can be at risk precisely by virtue of the level of maturity that they have attained. As an example, this point is of particular importance in preventing under-age military recruitment, where the standards relating to age may not be considered as locally relevant criteria in deciding who should be recruited.[7]

While age is a helpful, necessary factor in arriving at definitions of childhood and adolescence, it may prove counterproductive unless it is soundly embedded in a particular social, economic, political and cultural context. The establishment of a shared understanding of who is a child, the roles they perform, their protection needs, and the factors that describe the transition to adulthood must rest upon an appreciation of official or legal definitions, the views of the community and its leaders and, importantly, the views of children and adolescents themselves. Although the term 'child' is used throughout the chapter, in accordance with Article 1 of the Convention, the reader is asked to bear in mind that the consequences of insecurity will have a differential impact on children depending on their age and stage of development, and the contextual factors influencing the process of development.[8]

## A Model of Child Development

Simply stated, child development is concerned with how children grow and mature from birth, through childhood and adolescence. For all children, regardless of culture and background, aspects of their development will proceed along well-defined developmental pathways. Their bodies will mature, their brains and nervous systems will develop, and they will acquire the various competencies in language and other skills that they need to function and survive in the social and cultural environment that defines their childhood. Although 'general patterns of development can be predicted and observed across cultures and individuals … the expression of these universal patterns will always be embedded in, and shaped by, local conditions and cultural practices.'[9]

Historically, child development has been the domain of the social sciences, particularly psychology, and the health and educational sectors. Now, it is being increasingly acknowledged that there are clear implications for government, the security services and others. 'The catalogue of values that have to be defended as the key elements of the national security has been increasing in recent decades. Many new values that need protection in terms of ensuring security were added to the traditional ones. Not only are states supposed to defend their territorial integrity and political independence, but also they should protect such values as economic independence, cultural identity, and social stability.'[10] The concept of protection for children requires more than considerations to protect them from the physical harm that may result from situations of insecurity. It is also necessary to consider how insecure environments can affect their development.

*Understanding Child Development*

Understanding what is meant by normal development in any society enables us to address those factors in insecure environments that can affect children's developmental processes. The issue of context is one that arises in many discussions of children in 'adverse circumstances'. 'Optimal development is a result of the capacities inherent to the child and those available from his or her social and physical environment. Children's development evolves out of active interactions between the child, family, school, community, culture and larger political system.'[11]

Child development can be considered from the perspective of an 'ecological' model, which reflects the general framework of the Convention. It also reflects the interaction between genetic/biological factors and environmental factors that form a child's capacities, and emphasises that children play an active role in the creation of their identity.

Children are in continuous interaction with their environment, as represented in the following diagram.

**Diagram 3.1 The Child's Social Ecology**

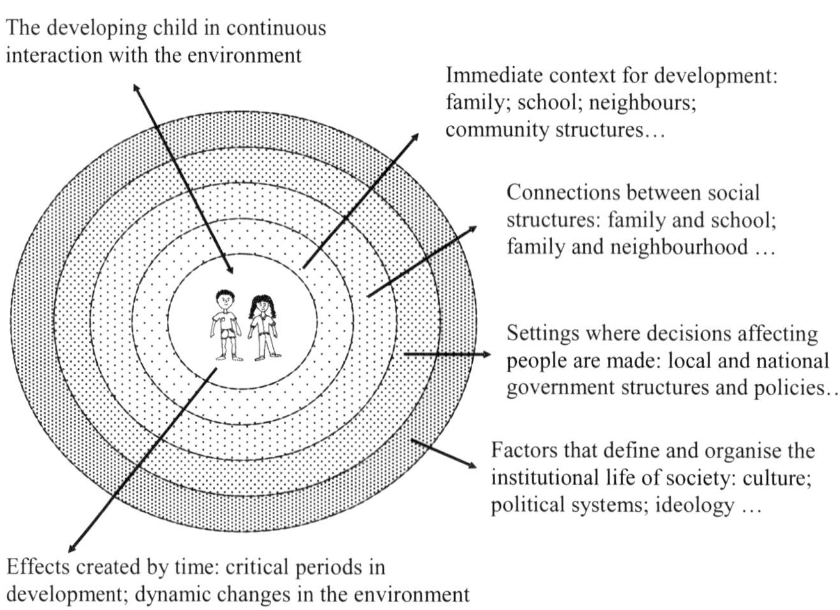

The theory of social ecology 'looks at a child's development within the context of the system of relationships that form his or her environment.'[12] Interpersonal relationships do not exist in a social vacuum but are embedded in the larger social structures. Given that the process of child development is influenced by an interaction between the economic, social and cultural factors that define the child's experiences, a model that enables us to understand this interactive process is of value in explaining how child development may be affected in insecure environments.

The ecology of human development acknowledges that humans do not develop in isolation, but in relation to their family and home, school, community and society. Each of these environments, which themselves are in a constant process of change, as well as interactions within and between these environments, is key to a child's development. The various levels of interaction can be described in the following way:

- The earliest and most immediate influences come from the family environment, and the social and community environment within which the family lives, including other families and children. Schools and religious institutions are other influences in this immediate environment.
- At the second level, there are connections between immediate environments in the child's experience: for example between the child's home and her school, between the child and her friends and their families, between the family and the religious group with which they are affiliated, and between the school and local community.
- The third level is comprised of external environmental settings, the larger political and social systems, which only indirectly affect development, such as the local community and the local authorities. The child does not actively participate in these settings, but they are where significant decisions are made affecting the individuals who do interact directly with the child.
- The influences that define and organise the institutional life of a society are found at the fourth level. These comprise, for example, the larger cultural context, including the values, customs, laws, beliefs and resources of a society; national economy; political culture; and regional and international factors.

Cutting across all four levels are time-related factors that contribute to the dynamic nature of the system, as it responds to changes and critical periods in the child's development, including situations of crisis for the family and the wider social network.

'The effective functioning of child-rearing processes in the family and other child settings requires public policies and practices that provide place, time, stability, status, recognition, belief systems, customs, and actions in support of child-rearing activities not only on the part of parents, caregivers, teachers, and other professional personnel, but also relatives, friends, neighbours, co-workers, communities, and the major economic, social, and political institutions of the entire society.'[13]

## Insecure Environments as the Context for Child Development

Insecure environments, particularly situations of conflict and displacement, are characterised by poverty, social and political instability, lack of institutional capacity and the breakdown of traditional value systems and social structures. They can result in extreme vulnerability for children and consequently adverse effects on their development. History is littered with examples of protracted armed conflicts during which children developed in situations where instability and insecurity were the norm. Many families and communities in countries in economic transition have faced an often abrupt transformation to a situation of economic and social insecurity, with children being adversely affected by the consequences of this transformation. Natural disasters can equally disrupt established traditional structures and mechanisms of child protection that had previously been vital to healthy child development.

In insecure environments a range of cultural and social factors can affect the ability of families and communities to care for children, increasing the stresses associated with family life and influencing the resources available to families. Families may experience difficulty in securing a livelihood, often becoming destitute and dependent on aid for survival. Family impoverishment may lead to the placement of children in institutions, child trafficking, sexual exploitation and child labour. The absence of social protection systems for children living in poverty is often a reason for admission into residential care. For example, in Central and Eastern Europe and former Soviet countries the transition to market economies has increased the numbers of children entering residential care for poverty-related reasons.[14] Economic considerations underline the need to consider children within the context of their families, and the need to implement initiatives to enable families to protect and care for their children. For the child growing up even in a situation of conflict, the family will have the most significant influence on development and will remain the child's greatest resource. The extent to which the physical and emotional well-being of the adults, upon whom children depend for nurturance and support, is affected by their experiences, can pose perhaps the greatest risk to child development in insecure environments.

In such contexts, children may not have even the bare necessities that provide the elements of everyday life and relationship that support children's development and achievement, including what we observe to be their resilience:

- At least one stable and affectionate caregiver with a long-term commitment to the child.
- Material and social support, as well as protection, for the child and caregiver provided by family, neighbours, community, and the state.
- Participation by the child and caregiver in meaningful social and cultural practices and institutions.[15]

Children living without the care and support of their families and communities will be deprived of even these 'bare necessities', and concerns for their development and initiatives to protect them from the risks inherent in insecure environments should be a priority. They will include:

- Separated and unaccompanied refugee and internally displaced children
- Children in institutions
- Child headed households
- Children associated with armed forces and groups
- Children living and working on the streets
- Trafficked children
- Children in detention

Where governments are unwilling, or unable, to protect their citizens, certain sectors of society will be the worst and most immediately affected. These will include those people already suffering discrimination or social marginalisation, many of whom will also be experiencing material poverty.

> Many of the defining features of emergencies – displacement, lack of humanitarian access, breakdown in family and social structures,

> erosion of traditional value systems, a culture of violence, weak governance, absence of accountability and lack of access to basic social services – create serious child protection problems. Emergencies may result in large numbers of children becoming orphaned, displaced or separated from their families. Children may become refugees or be internally displaced; abducted or forced to work for armed groups; disabled as a result of combat, landmines and unexploded ordnance; sexually exploited during and after conflict; or trafficked for military purposes. They may become soldiers, or be witnesses to war crimes and come before justice mechanisms. Armed conflict and periods of repression increase the risk that children will be tortured. For money or protection, children may turn to 'survival sex', which is usually unprotected and carries a high risk of transmission of disease, including HIV/AIDS.[16]

## Adolescents in Insecure Environments

It was noted earlier that many children live in situations where instability and insecurity is the norm. These 'children' develop into adolescents and young people in communities that have only ever experienced insecurity, and there is a justifiable concern that their situation is neither well understood, nor adequately addressed.

> In the eyes of the international community, which has reached tremendous heights of political consensus around the subject of 'innocent, vulnerable, children,' adolescents are woefully overlooked. In fact, for many decision-makers, adolescents do not seem like children at all, almost do not exist at all. They seem more like adults, able to care for themselves, or having more adult-like problems. And they may not look so innocent; they may be the perpetrators of violence. They may seem hard to deal with; they have opinions and can be demanding.[17]

It is probably safe to say that many people are frightened, or at least nervous of, adolescents who have had difficult and violent experiences that we do not necessarily share, and which we do not understand. 'The ... German philosopher Karl Liebknecht ... wrote: Whoever has the young has an army. Nothing better describes the exuberant power of the young to create a new world, and, equally, emphasises in graphic terms the potential of the young for destruction once they are disaffected. In a world whose population is steadily aging, it is in our own interests to ensure that we spawn a new generation of adults with a sense of community and obligation.'[18] How we set about this task is influenced by the particular context and available resources. It is also influenced to an important degree by our own attitudes towards adolescents and young people in general, and the extent to which we are prepared to engage them – to invite their participation – in developing long-term perspectives that are positive and meaningful to them.

One group of adolescents who have become the focus of considerable attention are 'child soldiers'. An aspect of their experience is the manner in which 'children and youth are used in conflicts in a political way only to be marginalised later and relegated to an apolitical sphere, especially during and after the peace process'.[19] This constitutes a 'lost opportunity to improve the social, economic and political lives of children and youth.'[20] The measure of disaffection and betrayal felt by young people in such circumstances is understandable. Unless it is addressed in insecure and unstable situations, the likelihood is that adolescents may contribute to the ongoing situation of insecurity. The following hopeful examples deserve consideration in other contexts.

**Box 3.2 Youth Organisations**

Organisations such as the Movement for Concerned Kono Youth (MOCKY) in Sierra Leone have developed as platforms aimed at articulating the needs of the youth with the potential of becoming political and social movements. MOCKY was formed to articulate the grievances of youth in the Kono region and channelling their energies in a constructive way. MOCKY has been credited with playing a very positive role in consolidating the peace in the area through mediation of disputes.

Other organisations such as YOSUPA (Youth for Sustainable Development), another local youth non-governmental organisation involved with peace projects immediately after the end of the war, reflect the dynamism and potential energy of young people to take responsibility for the future of Sierra Leone. It is this energy that needs to be nurtured and resources provided for the development of the young people of Sierra Leone in order for peace to be sustainable.

## Resilience

The construct of resilience has made a relatively recent entry into considerations of the processes involved in child development, particularly in situations of armed conflict and social instability. It has been defined as 'the manifestation of positive adaptation despite significant life adversity.'[21]

Resilience is a positive construct that focusses on people's strengths and resources and, with respect to children, what have been termed 'self-righting tendencies that move children toward normal adult development under all but the most persistent adverse circumstances.'[22] As such it contrasts with a 'deficit' model that predicts predominantly negative outcomes for children, focussing on the risks to people facing adversity. Research on and application of the concept of resilience grew out of observations of individuals, families and communities who, although considered to be 'at risk', were nevertheless thriving, doing well and constructing meaningful lives in situations of 'adversity'. In this sense, it goes beyond the notion of 'coping' with negative events. The term may be applied to communities as well as individuals, where it can incorporate the notion of 'social capital' – the degree of cohesion and solidarity that exists within communities, which can serve to protect children at risk, and which can provide for a reconstruction of community life, even where there have been periods of crisis and significant change.[23]

Work on the construct of resilience in the social sciences developed from the observation that certain people do well despite experiencing significant adversity. The International Resilience Project describes resilience as 'an individual's ability to overcome adversity, or difficult life challenges, and continue his or her normal growth and development'.[24] Perhaps one of the most important points to emerge in the recent studies on resilience is that it is a normal process, and not something exceptional. 'What began as a quest to understand the extraordinary has revealed the power of the ordinary. Resilience does not come from rare and special qualities, but from the everyday magic of ordinary, normative human resources in the minds, brains, and bodies of children, in their families and relationships, and in their communities.'[25] The International Resilience Project emphasises 'both the individual's role in nurturing and sustaining his or her well-being and the relational, social and cultural factors that must be available and accessible to individuals who face multiple risks.'[26] Resilience is not a personal attribute that some people have and others do not. It is considered to be a capacity that is innate to the process of human development, but that is nevertheless dependent on protective factors available to the child from their families and wider social environments.

Resilience refers to both individual qualities and social and environmental factors that can enable children to overcome the worst effects of adversity, and that may help a 'child or young person to cope, survive and even thrive in the face of great hurt and disadvantage.'[27] It is, however, important to stress 'that no child is, or can be rendered, invulnerable to emotional or physiological stress. Where adversities are continuous and extreme, and not moderated by factors external to the child, resilience will be very rare.'[28] This point is important to keep in mind, particularly when considering how children may be affected in insecure environments.

Resilience exemplifies human potential even in the most adverse of circumstances. It encourages a focus on the positive elements in people's experience, not only on solving 'problems'. It shifts the emphasis away from more deterministic approaches that focus on risks and adversity, predicting only negative outcomes from people's experience, and which portray them as helpless victims, rather than people with the capacity to deal with their adversities. Work on resilience has made it clear that there is not a neat, linear relationship between adversity and a negative outcome. In focussing on people's capacities to overcome adversity, however, it should not be seen as an excuse not to engage with communities experiencing adversity. Rather, the implications of the construct invite us to work with people to better understand how they have been affected, and what mechanisms they consider appropriate to address the consequences of their experiences.

## Risk and Protective Factors

In considering the relevance of the construct of resilience in insecure environments, it is worth reminding ourselves of the factors that can describe the context of insecurity:

- Poverty
- Social and cultural discrimination
- Social and political instability
- Lack of institutional capacity
- Breakdown of traditional value systems and social structures

In the application of resilience, particularly with children in situations of multiple risks to their development and well-being, there is a consideration of the risks that confront children and the protective factors that are available to them to mitigate the impact of risk. Protective factors are individual qualities or characteristics, and aspects of the social environment that buffer or moderate risk.

A resilience approach can be considered in two ways.[29] Firstly, as addressing risk factors through the identification of and response to specific actual or potential threats to children. This can be achieved in often straightforward ways. For example, in the course of developing a programme to prevent child sexual abuse in Cambodia, it was noted that individual children were selling shrimps on the beach – the fact that they were alone made them vulnerable to predatory advances from paedophiles who frequented the area, known for its sex tourism. It was suggested that children work in small groups and this simple intervention, reinforced by work with the children and their communities, served as a mechanism to reduce the risks to the children.[30]

Secondly, it can be considered as strengthening protective factors by improving the number and quality of structures and services available to support children and their families. This will very often consist of strengthening existing community resources, and reinforcing cultural norms and practices that promote resilience. An example of such a strategy is the prevention of child prostitution in impoverished communities through parent and community education, support to local non-governmental organisations and income-generation projects.

*Risk Factors*

Many aspects of insecure environments can be seen as risk factors for children, with consequences for their development:

- Traumatic experiences of violence, abuse, exploitation, separation, fear
- Loss of the family home, friends, familiar people and surroundings
- Loss of language and culture
- Lack of access to health facilities
- Poor diet and nutritional status
- Lack of opportunities for education
- Lack of opportunities for play and recreation
- Excessive burden of paid and/or unpaid domestic work
- Loss of self-respect and self-confidence
- Uncertainty about the future

Children's well-being is intrinsically linked with that of their parents. The risks to which parents or other caregivers are exposed will also affect the children. These may include:

- Poor health
- Anxiety
- Lack of access to health services
- Inadequate social support
- Separation from spouse
- Relationship problems and tensions in the marriage
- Unemployment and lack of access to economic opportunities
- Lack of material resources
- Concerns about the future

*Multiple Risk Factors*

Any discussion of resilience in the context of insecurity must highlight the fact that we are not seeking to create a 'risk-free' environment. All families and communities are confronted with risk in one way or another. What we must address is the fact that developmental harm is caused to children when there is an accumulation of risk factors. The presence of multiple risk factors, especially when they are linked with past traumatic experiences and current stresses on the part of both children and their parents, is likely to adversely affect the child's development, and in turn this places him at increased susceptibility to other risk factors.[31]

*Protective Factors*

Protective factors serve to shield both parents and children from the worst effects of risk factors and thereby contribute to resilience. They are considered to have 'a more profound impact on the life course of children who grow up under adverse conditions than do specific risk factors or stressful life events. They ... appear to transcend ethnic, social class, geographical, and historical boundaries.'[32] Some of these protective factors relate to the characteristics, assets or resources that an individual will bring to a particular situation:

- Cognitive competence – ability to think through problems, skills in communication, realistic planning
- A positive sense of self-esteem, self-confidence and self-control
- An active coping style rather than a passive approach – a tendency to look to the future rather than to the past

- A sense of structure and meaning in the individual's life, often informed by religious or ideological beliefs – a sense of coherence

For children, protective factors are found in their immediate social environment. The following examples have been identified in the course of work on resilience, and consideration should be given as to how these factors may function in situations of ongoing instability and insecurity:

- A stable emotional relationship with at least one parent or other trusted person.
- Good and consistent support and guidance from parents or other caregivers.
- Support from the extended family and friendship/community networks, teachers and others – the (re)establishment of a normal pattern of daily life.
- An educational climate which is emotionally positive, open and supportive.
- Appropriate role models who encourage constructive coping.

The social environment is also the source of protective factors for parents and other caregivers that will serve to enhance, or limit, resilience. These may include:

- A supportive marital relationship
- Support from the extended family and neighbours
- Supportive community structures
- Access to health and social support services
- Opportunities to (re)establish an acceptable and secure economic base for the family
- A secure physical environment

Resilience is not a 'soft' issue, but can be a powerful construct in developing approaches to people living in adversity. It is a matter of how we look at people and their response to their circumstances, for example reducing vulnerability through the involvement of communities.

> ... it is essential to recognise that humanitarian protection is not merely a legal and programming conversation between agencies, states and armed groups that is over the heads of protected persons. On the

> contrary, wherever access and contact permits, humanitarian protection work is also about working directly with protected persons to identify and develop ways that they can protect themselves and realise their rights to assistance, repair recovery, safety and redress ... It is vitally important that people in need of protection are not seen just as the objects of state power but also as the subjects of their own protective capabilities. In many wars, people survive despite the state. In any protection programme, protected persons must be recognised as protection actors as well as victims. States have obligations to protect them but the most critical protection strategies of civilians may often be their own.[33]

The extent to which resilience has meaning across cultures speaks to the point above. Complementing the social ecology model of child development, resilience is 'a culturally and contextually sensitive construct' related to individual, relational, community and cultural factors. As an aspect of understanding the effects of insecure environments, it will require efforts that are 'culturally embedded to capture the nuances of culture and context, while avoiding bias and designing interventions to promote how resilience is understood'.[34]

## Intersection of Child Development and Resilience with Children's Rights

As stated in the introduction of this publication, this chapter is framed within the four general principles of the Convention.[35] An understanding of the implications of these principles will facilitate a response to the circumstances of children in insecure environments. Any action will require:

- An assessment of the children's best interests
- The promotion of their survival and development
- Consideration of their opinions in decisions which affect them
- Efforts to avoid missing excluded or marginalised groups[36]

The Convention should not be considered as a remote or 'static' instrument of international law, but one that is dynamic and continuous, and reflects children's ongoing developmental process. The concept of the 'evolving capacities' of the child is one of the key features of Article 5 of the Convention. Evolving capacities refers to 'the process of maturation and learning whereby children progressively acquire knowledge, competencies and understanding'.[37]

A basic concept of the Convention is that 'all children should be allowed and supported to develop to their full potential. Understanding and knowledge of child development as a process is important for grasping the real significance of children's rights'.[38] Put simply, what children need to develop equates to their rights. States have an obligation to ensure that adequate resources are available to meet their commitments to children. That said, the ability, and often the willingness, of states to fulfil their obligations is not present. This is particularly the case in situations of insecurity, where recourse may be made to local and international organisations to fill the gap in providing services to prevent and address violations of children's rights.

Any agency or individual that has a role to play in promoting or supporting the healthy development of children is as such a 'duty-bearer' in the protection of children's rights. This role brings with it a number of obligations as described below.

**Diagram 3.3 Duties and Obligations in Child Protection**

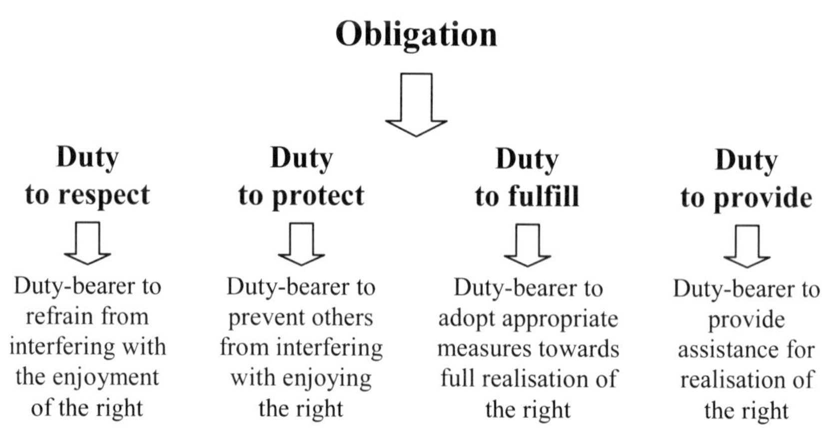


Human rights are linked to duties, accountability, obligation and responsibility. Duty-bearers are the actors collectively responsible for the realisation of human rights. Those who bear duties with respect to a human right are accountable if the right goes unrealised. When a right has been violated or insufficiently protected, not only has someone perpetrated a rights violation, someone or some institution has failed to perform a duty of protection.[39]

If we refer back to the diagram describing children's social ecologies, we can see that this is comparable with the following diagram that represents the environments in which children's rights are realised, and the individuals and communities of interest who have an influence on children's lives and who therefore constitute duty-bearers for different obligations towards children.

**Diagram 3.4 Duty-bearers at Local, National and International Levels**

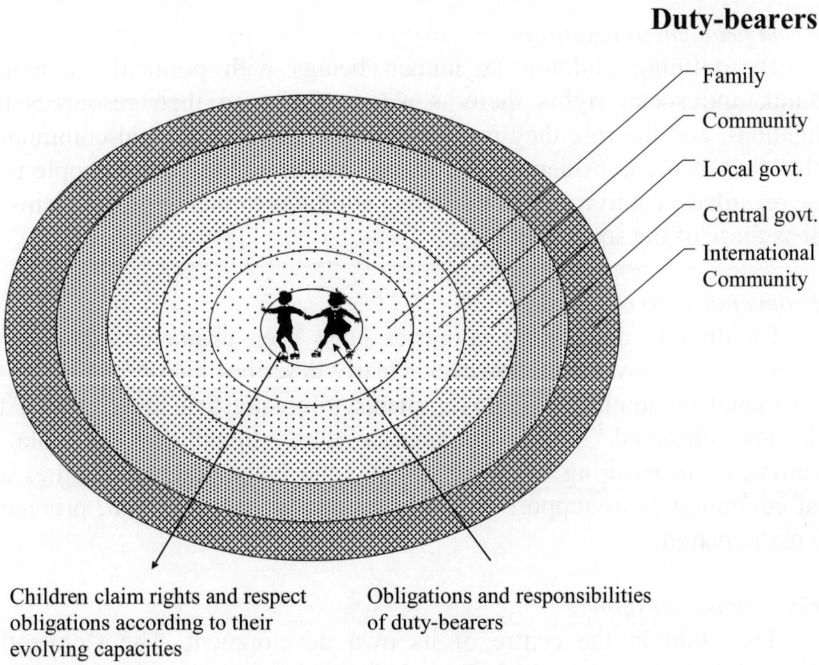


Since the ratification of the Convention there has been an increasing focus on establishing partnerships with communities, and viewing children as 'rights holders' rather than 'beneficiaries' of services to meet their needs.[40] The implications for change brought about by the ratification of the Convention were in many ways not anticipated. Organisations were required to rethink their way of working and to consider what it meant to work within a rights framework, as opposed to providing 'charitable' services to children in need.

There are five key areas in which our perceptions of and approaches to child protection and childhood development have changed over the last decade:

*1) From needs to rights*

The principle of non-discrimination employed in the Convention covers all children and implies that human rights cannot be divided. A needs approach focusses on an external assessment of what children need and are in a position to receive, an approach historically closely linked to charity. The rights approach is based on the Convention ratified by the international community defining what provisions must be made by parents, families, guardians, governments etc. in order to comply with children's rights.

*2) From problem to resource*

By defining children as human beings with political, economic, cultural, and social rights there is also a focus on their resources and obligations, and the role they may play in the family and local community. Rather than being considered a 'problem', children and young people need to be regarded as active agents in finding solutions to their own problems, as well as those of the society at large.

*3) From charity to obligation*

Children in developing countries have been characterised as 'poor victims'... The Convention, however, clearly describes the obligation of the international community and governments to ensure that the rights of the child are observed.[41] The Convention thus strengthens the role of governments in ensuring children's rights, and helps parents, families and local communities to support the child's survival, development, protection and participation.

*4) From object to subject*

The child in the centre of its own development. The Convention defines children's rights, including their right to play an active role in fulfilling these rights by the identification of their own needs and ways of meeting such needs. Children are thus no longer simply objects of international development aid, but active subjects in their own development.

*5) New areas of concern*

Children's participation, right of expression, and right to information and knowledge. Traditionally the planning of and preparations for child protection projects have focussed on adult views on a given problem. With the Convention children are increasingly being seen as active agents themselves. This change implies an increased focus on children's active participation in all stages of a given project – from planning to evaluation.

Child participation should not be promoted on the basis of 'political correctness', but rather because experience shows that it leads to the achievement of better project results and higher efficiency.

Summarising these more specific changes in our perceptions of children and how to work with them, the shift from regarding children as 'passive victims' to looking at them as 'active agents' is of paramount importance. It also marks a shift in focus from looking at children's 'vulnerability' to explore how we may support and develop children's 'resiliency' and general coping strategies. Finally there has been a shift in emphasis from merely 'rescuing' or 'saving' children, to approaches in which the involvement and empowerment of children is seen as part and parcel of the solution to their problems.'[42]

## A Framework for Action

Promoting and protecting children's rights, and working to promote resilience, provides a framework for action to promote positive child development in situations of insecurity. If we accept that resilience can indeed be a reality of life, this implies for us a measure of obligation to understand the processes that lead to certain children being resilient and the identification of strategies to enhance this capacity in other children. It is important to remember that in 'persistent adverse circumstances' the development of resilience will be compromised. Thus, strategies need to be defined with respect to the environments that impact on child development in different situations of insecurity.

Resilience is a continuous process, an interaction between individuals, social systems and their environment. It therefore varies depending on the particular context or stage in life. In a comparable way the Convention implicates all levels of society, from the individual to state services, and the international level, emphasising the 'progressive realisation' of children's rights. It provides us with 'a set of guiding principles … and in its clarification of children's human rights sets out the necessary environment and means to enable every human being to develop to their full potential.'[43]

A resilience perspective gives us a particular view on how to put the principles of the Convention into practice. But it is not a panacea, a remedy that will solve all problems and difficulties. Both the Convention and the concept of resilience are reference points to guide action in a given situation, and must be put into practice in a way adapted to local contexts and challenges. Neither one is a 'technique' that can be applied regardless of circumstances.

**Diagram 3.5 Dimensions of Political Change Affecting Children**

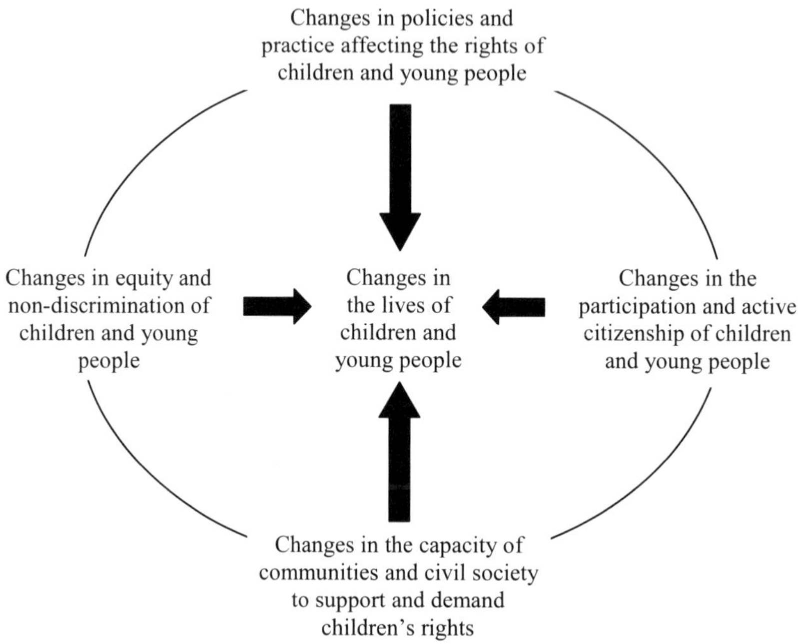


A rights-based approach to the situation of children in insecure environments complements the dynamism of the two constructs of child development and resilience, and can influence and monitor change in children's lives. A rights-based approach monitors different dimensions of change: changes in children's lives, policies and practices, equity, participation and empowerment.[44]

## Conclusion

Situations of insecurity can have a negative impact on the process of child development, but this impact can be mediated by a range of social, cultural and political factors in the child's experience, and by the capacities of the individual child and groups of children. This latter point is of special importance in considering the experiences of adolescents and the positive contribution they are capable of making – if given the opportunity – in reconstructing their communities following periods of adversity.

This chapter has outlined the constructs of child development and resilience, and discussed issues that affect children's development in insecure environments and how this process may be facilitated. This requires a framework that can take full account of the context in which children are developing and which is informed by international standards for child protection, in particular for children experiencing adversity and insecurity. The inter-connectedness of resilience and children's rights can inform the development of an operational framework that not only addresses the immediate consequences of insecurity, but creates a foundation for an environment where children's rights are respected and not violated. This will necessitate planning and consultation with families, communities and structures in civil society, taking account of local understandings of childhood, and promoting local understandings of resilience.

## Endnotes

1 Geneva Centre for the Democratic Control of Armed Forces (DCAF), *Women in an insecure World Factsheet* (Geneva: DCAF, 2007).

2 Discussion of the validity and appropriateness of 'mental health' programmes in situations of conflict and forced migration are numerous, and beyond the scope of this chapter. See for example, Derek Summerfield, 'Discussion Guide 1: The Nature of Conflict and the Implications for Appropriate Psychosocial Responses' in *Refugee Experience-Psychosocial Training Module* (Oxford: Refugee Studies Centre, 2001). Vanessa Pupavac, 'Therapeutising refugees, pathologising populations: international psychosocial programmes in Kosovo', *UNHCR Working Paper* No. 59 (August 2002).

3 The Psychosocial Working Group, 'Psychosocial Intervention in Complex Emergencies: A Framework for Practice' (2003), http://www.forcedmigration.org/psychosocial/papers/Conceptual%20Framework.pdf (accessed October 2008).

4 Margaret McCallin, 'Understanding the Psychosocial Needs of Children and Adolescents' in *The Refugee Experience: Psychosocial Training Module*, eds. Maryanne Loughry and Alastair Ager (Oxford: Refugee Studies Centre, 2001).

5 United Nations High Commissioner for Refugees (UNHCR)/International Save the Children Alliance, Action for the Rights of Children (ARC), 'Resource Pack on Child Soldiers' (2002), http://www. savethechildren.net/arc/files/main.html (accessed October 2008).

6. Jason Hart and Bex Tyrer, 'Research with Children Living in Situations of Armed Conflict: Concepts, Ethics and Methods' *RSC Working Paper* No. 30 (May 2006), http://www.rsc.ox. ac.uk/PDFs/workingpaper30.pdf (accessed October 2008).

7 Margaret McCallin, A Framework for Developing Local Initiatives to Prevent Under-Age Military Recruitment (International Save the Children Alliance, 2002,).

8 'For the purposes of the present Convention, a child means every human being below the age of eighteen years unless under the law applicable to the child, majority is attained earlier.' United Nations Convention on the Rights of the Child, Article 1 (1989).
9 UNHCR/International Save the Children Alliance, ARC, 'Resource Pack on Child and Adolescent Development'.
10 Anna Kicinger, 'International Migration as a Non-Traditional Security Threat and the EU Responses to this Phenomenon' *CEFMR Working Paper* 2 (Warsaw Central European Forum for Migration Research, 2004).
11 Paul Bouvier, 'Resilience: A Different Way of Looking at Things' in *Child Rights and Resilience* (Geneva: International Catholic Child Bureau, 2007), http://www.crin.org/docs/Resiliance.doc (accessed October 2008).
12 Dede Paquette and John Ryan, 'Bronfenbrenner's Ecological Systems Theory' (2001), http://pt3.nl.edu/paquetteryanwebquest.pdf (accessed October 2008).
13 Elizabeth Jareg, 'Crossing Bridges and Negotiating Rivers: Rehabilitation and Reintegration of Children Associated with Armed Forces' (2005), http://www.child-soldiers.org/resources/ psychosocial (accessed October 2008).
14 International Save the Children Alliance, *A Last Resort: The growing concern about children in residential care* (London: International Save the Children Alliance, 2003), http://www. scslat.org/search/publieng.php?_cod_19_lang_e (accessed October 2008).
15 Linda Richter, 'Empathic Care: Between Child Rights and Resilience' in *Child Rights and Resilience* (Geneva: International Catholic Child Bureau, 2007).
16 Inter-Parliamentary Union (IPU) and UNICEF, *Child Protection: A Handbook for Parliamentarians* (Switzerland: IPU and UNICEF, 2004).
17 Women's Commission for Refugee Women & Children, 'Untapped Potential: Adolescents affected by armed conflict: A review of programs and policies' (USA: 2000).
18 Laurence Brockliss and George Rousseau, 'The History Child' Oxford Magazine, Michelmas Term (2003).
19 Angela McIntyre and Thokozani Thusi, 'Children and Youth in Sierra Leone's Peace-Building' *African Security Review* 12, No. 2 (2003).
20 Ibid.
21 Suniya S. Luthar, *Resilience and vulnerability: Adaptation in the context of childhood adversities* (New York: Cambridge University Press, 2003). Referenced in Paul Bouvier, 'Resilience: A Different Way of Looking at Things' in *Child Rights and Resilience*.
22 Emmy Werner and Ruth Smith, *Overcoming the Odds: High Risk Children from Birth to Adulthood* (Ithaca and London: Cornell University Press, 1992).
23 World Health Organisation (WHO), 'Chapter Three: Child abuse and neglect by parents and other caregivers' in *World report on Violence and Health* (Geneva: WHO, 2002).
24 International Resilience Project, *Project Report: January 2006* (2006), http://www. resilienceproject.org/documents/2006_reports/mainreport.pdf (accessed October 2008).
25 Anne S. Masten, 'Ordinary magic: Resilience processes in development' *American Psychologist* 56 (2001): 227-238, reprinted in *Annual progress in child psychiatry and child development*, eds. M. E. Hertzig and E. A. Farber (New York: Routledge, 2002).
26 International Resilience Project (2006).
27 Robbie Gilligan, 'Beyond permanence? The importance of resilience in child placement and planning' in *Signposts in adoption: Policy, practice and research issue*, eds. Malcom Hill and Martin Shaw (London: BAAF, 1998).
28 Tony Newman, 'Limits to the Concept of Resilience' in Child Rights and Resilience (Geneva: International Catholic Child Bureau, 2007).

29 UNHCR/International Save the Children Alliance, ARC, 'Resource Pack on Child and Adolescent Development'.
30 Personal anecdote related to the author.
31 Margaret McCallin, 'The Impact of Current and Traumatic Stressors on the Psychological Well-being of Refugee Communities' in *The psychological well-being of refugee children: research, practice and policy issues*, 2nd edition, ed. Margaret McCallin (Geneva: International Catholic Child Bureau, 1996).
32 Emmy E. Werner and Ruth S. Smith, Overcoming the Odds: High Risk Children from Birth to Adulthood.
33 Hugo Slim and Andrew Bronnick, *Protection: An ALNAP guide for humanitarian agencies* (London: Overseas Development Institute, 2005).
34 International Resilience Project (2006).
35 IPU and UNICEF, *Child Protection: A Handbook for Parliamentarians*. Recognition of the child's right to protection is not limited to the Convention on the Rights of the Child. There are a number of other instruments, both those of the UN and those of other international bodies, which also lay out these rights. These instruments include: The African Charter on the Rights and Welfare of the Child of the Organisation for African Unity (now African Union) of 1990; the Geneva Conventions on International Humanitarian Law (1949) and their Additional Protocols (1977); the International Labour Convention No. 138 (1973), which states that, in general, persons under the age of 18 may not be employed in jobs that are dangerous to their health or development, and International Labour Convention No. 182 (1999) concerning the Prohibition and Immediate Action for the Elimination of the Worst Forms of Child Labour; the Protocol to Prevent, Suppress and Punish Trafficking in Persons, Especially Women and Children to the UN Convention on Transnational Organised Crime (2000).
36 International Save the Children Alliance, Child Rights Programming: How to Apply Rights-Based Approaches in Programming. A Handbook for International Save the Children Alliance Members (Stockholm: Save the Children Sweden, 2005).
37 Bernard van Leer Foundation, 'A Guide to General Comment 7: Implementing Child Rights in Early Childhood' (The Hague: Bernard van Leer Foundation 2006).
38 International Save the Children Alliance, *A Last Resort*.
39 UN System Staff College, Powerpoint Presentation - 'Introduction to Human Rights Based Approach to Programming' (CCA/UNDAF Orientation, Jordan, 6 March 2006), http://www.unssc.org/web1/programmes/rcs/cca_undaf_training_material/teamrcs/file2.asp?ID=2069 (accessed October 2008).
40 See for example, Julian Y. Kramer, 'Child Rights Programming: Experiences from Save the Children Norway', Paper presented to the DSA NGO Study Group (November 2002).
41 UN Convention on the Rights of the Child, Article 4.
42 Peter Crawford, 'Strategies for improved social protection in Asia: Child Protection (Project and Programme Issues)', paper presented at the Asia and Pacific Forum on Poverty: Reforming Policies and Institutions for Poverty Reduction, held at the Asian Development Bank (Manila, 5-9 February 2001).
43 UNICEF, 'Understanding the Convention on the Rights of the Child', http://www.unicef.org/crc/index_understanding.html (accessed October 2008).
44 Joachim Theis, 'Rights-based Monitoring and Evaluation: A Discussion Paper' (Save the Children, April 2003), http://portals.wi.wur.nl/files/docs/ppme/rights_based_monitoring_evaluation%5B1%5D.pdf (accessed October 2008).

# Chapter 4

# Creating a Secure Environment for Children

*David Nosworthy*

The challenge that faces the security sector in ensuring the protection of children is, on the face of it, a daunting one not only due to the range of issues that impact on children's well-being, but also the sheer scale of some of the protection challenges such as child labour, and the depth and sensitivity associated with various forms of abuse such as domestic violence that has its roots within the confines of the family.

As outlined in the first part of this publication the actions of the security sector towards children are best guided by reference to the existing human rights framework. This international legal framework, once integrated into national/domestic law, provides a comprehensive set of standards that deal with all aspects of children's protection. Coupled with an understanding of child development and the inherent resilience of children and youth, we can begin to see an approach emerge that values and respects today's children as citizens in their own right and active agents in their social surroundings.

The security sector has a key role to play, working alongside others, to both reduce risk factors that impact on children and their lives, and to strengthen protective factors within and around the child's environment with the aim of assisting all children to achieve positive outcomes. But, it is also important to remember that the security sector's responsibilities extend to not only protecting children's rights from the actions of others, but also ensuring that its own actions do not infringe the rights of children.

The United Nations Children's Fund (UNICEF) works with national governments in fulfilling their obligations under international law. As part of their child protection policy they have developed an approach that aims to build a protective environment around children, essential to enabling them to develop to the fullest of their abilities and capacities. This chapter reviews this approach and its implications for the security sector and considers the linkages to areas of intervention that are required to realise and protect children's rights.

As mentioned, the security sector must focus on ensuring that its own actions are not infringing the rights of children. An important element of this is the 'duty of care', which can be conceptualised as the procedures and mechanisms that govern security sector engagement with children whether as victims, witnesses or offenders (and across a range of settings) and assure that its actions are in keeping with the rights of the child.

To set the scene for this discussion it is first useful to reflect on some of the challenges that children face to their security as a result of acts of both commission and omission on the part of a range of security actors. Key to guaranteeing the security of children and protecting their rights under these circumstances are the police and justice systems but, as mentioned earlier when considering the broader definition of the parties that constitute the security sector, a whole range of additional actors will have a role to play and must be considered in policy formulation and planning.

## A Systems Approach to Child Protection – the Protective Environment[1]

The scale, nature and urgency of child protection issues make them particularly challenging. Yet there are numerous examples across many countries of the varied ways in which governments, civil society actors, communities and children themselves have helped prevent and respond to violence, abuse and exploitation. For children's rights to be systematically respected, child protection responses have to be holistic, recognise the duties of all people at all levels, and be applied to all children in all circumstances without discrimination. While there is no legal definition of what constitutes a protective environment, it should address at least the following elements:

*a) Governmental commitment to fulfilling protection rights*

Government interest in, recognition of and commitment to child protection is an essential element for a protective environment. This includes ensuring that adequate resources are made available for child protection, for example, for programmes to combat child labour. It also includes political leaders being pro-active in raising protection on the agenda and acting as advocates for protection.

*b) Attitudes, traditions, customs, behaviour and practices*

In societies where attitudes or traditions facilitate abuse – for example, regarding sex with minors, the appropriateness of severe corporal punishment, the application of harmful traditional practices or differences in the perceived status and value of boys and girls – the environment will not be protective. In societies where all forms of violence against children are taboo, and where the rights of children are broadly respected by custom and tradition, children are more likely to be protected.

*c) Open discussion of, and engagement with, child protection issues*

At the most basic level, children need to be free to speak about child protection concerns affecting them or other children. At the national level, both media attention and civil society engagement will be vital to child protection efforts. Partnerships among actors at all levels are essential for an effective and co-ordinated response.

*d) Legislation and enforcement*

An adequate legislative framework, consistent implementation, accountability and a lack of impunity are essential elements of a protective environment.

*e) Capacity*

Parents, health workers, teachers, police, social workers and many others who care for and live, deal and work with children need to be provided with the necessary skills, knowledge and authority, and have the motivation to identify and respond to child protection problems. There are other broader types of capacity that relate to the protective environment, including the provision of education and safe areas for play.

*f) Children's life skills, knowledge and participation*

If children are unaware of their right not to be abused, or are not warned of the dangers of, for example, trafficking, they are more vulnerable to abuse. Children need information and knowledge, commensurate with their evolving capacities, to be equipped to protect themselves. Children also need to be provided with safe and protective channels for participation and self-expression. Where children have no opportunities for participation and feel excluded, they are more likely to become involved in crime or other negative behaviours.

*g) Monitoring and reporting*

A protective environment for children requires an effective monitoring system that records the incidence and nature of child protection abuses and allows for informed and strategic responses. Such systems can be more effective where they are participatory and locally owned. It is a responsibility of government to make sure that every country knows the situation of its children with regard to violence, abuse and exploitation.

*h) Services for recovery and reintegration*

Child victims of any form of neglect, exploitation or abuse are entitled to care and non-discriminatory access to basic social services. These services must be provided in an environment that fosters the health, self-respect and dignity of the child.

There are a number of ways to build a protective environment for children. These include:

- Addressing and mitigating the impact of economic and social poverty.
- National advocacy and initiating dialogue at all levels, from government down to communities, families and children themselves.
- Seeking societal behaviour change, challenging attitudes and traditions that can underpin child protection abuses and supporting those that are protective. This might involve national campaigns or working closely with the media.
- Strengthening capacity to assess and analyse protection issues. Without knowing what is happening, governments and other actors will be disadvantaged in responding to protection problems.
- Putting mechanisms in place and providing resources so that those caring for and living and working with children have the skills and knowledge to do so in a way that ensures their protection through education and training.
- Recognising that legal standards are particularly important to child protection, and that they need to be known, understood, accepted and enforced. This can involve legislative reviews, revision of laws or even the creation of new laws. It also involves scrutiny of the actual practices of those governed by the laws to ensure that they are respected.
- Developing and reviewing national monitoring systems to ensure that they properly cover child protection issues. In particular, this may involve disaggregation of national statistics to ensure that patterns of discrimination become apparent.

- Ensuring access to services for recovery and reintegration for children who have suffered abuses.
- Promoting child participation and strengthening children's own resilience.

At the same time, it is not effective to address protection as a separate and stand-alone issue. Given the relationships between child protection and other areas, it is valuable to consider the protection aspects of any issue being considered. For example:

- When considering education policy, it is necessary to consider safety and security in schools and to discourage the use of corporal punishment. This might include initiatives to address violence among children in schools, such as bullying.
- When considering the care practices of family and early childhood, parents should be discouraged from using violent forms of discipline and encouraged to ensure that their child's birth is registered.
- Any consideration of HIV/AIDS is incomplete without considering the stigma often attached to children affected by HIV/AIDS, as well as the increased protection risks faced by vulnerable children who have been orphaned by AIDS. Thus, an appropriate response to child protection involves understanding it both as an issue in its own right and as a consideration with regard to other issues. It also requires that every actor plays his or her part in ensuring a protective environment for children.

## A Review of the Legal Framework

In reaffirming the language of the United Nations Charter, the United Nations Convention on the Rights of the Child (the 'Convention') is clearly stating that the protection of the dignity and worth of the human person applies to all, including persons under 18 years.

> … the peoples of the United Nations have, in the Charter, reaffirmed their faith in fundamental human rights and in the dignity and worth of the human person, and have determined to promote social progress and better standards of life in larger freedom.[2]

When the UN Charter spoke of social progress in 'larger freedom', not only did this include the basic political freedoms to which all human beings are entitled, but it went beyond to encompass what President Franklin Roosevelt called 'freedom from want' and 'freedom from fear.'[3] Nowhere are these considerations more pertinent for human development than in relation to children and the aspirations that they embody for the future.

Former UN Secretary-General Kofi Annan developed the notion highlighting the interdependent nature of security, development and human rights for achieving larger freedom. As he stated, 'we will not enjoy development without security, we will not enjoy security without development, and we will not enjoy either without respect for human rights'.[4] Freedom from fear was linked to a vision of collective security. This notion provides a clear call and broad agenda for a vision of security that protects the security of all individuals, as well as that of the state.

As mentioned previously, children share basic human rights with all other persons and this section will explore some of the key instruments that apply to children, beyond of provisions of the Convention. The legal framework for the protection of children from abuse and exploitation is detailed in various instruments that differ in the nature of their obligations. Treaties, such as conventions or covenants, are formal legal texts to which states become parties. They are considered as 'hard law', and create legal binding obligations. Other instruments, such as declarations, principles or rules, are non-binding on states, and are often referred to as 'soft law'. However, their provisions are often more detailed than those found in treaties, and as such complement hard law. These instruments represent authoritative standards as states have participated in their elaboration and as such they reflect an international consensus on protection issues related to children.[5]

In addition, regional instruments can be particularly useful, especially where their provisions provide a stronger protection regime for children, examples being the African Charter on Human and Peoples' Rights, the African Charter on the Rights and Welfare of the Child, the European Convention for the Protection of Human Rights and Fundamental Freedoms, the American Convention on Human Rights, and the Arab Charter on Human Rights.

In ratifying treaties, states make a commitment to integrate all provisions into national law. This in turn defines intervention procedures for national and local authorities, including complaint or representation procedures, investigative measures, referral mechanisms, rehabilitation and follow-up, and educational measures required.

As already stressed, if law enforcement responses are not accompanied by respect for human rights they risk endangering child victims. In order to respond appropriately, relevant security sector actors must be informed on all aspects of child protection. They require knowledge and understanding of child rights and specific needs, and need to be familiar with referral procedures to organisations providing assistance and services to child victims. International instruments underline the obligation of states to train their law enforcement officials in both the prevention of child abuse, as well as in human rights and child-sensitive issues.

Children may come into contact with the formal criminal justice system on a number of levels. While the police are likely to be the first point of contact, this may involve a range of other local law enforcement and justice actors, all of who have an obligation to protect and promote the rights of the child at all times, as well as reinforce the child's respect for the human rights and fundamental freedoms of others. Children may appear in the justice system as child offenders ('children in conflict with the law'), or as child victims of crime or abuse. Whether children are offenders or victims they hold the same basic human rights as adults, and have additional rights as children.

In addition however, it is vitally important that law enforcement officials remember that the children they encounter may also be witnesses of crime. In order to address the special protections needs of child witnesses and child victims, both in terms of procedures and safeguards, the United Nations has developed the United Nations Guidelines on Justice in Matters involving Child Witnesses and Victims of Crime (2005).

For child victims, the Guidelines stress that 'professionals should develop and implement comprehensive and specially tailored strategies and interventions in cases where there are risks that child victims may be victimised further'.[6] Such strategies may be based on government, local authority or civil society initiatives. The Guidelines place great emphasis on training, education and information of professionals working with child victims and witnesses, including those from the security sector, and stipulate in detail the elements of such training. A multidisciplinary and co-operative approach between professionals and institutions is essential to help familiarise children with the array of services that should be available, such as victim support, economic assistance, counselling, education, health, legal and social services.

**Box 4.1 Guidelines on Justice in Matters involving Child Victims and Witnesses of Crime**[7]

Training, education and information should include:

- Relevant human rights norms, standards and principles, including the rights of the child
- Principles and ethical duties of their office
- Signs and symptoms that indicate crimes against children
- Crisis assessment skills and techniques, especially for making referrals, with an emphasis placed on the need for confidentiality
- Impact, consequences, including negative physical and psychological effects, and trauma of crimes against children
- Special measures and techniques to assist child victims and witnesses in the justice process
- Cross-cultural and age-related linguistic, religious, social and gender issues
- Appropriate adult-child communication skills
- Interviewing and assessment techniques that minimise any trauma to the child while maximising the quality of information received from the child
- Skills to deal with child victims and witnesses in a sensitive, understanding, constructing and reassuring manner
- Methods to protect and present evidence and to question child witnesses
- Roles of, and methods used by, professionals working with child victims and witnesses

The remainder of this section will look more specifically at instruments that relate to children and that complement the Convention on the Rights of the Child (the 'Convention'). Due to the direct implications to the activities of the security sector, special attention is paid to children in conflict with the law, and provisions aimed at identifying and responding for child victims will be considered under two areas of intervention that address violence against children and contemporary forms of slavery.

### *Children in Conflict with the Law*

The term 'children in conflict with the law' refers to anyone under 18 who comes into contact with the justice system as a result of being suspected or accused of committing an offence.[8] Many of these children will have only committed petty crimes or minor offences such as vagrancy, truancy, begging or alcohol use (status offences, that would normally not be considered criminal when committed by adults), but their experiences of the justice system could have long-term and profound effects on their future lives and their interactions with the law.

Recognising the special protection needs of children, the administration of juvenile justice and the prevention of juvenile delinquency are subject to the provisions of a comprehensive set of international instruments consisting of human rights guarantees that are applicable to all persons, and a series of child-focussed norms and standards. The reference point for the latter is the Convention along with three 'soft law' instruments, namely the United Nations Standard Minimum Rules for the Administration of Juvenile Justice ('Beijing Rules')[9], the United Nations Guidelines for the Prevention of Juvenile Delinquency ('Riyadh Guidelines')[10], and the United Nations Rules for the Protection of Juveniles Deprived of their Liberty[11].

Each of these instruments, in particular the Riyadh Guidelines, aims to provide guidance on policies to prevent children from coming into contact with the formal legal system, preferring alternative interventions involving families, schools and communities. They call for the adoption of a child-oriented juvenile justice system, which recognises the child as a subject of fundamental rights and freedoms, and stress the need for all actions concerning children to be guided by the best interests of the child as a primary consideration. The ultimate aim is to encourage a process of behavioural change to promote the child's successful reintegration and constructive role in society. The Beijing Rules envisage this system as being an integral part of the national development process of each country, within a comprehensive framework of social justice for all juveniles (Rule 1.4).

As such, diversion away from formal judicial proceedings is encouraged for all but the most serious offences and, in particular, when dealing with first time offenders. Such alternatives aim to avoid institutionalisation of children and may include care, guidance and supervision orders, counselling, probation, foster care, education or vocational training, restitution, and compensation of victims. However, it is important not to overlook the fact that these alternative solutions also need to provide legal safeguards and protect the rights of the children involved.

Institutionalisation of children is generally associated with negative outcomes and, as such, detention or imprisonment should only be used as a measure of the last resort and be for the shortest appropriate period of time possible.[12] One of the major concerns associated with depriving children of their liberty is that in such circumstances they are often more susceptible than adults to abuse and violation of their rights. Abuses of this principle tend to be most prevalent in the context of pre-trial detention.

A core element of the juvenile justice system is the establishment of a minimum age of criminal responsibility (the age below which a child cannot be held responsible in a penal law procedure). Aware that in some countries the minimum age has been set as low as seven years, the Committee on the Rights of the Child has concluded that a minimum age below 12 years is not reasonable, and at the same time has called for states to aspire to an age limit even higher than 12 years.[13]

Administration of the juvenile justice system directly implicates a number of actors within the formal security sector, including police, law enforcement officials, judges and magistrates, prosecutors, lawyers and administrators, prison officers, and other professionals working in institutions where children are deprived of their liberty. Interestingly, international instruments not only highlight that law enforcement officials working with children should be specifically trained, but also that they be personally suited to the role.[14]

The Convention and other instruments protect children against abuse and ill treatment. This is particularly relevant for children deprived of their liberty, where an important consideration is that of the 'duty of care'. While in custody, juveniles should receive all necessary protection and individual assistance appropriate to their age, sex and personality, whether social, educational, vocational, psychological, medical or physical. Personnel of detention facilities should ensure the full protection of the physical and mental health of juveniles, including protection from physical, sexual and emotional abuse and exploitation, and should take immediate action to secure medical attention whenever required.[15]

In addition, there is an absolute prohibition against torture, cruel, inhuman or degrading treatment or punishment under any circumstances, including prohibition of corporal punishment, whether imposed as punishment for an offence or as an educative or disciplinary measure.[16] Disciplinary procedures should respect the child's dignity and be designed to instil in the child a sense of justice, self-respect and respect for human rights.[17] Any use of physical restrains and force on children should be exceptional, employed only when all other control measures have been exhausted, and should be employed for the shortest period of time. Disciplinary measures that are prohibited for juveniles include inter alia closed or solitary confinement, reduction of diet, restriction or denial of contact with family members, and a requirement to work.[18] International law also puts firm restrictions on penal sanctions for children. They shall never be subjected to capital punishment or to life imprisonment without chance of release for offences committed below 18 years of age.[19]

Accountability measures in the juvenile justice system are essential for ensuring proper implementation of procedures and safeguards within the system, including the responsibility of the personnel of detention facilities to report suspected cases of serious violations of child rights.

*Domestic and Institutional Violence*

> States Parties shall take all appropriate legislative, administrative, social and educational measures to protect the child from all forms of physical or mental violence, injury or abuse, neglect or negligent treatment, maltreatment or exploitation, including sexual abuse, while in the care of parent(s), legal guardian(s) or any other person who has the care of the child. (Convention, Article 19).

Police are in a position of special responsibility regarding the response to violence, as they are generally the first to be called and to intervene at a scene. If concerns about the safety of a child are identified, Emergency Protection Orders may be obtained to protect children from violence, but it is also worth noting that in many jurisdictions the police are the only body entitled to remove a child from its immediate carers for its protection without prior recourse to judicial procedure.

It is the duty of governments to protect children from abuse and neglect, including abuse happening within the family, as well as other caring environments, such as foster care, day care, schools and institutions. This duty takes on added significance when not respected, as it often deprives the child of access to help, and the mistreatment or abuse may then continue undetected for long periods of time.

Parents and legal guardians bear the primary responsibility for the upbringing and development of children. States in turn are responsible for ensuring that children's rights are realised, and as such for the development of institutions, facilities and services for the care of children.[20] Programmes to address violence against children will require multidisciplinary approaches, and broad consideration of the following elements: procedures for prevention, identification, reporting, referral, investigation, treatment and follow-up of instances of child maltreatment; and, as appropriate for judicial involvement.[21] Prevention is crucial, and covers not only parents' education and support to parenting but also development of family planning services, establishment of health care systems capable of providing regular checks for every pre-school child and providing special support to vulnerable families.

Traditionally, the privacy of a family was considered sacrosanct and intervention on the part of state institutions was minimal. However, since the early 1990s there has been a growing awareness and acknowledgement of the existence of child abuse, including within the family, and international law has increasingly called on states to ensure that parental power is not abused and that parental responsibilities are exercised properly. However, securing children's rights at the family level still represents a significant challenge requiring a balance between the rights of the child, the rights and responsibilities of parents or other caregivers, and the obligations of the state.

A key responsibility of the state is to ensure that systems for the monitoring, reporting and investigation of ill treatment of children exist, and that they are able to identify children at risk and provide appropriate services to reduce those risks. The accountability of persons within the public sector who occupy positions of responsibility for the protection of children must be required to account for any failure to protect vulnerable children from deliberate harm or exploitation.[22]

Such system should involve all sectors of society, including policy-makers, health professionals, teachers, legal professionals, law enforcement officials, mass media, civil society, religious and community leaders, parents and children themselves. Meaningful child participation is crucial, in particular assessing children's views and perceptions of their experience, rather than focussing only on the material circumstances of the families.

Having said this, physical assault against a child constitutes child abuse. In this sense, punitive corporal punishment, whether in the family or in institutions, is incompatible with the child's right to physical integrity. Regarding corporal punishment in schools, the Convention states that all appropriate measures shall be taken 'to ensure that school discipline is administered in a manner consistent with the child's human dignity …'.[23]

Also, a range of traditional practices may need to be reviewed to determine whether they involve any form of physical or mental violence. When these traditional practices are beneficial, or harmless, they are a way of maintaining a community's identity and preserving its culture. However, some traditional practices are harmful to health, well-being and development; most often, girls and women are affected including by practices such as female genital mutilation and early childhood marriage. These practices are internationally condemned due to the grave health risks they may entail as well as the human rights principles they violate.

Disabled children may be particularly vulnerable to abuse due to difficulties in communication, and the fact that many of them are abandoned to placement in institutions. The UN Standard Rules on the Equalisation of Opportunities of 1994 noted that persons with disabilities are particularly vulnerable to abuse in the family, community and institutions.

In all cases of abuse, neglect and exploitation, Article 39 of the Convention notes that the state has an obligation to ensure that child victims (of armed conflicts, torture, neglect, maltreatment or exploitation) receive appropriate treatment for their physical and psychological recovery and social reintegration in an environment that fosters the health, self-respect and dignity of the child victim.

The death or serious injury of any child should result in rigorous routine investigation, the standard of investigation of offences against children being as rigorous as those for similar crimes against adults.

*Addressing Contemporary Forms of Slavery*

The Universal Declaration of Human Rights and the International Covenant on Civil and Political Rights include provisions prohibiting slavery.[24] The Supplementary Convention on the Abolition of Slavery, the Slave Trade, and the Institutions and Practices Similar to Slavery (1956, article 1), covers, 'any institution or practice whereby a child or young person under the age of 18 years is delivered by either or both of his natural parents or by his guardian to another person, whether for reward or not, with a view to the exploitation of the child or young person or of his labour.'

Included among the abuses that constitute contemporary forms of slavery are exploitative child labour, the sale of children, child prostitution and child pornography, and the trafficking in persons (also included is the recruitment of children into armed service, which will be considered in more detail in part three of this publication).[25] One of the features of these slavery-like practices is that they tend to be clandestine in their nature and as such notoriously difficult to monitor. For criminal gangs operating outside of the law, these gross abuses of child rights simply represent lucrative activity that often ends up merging with other criminal activity that they are involved with, such as the drugs trade. The reach of organised crime means that both victims and witnesses are often reluctant to come forward or pursue prosecutions. Intimidation may stretch to establishing influence over the local authorities who are ostensibly charged with maintaining order and providing public security. The resources at the disposal of these criminal gangs also mean that if a particular activity becomes compromised, they simply move on to some other exploitative activity.

One of the most pernicious features of these modern forms of slavery is that the victims tend to be targeted from what are essentially already the most deprived segments of society. The victims of such exploitation are also likely to experience multiple abuses, there being no distinction between crimes and victims in the criminal netherworld that exists beyond the state.

This section expands on the implications of contemporary slavery for children and the legal framework that exists to protect them.

*a) Exploitative child labour*

Many children around the world perform work-like activities and, within certain limits and with safeguards, this can contribute to their development and be a constructive, even educational, experience. However, a distinction needs to be made between child work that may be beneficial to the child, and the worst forms of child labour that impact negatively on the child's well-being and health. The reality is that millions of children are being exploited for their labour, either inadequately recompensed or forced to work in unacceptable or dangerous conditions.

**Box 4.2 The Challenge of Child Labour**

- In 2004, 218 million children were believed to be engaged in child labour, excluding child domestic labour.
- Some 126 million children aged 5-17 are believed to be engaged in hazardous work.
- It is estimated that children represent 40-50 percent of all victims of forced labour, or 5.7 million children are trapped in forced and bonded labour.
- Children working in the home of a third party or 'employer' are extremely vulnerable to exploitation and abuse. ILO estimates that more girls under age 16 are in domestic service than in any other category of work or child labour.

Source: UNICEF Child Protection Information Sheet, http://www.unicef.org.

Exploitative child labour represents a step beyond acceptable limits and will impact negatively on children's healthy development, rob them of an education, and as such carry a long-term cost for society.

National labour laws should define a range of protective measures for children including minimum age for admissions to employment, appropriate regulation of the hours and conditions, and provide for appropriate penalties or other sanctions to ensure effective enforcement. In practice, however, many countries that have signed international conventions in respect of child labour simply do not have the structure and mechanisms for monitoring and enforcement.

International Labour Organization (ILO) Convention No. 29 (1930) on Forced Labour covers problems such as the exploitation of children through debt bondage and 'other contemporary forms of slavery', including child prostitution. The ILO Convention No. 138 (1973) on Minimum Age, upheld by the Committee on the Rights of the Child as an appropriate standard, provides principles that apply to all sectors of economic activity. Ratifying states are to fix a minimum age for admission to employment or work, undertake to pursue a national policy designed to ensure the effective abolition of child labour, and raise progressively the minimum age for admission to employment or work to a level suitable with the fullest physical and mental development of young persons.

In November 2000, ILO Convention No. 182 concerning the Prohibition and Immediate Action for the Elimination of the Worst Forms of Child Labour entered into force. It applies to all young persons under the age of 18, and defines the worst forms of child labour including child slavery, child prostitution or pornography, the use of a child in illicit activities, and work which is likely to harm the health or safety of a child. Regarding this last category, the types of work referred to 'shall be determined by national laws or regulations or by the competent authority, after consultation with the organisations of employers and workers concerned'.[26] ILO Recommendation No. 190 concerning the prohibition and immediate action for the elimination of the worst forms of child labour contains a listing of types of work that should be considered when determining at the country level what constitutes hazardous work.

*b) Sale of children, child pornography and child prostitution*

The exploitation of children includes practices such as the sale of children for sexual purposes, child prostitution and pornography. In some instances the term commercial sexual exploitation of children has been used to underline its commercial characteristic.[27] These forms of exploitation often overlap and are combined with other abuses such as forced labour or human trafficking. The child vulnerable to, or experiencing, one form of abuse is likely susceptible to others. With the widespread practice of sex tourism, availability of child pornography on the internet and increasing international trafficking of children, an Optional Protocol to the Convention on the Rights of the Child on the Sale of Children, Child Prostitution and Child Pornography (the 'Optional Protocol' for the remainder of this chapter) was adopted in 2000 to extend the measures that States Parties should undertake in order to guarantee the protection of the child.[28]

The Optional Protocol prohibits the sale of children, child prostitution and pornography. It specifies a series of acts and activities that States Parties must ensure are covered in criminal or penal law, whether offences are committed domestically or transnationally, or on an individual or organised basis. The Optional Protocol calls on the state to make such offences punishable by appropriate penalties that take into account their grave nature.[29] This is an important provision as crimes pertaining to the sale of children, child pornography and prostitution have often been associated with impunity and a perception that the justice system is ineffective, corrupt or insensitive to children's concerns.[30] It stresses the importance of international co-operation to apply the principle of extraterritoriality, i.e. that nationals of a State Party, committing a sexual offence against children in another country, can be prosecuted in their own country.

The **sale of children** is defined as 'any act or transaction whereby a child is transferred by any person or group of persons to another for remuneration or any other consideration'.[31] This thereby obliges states to criminalise the offering, delivering or accepting of a child for the purpose of sexual exploitation, transfer of organs or forced labour, as well as improperly inducing consent for adoption. **Child prostitution** means 'the use of a child in sexual activities for remuneration or any other form of consideration'[32] and that the offering, obtaining, procuring or providing of a child for prostitution should be criminalised. **Child pornography** means 'any representation, by whatever means, of a child engaged in real or simulated explicit sexual activities or any representation of sexual parts of a child for primarily sexual purposes'.[33] Here, States Parties are obliged to criminalise a wide range of acts, including producing, distributing, disseminating, importing, exporting, offering, selling or possessing child pornography.

Age again becomes an important issue in relation to the protection of a child from prostitution and pornography in terms of the age of consent to sexual activity. While the Convention on the Rights of the Child (the 'Convention') and the Protocol protect all children under the age of 18, national legislation sometimes provides for lesser protection to children above the age of consent, even if they are legally protected against forced and remunerated activities. As mentioned earlier in this publication, the issue of a lower age of consent should not affect the child's access to the support they require, as they continue to benefit from the protection of the Convention and the Optional Protocol up to the age of 18. In the same vein, the Special Rapporteur on the sale of children, child prostitution and child pornography has recommended that a child under 18 should not be considered as able to consent to engagement in pornography, prostitution or trafficking.[34]

The Optional Protocol stipulates in detail the rights of child victims of sexual exploitation during the criminal justice process. These provisions have a direct relevance to the security sector, including police, judges, court staff, prosecutors, prison guards, child welfare staff and all others who, within the context of their work, are in contact with child victims of sexual exploitation, or who are responsible for addressing the needs of children within the criminal justice system. The provisions include obligations for the protection of child victims, similar to the general protective measures of child victims of crime, such as: an obligation to adapt procedures to reflect the special needs of children; to protect the privacy, identity and safety of the child; to properly inform child victims at all stages of the process; to avoid unnecessary delays; and to provide appropriate support services to child victims. Insensitive handling by indifferent or untrained police officers can give rise to secondary or multiple victimisation of the child.

While considering the first reports of States Parties on the implementation of the Optional Protocol, the Committee on the Rights of the Child referred on several occasions to the Guidelines on Justice in Matters involving Child Victims and Witnesses of Crime[35], and recommended to states that they use these Guidelines in implementing the Optional Protocol.[36]

The security sector is a key duty-bearer in terms of both prevention and protection of child victims of such exploitation. As observed by the Special Rapporteur, 'the child's first impression in the hands of police sets the tone of trust or mistrust, co-operation or withdrawal, and a feeling of security and elation that at least somebody cares or a feeling of bewilderment and despair that the ultimate recourse under the rule of law is not made available to them'.[37] This has led to the recommendation that the justice system strengthen its victim focus when dealing with cases of sexual exploitation. The Committee on the Rights of the Child has also stressed a non-punitive approach to victims.[38] According to the Convention and the Optional Protocol, child victims of sexual exploitation should be protected from reprisals and be provided with support and rehabilitation 'to promote their physical and psychological recovery and social reintegration'.[39] Child-friendly and child-sensitive procedures should be applied by all actors, including the security sector, in order to fulfil this obligation.

*c) Trafficking in persons*

Population movement in general represents one of the major challenges for the security sector, in particular illegal migration. Trafficking and smuggling activities have both become widely associated with economic migration and, as such, big business for the criminal elements involved. One of the challenges for the security sector is differentiating between economic migration and the smuggling/trafficking of adults and adolescents above the minimum working age. In addition, for younger children there can be considerable difficulties associated with even detecting their illegal movement across borders. Not only do such illegal movements present major challenges but the very efforts to address or combat them risk infringing (or at minimum compromising) the basic human rights of innocent individuals – the implications for asylum seekers being particularly acute.

In 1998, the UN General Assembly established an Ad Hoc Committee, open to all states, for the purpose of elaborating an international convention against transnational organised crime. The resulting United Nations Convention against Transnational Organised Crime was adopted by the General Assembly at its Millennium meeting in November 2000. Also, two protocols were adopted detailing measures to be taken by countries to combat smuggling of migrants and the trafficking of women and children for exploitation.

Trafficking in persons is defined in the Protocol to Prevent, Suppress and Punish Trafficking in Persons, Especially Women and Children, supplementing the United Nations Convention against Transnational Organised Crime (2000),[40] including a specific reference to clarify that, for children, an act of trafficking is not dependent on the use of force or coercion. The Protocol details measures as to how countries can improve co-operation on such matters as extradition, mutual legal assistance, transfer of proceedings, and joint investigations. Parties to the treaty would also provide technical assistance to developing countries to help them take the necessary measures and upgrade their capacities for dealing with organised crime.

While the Convention against Transnational Organised Crime also has a supplementary Protocol against the Smuggling of Migrants by Land, Sea and Air, in regard to children the very act of recruitment, transportation, transfer, harbouring or receipt of a child makes the offence one of trafficking.

It is also worth noting that the Rome Statute of the International Criminal Court recognises human trafficking as a crime against humanity, and a war crime in certain circumstances. ILO Convention 182 on the Worst Forms of Child Labour[41] includes trafficking in children as a form of slavery or practice similar to slavery.

**Box 4.3 Protocol to Prevent, Suppress and Punish Trafficking in Persons, Especially Women and Children (Article 3)**

Use of terms for the purposes of this Protocol:

- 'Trafficking in persons' shall mean the recruitment, transportation, transfer, harbouring or receipt of persons, by means of the threat or use of force or other forms of coercion, of abduction, of fraud, of deception, of the abuse of power or of a position of vulnerability or of the giving or receiving of payments or benefits to achieve the consent of a person having control over another person, for the purpose of exploitation. Exploitation shall include, at a minimum, the exploitation of the prostitution of others or other forms of sexual exploitation, forced labour or services, slavery or practices similar to slavery, servitude or the removal of organs.
- The consent of a victim of trafficking in persons to the intended exploitation shall be irrelevant.
- The recruitment, transportation, transfer, harbouring or receipt of a child for the purpose of exploitation shall be considered 'trafficking in persons'.
- 'Child' shall mean any person under eighteen years of age.

The Convention on the Rights of the Child (the 'Convention') calls for children to be protected from all forms of exploitation.[42] Concerning trafficking, States Parties are obliged to take all appropriate national, bilateral and multilateral measures to prevent trafficking in children for any purposes, or in any form.[43]

Human rights law focusses on the rights of victims of trafficking, stressing that child victims of trafficking are entitled to special protection and assistance, and that anti-trafficking measures should not adversely affect the human rights and dignity of the victims involved. As such, victims should never be subjected to criminal prosecution or sanctions for offences related to their situation as trafficked children. For example, girls who are trafficked into the sex industry should not be penalised on charges of prostitution, illegal stay or use of false visas, as happens in many countries.[44] Promoting their physical, psychological and social recovery will require consideration of appropriate housing, counselling and information, access to health care, psychological support, legal assistance as well as educational opportunities. These provisions should apply to all victims of trafficking regardless of whether they were trafficked internally or across borders, or whether a criminal group or individual were responsible.

States Parties to human rights treaties must ensure that national legislation, as well as its application, is in accordance with applicable international law. This obligation should be reflected in anti-trafficking laws and other legislation relevant to the issue. In particular, States Parties should provide or strengthen training for law enforcement, immigration and other relevant officials in the prevention of trafficking in persons. The training should focus on methods used in preventing trafficking, prosecuting the traffickers and protecting the rights of the victims (including protecting the victims from the traffickers). The training should also consider human rights and child and gender issues, and encourage co-operation with non-governmental organisations and other elements of civil society.[45]

The Recommended Principles and Guidelines on Human Rights and Human Trafficking[46] (henceforth the 'Trafficking Guidelines') elaborated by the Office of the High Commissioner for Human Rights, provide more detailed guidance on the prevention of trafficking and the protection of its victims. Whilst the Trafficking Guidelines are not legally binding they contain important standards with respect of victims of trafficking, including children. Because of the increased vulnerability to exploitation of trafficked children, they require that children are dealt with separately from adult trafficked persons in terms of policies, programmes and interventions.

A key provision of the Trafficking Guidelines is the need for the rapid identification of child victims. This is particularly relevant for security sector actors such as border guards, police or immigration officials involved in the detection, reception and processing of irregular migrants. Identification of a child as a victim of trafficking, and not as an illegal migrant, lowers the risk of child's immediate expulsion, retaliation or re-trafficking. A failure to identify a trafficked child correctly is likely to result in a further denial of that child's rights and lead to his or her abuse and exploitation. Where there are reasonable grounds to believe that he or she may be a victim of trafficking, it is important that the child receive appropriate assistance. Verifying an individual's age can be particularly difficult but, for example, the Council of Europe Convention against Trafficking in Human Beings[47] requires States Parties to presume that a victim is a child if there are reasons for believing that to be so. The importance of pro-active identification measures cannot be underestimated, including co-ordinated information sharing between agencies. For example, social services, labour inspectors, and health and education authorities should contact the relevant law enforcement authorities where there is knowledge or suspicion that a child is or has been exploited or trafficked, or is at risk of exploitation and trafficking.[48]

Security sector actors will also be involved in the identification and implementation of durable solutions for a child victim of trafficking. They should co-operate with the child's guardian, social services and other partners in order to determine the solution most adapted to the child and his or her situation, and which is in the best interests of a child. Such solutions may be voluntary return to the country of origin, local integration or resettlement to a third country. If the child was not accompanied by parents or relatives, one of the most complex activities in such instances will be the identification of the family and reunification, if appropriate. Whatever solution is identified as the most suitable, an individual integration plan should always be elaborated for each child.[49]

## Conclusion

As a major element of building a protective environment for children, the security sector holds a key role in terms of its responsibility for ensuring that children have a secure environment. Not only does the security sector have a central function to fulfil in reducing or removing threats to children's healthy development, but it is also importantly placed to promote actions that strengthen the protective factors around children.

In reviewing the legal framework established in international law, this chapter has outlined some of the standards that exist to guide the security sector in terms of defining policies and actions aimed at protecting and promoting the rights of the child. Understanding these responsibilities is as much about assessing the systems requirements that will ensure the protection of children as it is the identification of specific threats. Recognition of these systems requirements should be an integral part of security sector reform activities.

Associated with the various elements of a protective environment is a series of responses that relate to the actions of a range of security sector actors, and are applicable regardless of the threat facing children. These responses can be considered under the following six broad categories, and assessment of each is a helpful basis for guiding policy formulation and planning when responding to child protection concerns.

- Develop preventive strategies to stop the occurrence of the abuse in the first place.
- Put in place pro-active detection and identification measures including opportunities for children to seek direct help.
- Provide appropriate protection and assistance services for victims and witnesses, and for child offenders.

- Implement durable solutions that enable children to successfully reintegrate into society.
- Address impunity by ensuring that perpetrators are prosecuted.
- Establish robust monitoring and reporting mechanisms.

## Endnotes

1 Adapted from Inter-Parliamentary Union (IPU) and UNICEF, *Child Protection: A Handbook for Parliamentarians* (Switzerland: IPU and UNICEF, 2004). See also UNICEF Child Protection Strategy, UNICEF Executive Board Annual Session 2008, UN doc. E/ICEF/2008/5/Rev.1 (New York: June 2008).

2 United Nations Convention on the Rights of the Child, Preamble (November 1989), http://untreaty.un.org/English/TreatyEvent2001/pdf/03e.pdf (accessed October 2008).

3 Kofi A. Annan, 'In Larger Freedom: Decision Time at the UN' *Foreign Affairs* (May/June 2005), http://www.foreignaffairs.org/20050501faessay84307/kofi-annan/in-larger-freedom-decision-time-at-the-un.html (accessed October 2008).

4 UN General Assembly, *In larger freedom: towards development, security and human rights for all*, Report of the Secretary-General, UN Doc. A/59/2005 (New York: March 2005).

5 United Nations High Commissioner for Refugees (UNHCR)/International Save the Children Alliance, Action for the Rights of Children (ARC), 'Resource Pack on Abuse and Exploitation' (2001), http://www. savethechildren.net/arc/files/main.html (accessed October 2008).

6 UN Economic and Social Council, Guidelines on Justice in Matters involving Child Victims and Witnesses of Crime, Resolution 2005/20, Note 8 (July 2005).

7 Ibid.

8 UNICEF, 'Child Protection Information Sheet: Children in Conflict with the Law' (May 2006), http://www.unicef.org/protection/files/Conflict_with_the_Law.pdf (accessed October 2008).

9 UN General Assembly, *UN Standard Minimum Rules for the Administration of Juvenile Justice* ('The Beijing Rules'), adopted by Resolution 33, UN doc. 40/33 of 29 November 1985.

10 UN General Assembly, *UN Guidelines for the Prevention of Juvenile Delinquency*, Resolution 112, UN doc. 45/112 (New York: December 1990).

11 UN General Assembly, *UN Rules for the Protection of Juveniles Deprived of their Liberty*, adopted by General Assembly, Resolution 113, UN doc. 45/113 (December 1990).

12 UN Convention on the Rights of the Child, Article 37(b).

13 Committee on the Rights of the Child, Children's Rights in Juvenile Justice, General Comment No. 10, UN doc. CRC/C/GC/10 (February 2007).

14 UN Standard Minimum Rules for the Administration of Juvenile Justice; UN Rules for the Protection of Juveniles Deprived of their Liberty.

15 Ibid.

16 UN Convention on the Rights of the Child, Article 37(a); International Covenant on Civil and Political Rights (ICCPR), Article 7 (1996); UN Convention against Torture and Other Cruel, Inhuman or Degrading Treatment or Punishment, Article 2 (1984); African Charter

on Human and Peoples' Rights (1981); Council of Europe, Convention for the Protection of Human Rights and Fundamental Freedoms as amended by Protocol No. 11, Article 3 (1950).

17 UN Rules for the Protection of Juveniles Deprived of their Liberty, Rule 66.

18 UN Rules for the Protection of Juveniles Deprived of their Liberty.

19 UN Convention on the Rights of the Child, Article 37(a); ICCPR Article 6(5); ACHR, Article 4(5).

20 UN Convention on the Rights of Child, Article 18(2).

21 UN Convention on the Rights of Child, Article 19(2).

22 For example, The Victoria Climbié Inquiry (presented to the UK Parliament, 2003) into the 'individual, collective and institutional failures in the system' in preventing the murder of 8-year-old Victoria, caused by severe domestic violence, suggested that the 'single most important change in the future must be the drawing of a clear line of accountability, from top to bottom, without doubt or ambiguity about who is responsible at every level for the well-being of vulnerable children', http://www.victoria-climbie-inquiry.org.uk/finreport/finreport.htm (accessed October 2008).

23 UN Convention on the Rights of the Child, Article 28(2).

24 Universal Declaration of Human Rights, Article 4 (December 1948); ICCPR, Article 8.

25 Office of the High Commissioner for Human Rights, 'Contemporary Forms of Slavery', Fact Sheet No. 14 (1991), http://www.ohchr.org/Documents/Publications/FactSheet14en.pdf (accessed October 2008).

26 International Labour Organisation (ILO) Convention No.182 concerning the Prohibition and Immediate Action for the Elimination of the Worst Forms of Child Labour (Geneva, 1999).

27 This is especially so since the First World Congress against the Commercial Sexual Exploitation (Stockholm, 1999). Its Declaration and Agenda for Action note that, 'The commercial sexual exploitation of children is a fundamental violation of children's rights. It comprises sexual abuse by the adult and remuneration in cash or kind to the child or a third person or persons. The child is treated as a sexual object and as a commercial object. The commercial sexual exploitation of children constitutes a form of coercion and violence against children, and amounts to forced labour and a contemporary form of slavery', http://www.csecworldcongress.org/PDF/en/Stockholm/Outome_documents/Stockholm_Declaration_1996_EN.pdf (accessed October 2008).

28 Optional Protocol to the Convention on the Rights of the Child on the sale of children, child prostitution and child pornography (adopted and opened for signature, ratification and accession by General Assembly Resolution 263, UN doc. A/RES/54/263 (25 May 2000 entered into force on 18 January 2001).

29 Article 3(3) of the Optional Protocol.

30 See for example, UN Special Rapporteur on the sale of children, child prostitution and child pornography, UN doc. E/CN.4/1997/95 (February 1997), 22.

31 Article 2(a) of the Optional Protocol.

32 Article 2(b) of the Optional Protocol.

33 Article 2(c) of the Optional Protocol.

34 UN Special Rapporteur on the sale of children, child prostitution and child pornography.

35 UN Economic and Social Council, Guidelines on Justice in Matters involving Child Victims and Witnesses of Crime.

36 Committee on the Rights of the Child, Forty-first Session, CRC/C/OPSC/AND/CO/1, para. 19 (Geneva: March 2006).

37 UN Special Rapporteur on the sale of children, Note 11, 23.

38 Rachel Hodgkin and Peter Newel, *Implementation Handbook for the Convention on the Rights for the Child*, Note 12 (New York: UNICEF, 2002), 515.

39 UN Convention on the Rights of the Child, Article 39.

40 UN General Assembly, Protocol to Prevent, Suppress and Punish Trafficking in Persons, Especially Women and Children, supplementing the United Nations Convention against Transnational Organised Crime, Protocol adopted by Resolution A/RES/55/25 (15 November 2000, entered into force 25 December 2003).

41 ILO Convention No. 182 concerning the Prohibition and Immediate Action for the Elimination of the Worst Forms of Child Labour, Article 3.

42 UN Convention on the Rights of the Child, Article 32 on economic exploitation, Article 33 on the illicit use of narcotic drugs, Article 34 on sexual exploitation and abuse and Article 36 on all other forms of exploitation.

43 UN Convention on the Rights of the Child, Article 35.

44 UN Special Rapporteur on the sale of children, Note 5, para. 10.

45 UN General Assembly, Protocol to Prevent, Suppress and Punish Trafficking In Persons, Article 10(2).

46 Office of the High Commissioner for Human Rights, *Recommended Principles and Guidelines on Human Rights and Human Trafficking*, text presented to the Economic and Social Council as an addendum to the report of the UN High Commissioner for Human Rights, UN Doc. E/2002/68/Add.1 (20 May 2002).

47 Council of Europe, 'Convention on Action against Trafficking in Human Beings' *Council of Europe Treaty Series*, No. 197 (16 May 2005).

48 UNICEF, Guidelines for the Protection of the Rights of Children Victims of Trafficking in Southeastern Europe, para. 3.1.1 (Geneva: UNICEF Regional Office, 2003).

49 UNICEF, 'Reference Guide on Protecting the Rights of Child Victims of Trafficking in Europe', http://www.unicef.org/ceecis/UNICEF_Child_Trafficking_low.pdf (accessed October 2008).

# Part III

# The Security Sector and the Protection of Children's Rights

# Chapter 5

# Civil Society and the Security Sector

*Eden Cole and David Nosworthy*

## Introduction[1]

Not only is there a strong moral argument associated with the need for guaranteeing children's safety and security, there is an international legal framework that binds states to respecting the rights and dignity of each and every individual within society.

Unfortunately, states do not always live up to their obligations, and one of the challenges specifically related to children is that they do not have a political voice by which to express discontent and demand accountability. In effect, it falls to civil society organisations to provide this key oversight function by monitoring the situation of children and ensuring that state institutions live up to their responsibilities to provide appropriately and effectively for children's protection. What is particularly challenging in this context is the wide range of actors who will be required to collaborate in guaranteeing a protective environment for children, including their families, communities and local authorities. Child protection can no longer be seen as simply referring to social or welfare services, or health and education, but extends to a range of security and administrative actors who have a responsibility to protect, and who have, through their day-to-day activities, dealings that have a direct bearing on the lives of children.

Civil society organisations (CSOs) can also provide the important link between children and the relevant state bodies, acting as interlocutors in relation to representing the security concerns of children, and as intermediaries because of the key role that they often play in service delivery. CSOs are very often responsible for establishing or running the independent structures that provide contact points for young people seeking assistance, support or advice, whether in the form of telephone help-lines, youth clubs or other targeted programmes on behalf of children and youth.

They also have a major role to play in monitoring, reporting and insisting on the accountability of key duty-bearers.

The specific engagement of CSOs in the security policy domain contributes to accountability and the maintenance of good governance by their acting as government watchdogs and an index of public contentment with security sector activity. Actions such as monitoring government performance, policy, compliance with laws and upholding of human rights all contribute to this process. In addition, advocacy by civil society groups representing the interests of local communities and groups of like-minded individuals helps to give voice to often marginalised actors and opens up the policy process to a wider set of perspectives. In this way, CSOs have a vital role to play, not only in established democracies but also in post-conflict and undemocratic states, where the activities and inputs of CSOs can contribute to redefining the political decision-making process.

This chapter will explore the terms and concepts surrounding civil society and public oversight, and the roles that civil society can play in providing checks and balances that reflect child protection concerns in security governance and security sector reform (SSR).

## Civil Society and Public Oversight of the Security Sector

### *Defining Civil Society and Capacities*

While there is no commonly agreed single definition, civil society generally refers to the sphere of collective actions by citizens that develop around shared interests, purposes and values. The term is a materialisation of the way in which citizens associate in order to manage their lives, voice opinions, pursue interests, exchange information and mediate differences, creating patterns of relationships and social institutions that are as diverse as the people who establish them at local, national, regional and international levels.

Civil society is, therefore, the coming together of individuals to form a diversity of non-state actors and associations such as non-governmental organisations (NGOs), social groups and networks. Sometimes these groups may be motivated by specific interests or issues – they are not purely driven by private or economic interests as corporate entities are. They are autonomous and interact in the public sphere.

Although they are independent from the state, CSOs interact with the state and the political sphere. By helping to build trust among different social groups, encouraging dialogue between members of society and state institutions and governmental authorities, and representing the interests of local communities, many CSOs are recognised as improving the quality of civic life in their polity, as well as societal governance itself. CSOs are also engaged in the important tasks of monitoring government policies and actions, as well as advocacy.

A dynamic relationship between civil society, government and state agencies is based on a constant interest in transparency and accountability manifested in the principle of open government. Openness has a beneficial effect on governance in democracies. Interested citizens often do not seek access to information to which they have a right because they are unaware of its existence. Having a more engaged and informed citizenry enables fuller discussion of policy and policy alternatives. Introducing and engaging children and youth in this process is a vital step toward strengthening and promulgating the very notion of democracy. This is nowhere more relevant than in the local political arena where the issues relate directly to the experiences and realities of the populations day to day lives. A key role can be played by CSOs such as specialised NGOs, which can stimulate debate and focus public attention on policy issues. Active citizens and groups in civil society can also help to ensure that information about public issues and public policies is more fully disseminated and analysed, therefore providing more possibilities for participation in the deliberative process, not least through the use of local, national and international media to ensure maximum exposure.

NGOs and other civil society groupings need to be recognised as more than simply alternative welfare service providers and their key role in security matters needs to be acknowledged in policy development, planning and implementation. The importance of engaging civil society and accepting them as equal partners in democratic government is becoming increasingly recognised and promoted by the international community.

Adopting a rights-based approach can significantly strengthen communities' and civil societies' ability to hold governments accountable for the fulfilment of children's rights. In this regard the UN treaty body responsible for overseeing the implementation of the United Nations Convention on the Rights of the Child (the 'Convention') has 'systematically and strongly' encouraged NGOs to submit reports.

**Box 5.1 The UN Committee on the Rights of the Child – Participation of NGOs**

All States Parties are obliged to submit regular reports to the Committee on how the rights are being implemented. The Committee examines each report and addresses its concerns and recommendations to the State Party in the form of 'concluding observations'. Often referred to as Alternative Reports, NGOs and national human rights institutions are encouraged to provide documentation or other information to the Committee in order to develop a comprehensive picture as to how the Convention is being implemented in a particular country. Based on the written information submitted, the Committee will issue a written invitation to selected NGOs to participate in the pre-sessional working group of the Committee, which provides a unique opportunity for dialogue with partners regarding the implementation of the Convention by the States Parties.

Source: UN Committee on the Rights of the Child – Working Methods.

### *The Rationale for Public Oversight of the Security Sector*

According to the human security doctrine, security is considered to be a public good that should be responsive to the immediate needs of the people and developing trends, as well as subject to democratic, civilian oversight. To imagine that civil society is not a key actor in security provision misses the point of the collective responsibility involved in providing for the security of all individuals within a society. Civilians understand security matters because they are the ultimate end-users or beneficiaries of public security services and experience them on a day-to-day basis. Therefore, they can play a vital role in making the security sector not only more accountable, but also more effective in protecting citizens.

Moreover, as it is citizens who pay for the provision of security services via taxation, those relevant agencies should be subject to public scrutiny to ensure that they address the needs of the people rather than a narrow group. As with many public services, the state is the most legitimate platform for the provision of security (although it is open to debate as to whether it is always the most efficient) – civil society has a crucial role to play in ensuring that public resources are allocated efficiently and effectively.

A basic tenet of security provision is that the state should retain the monopoly on the 'use of force' although increasingly various tasks are being outsourced to private companies on license. While the mandate and actions of these companies remain monitored and controlled by state authorities, this raises another layer of challenges for CSOs in terms of ensuring monitoring and oversight. Via various feedback loops – campaigning, media, institutional and official platforms – including participatory involvement in advisory boards, CSOs can guarantee that agencies providing security become more effective through consistent scrutiny of their policy and actions. It should also be borne in mind that at times non-state actors may actually be responsible for security provision to the population, but again civil society should be ensuring that it is in a position to monitor and hold accountable those involved in any transgressions or violations.

**Box 5.2 The Private Sector as Service Provider**

Paul Hunt … speaking in a personal capacity … noted that a state could not privatise its international human rights obligations, and must take reasonable measures to ensure that privatised services were consistent with international human rights – for instance, non-discriminatory and within the reach of all sectors of society. He furthermore emphasised the need to ensure accountability, and the corresponding requirement of adequate monitoring and setting of indicators and benchmarks. Finally, he noted that national policies, including privatisation, should be preceded by an independent, objective and publicly available assessment of the impact on the respective right.

Source: UN Committee on the Rights of the Child, The Private Sector as Service Provider (Unedited), http://www.unhchr.ch/html/menu2/6/crc/doc/days/service.pdf

Civil society's role in oversight of the security sector is closely linked to democracy and can be seen as a means of strengthening democratic processes. It involves an expansion of democratic participation in the political process. The capacity of civil society to improve quality of civic life includes the area of security policy and governance. In both democratic and non-democratic polities, security policy has historically been the preserve of political and security elites.

The spread of democratic principles of government and the acceptance of the broader, less militarised and more complex understanding of security as 'human security' – crucially, of the provision of security as a public good – have challenged the notion of security as an exclusive sphere dominated by military concerns, and supplanted it. One of the most fundamental functions of the state is to provide for the security of its citizens. The democratic state has a duty to provide security that is effective, transparent and accountable to its citizens.

The Organisation for Economic Co-operation and Development – Development Assistance Committee (OECD DAC) encourages its members to 'support civil society efforts to create a pro-reform environment for democratic governance of the security system.'[2] This includes identifying entry points and developing methods of working through local actors to build on existing initiatives. While the development community has tended to come to see NGOs and other civil society organisations as alternate service providers and channels for donor assistance, they can also play an important role in the broader policy process. For example, members of the OECD are instructed to support the involvement of civil society groups as 'policy interlocutors who can contribute to and raise awareness on security decision-making as well as make practical suggestions to help sustain the reform process.'[3]

**Box 5.3 Reasons for Civil Oversight**

- Representing the opinions of civil society in security policy formulation
- Enhancing dialogue and understanding between public and security institutions
- Ensuring transparency and accountability of government
- Maintaining sustained policy scrutiny
- Promoting a responsive government
- Providing specialised information to policy development
- Providing a conduit for information sharing with communities

Establishing local ownership of SSR has become a concern in circles working on this issue. While local ownership is much vaunted as a guiding principle of SSR activities, its realisation in practice is somewhat more patchy. Local ownership implicitly involves civil society, both in representing the views of local communities to policy-makers addressing reforms that respond to local conditions and needs, and in monitoring the implementation of those reforms. Civil society groups, especially in rural areas and provinces far from capital cities, play a vital role not only in bringing the needs of local communities to the attention of central political and policy elites, but as the primary security providers on the ground. The challenge is that a wide divide often exists between what seems to be local ownership when engaging local actors at the national level, and what constitutes local ownership in terms of the often excluded and disenfranchised communities who are at the receiving end of insecurity.

Unfortunately, SSR programmes have until this point tended to focus on reforming state institutions with little effort to systematically involve all levels of civil society – this despite the fact that effective programmes require local participation and ownership to build confidence and ensure that programmes respond adequately to the needs of the population.

Where there has been attention to 'local ownership' in reality it has rarely filtered down beyond 'national ownership'. One of the key priorities for moving forward SSR programmes must be about how to get beyond discussion at the level of national and provincial capitals, to engaging with affected communities on the identification and response to security threats. Establishing national ownership of the process is the first key step, but this needs to be complemented by efforts to guarantee meaningful local ownership at community level, and for this civil society will be the key – perhaps only – credible interlocutor.

### *Civil Society's Role in Security Sector Oversight*

Civil society has an important role to play in public oversight of the security sector. NGOs and community groups can raise public and political awareness of key issues, concerns and interests, especially those facing their members or local communities. In this way they can improve the quality of government policy in terms of responsiveness and hold government accountable.

CSOs are often more aware of local needs and conditions than governments and their local agencies. They can provide detailed information on the needs and interests of specific communities to public authorities. They can also provide valuable expertise on specific issues and social groups. Some CSOs, for example, may deal with marginalised or vulnerable groups such as asylum-seekers, indigenous people, and women and children who tend to have little or no voice in national discourse or public policy making processes and who may face particular challenges in terms of security and justice.

Moreover, the special knowledge and expertise of certain civil society actors can be a supplementary, or alternative, source of information for government and security bureaucracies on policies and budgets. As an alternate source of information and independent analysis, civil society can challenge entrenched attitudes and assumptions that may be influenced by bureaucratic political considerations or industrial interests. By injecting a broader range of perspectives from society on security policy issues, civil society groups also broaden the legitimacy and responsiveness of security policy processes and policy outcomes. CSOs can also provide feedback on policies and the ways that they are implemented.

**Box 5.4 Getting to Grips with Gang Crime**

Rizwan Darbar, 17, was stabbed in West Ham Park, Plaistow, east London, on Sunday as he intervened in the robbery. He is the 20th teenager to have died as a result of gun or knife-related crime in London this year. Source: BBC, Oct. 2007.

These tragic events have increased anxiety locally – chiefly among young people themselves, with many saying they feel unsafe on the streets, and travelling to and from school. In London, there is considerable work going on between the Youth Justice Board (YJB), youth offending teams (YOTs), criminal justice agencies, children's services and the Voluntary and Community Sector (VCS) to develop responses encompassing prevention, community interventions and enforcement.

Multi-faceted prevention programmes and community engagement are key to addressing an apparently increasing problem. Children's services and schools have a vital role to play in early identification, challenging the lure of gang activity, and providing appropriate role models for young people.

Source: Youth Justice Board for England and Wales, The Magazine for Youth Justice. June/July 2007. Getting to Grips with Gang Crime.

It is in the nature of many citizen mobilisations and CSOs to form in response to a very specific pressing issue and to dissolve once the problem is resolved. For citizen mobilisations to become movements or sustainable CSOs and to serve as an ongoing source of influence or input into government decision-making and public debate, they must be focussed on more than a single issue, or on one which has broader scope. They require solid leadership and an ability to inform and engage the public and state policy-makers and opinion-leaders on policy issues. There is a role for both groups in affecting security oversight in so far as they can decisively influence government policy in both the long and short term. These requirements for CSO sustainability explain the effort directed towards CSO capacity-development in many donor programmes.[4]

In some states, civil society has, at times, played an adversarial role vis-à-vis the state in response to what it perceives as repressive, undemocratic or simply wrong actions taken in the security field. Mass protests against a country's involvement in a war or internal security operation that many of its citizens consider to be illegitimate are useful in drawing public attention to issues.

**Box 5.5 Civil Society Contributions to Security Sector Governance and Security Sector Reform**

- Facilitating dialogue and debate on policy issues
- Educating politicians, policy-makers and the public on special issues of concern
- Empowering groups and the public through training and awareness-raising on specific issues
- Sharing specialised information and knowledge of local needs and conditions with policy-makers, parliamentarians and the media
- Improving the legitimacy of policy processes through broader inclusion of societal groups and perspectives
- Encouraging security policies that are representative of and responsive to local communities
- Representing the interests of groups and communities in the policy environment
- Putting security issues on the political agenda
- Providing a pool of independent expertise, information and perspectives
- Undertaking policy-relevant research
- Promoting transparency and accountability of security institutions
- Monitoring reform implementation
- Creating platforms that decisively affect the policies and legitimacy of executive-level bodies in the interests of the public good
- Facilitating democratic change by protecting international human rights standards under democratic and undemocratic regimes
- Creating and mobilising a critical mass of systematic public opposition to undemocratic and unrepresentative local and national government

Two famous cases in point are the mass protests in the United States against the Vietnam War in the 1960s to communicate to the public information that was being withheld by the government, and in the 1970s the Mothers of the Plaza de Mayo in Argentina to protest against and demand justice for the youths who disappeared during the Argentine military dictatorship. A vibrant civil society contributes to the quality of a polity not only by offering alternate perspectives on issues that are of critical importance to society, but also by providing workable alternative solutions to problems. The OECD DAC has concisely asserted that:

> Given the weakness of state capacity in many countries, it is particularly important that civil society groups develop the capacity to go beyond denouncing governments for their failings and make practical suggestions that will help to sustain the reform process.[5]

Developing an oversight role and the capacity to engage constructively in dialogue with state actors is enabled through recognising that the state is not the 'enemy', but a key partner in the aim of transforming and assisting in becoming more efficient, just and responsive. Just as governments and regional/international organisations must make the effort to open up space in policy consultations to interact with CSOs, civil society must also engage with government and state bureaucracies. Content variables aside, civil society groups can perform these roles in post-conflict, transition, developing and developed states.

A generally acknowledged precondition for effective SSR tends to be a willingness on the part of state authorities to reform and, as such, the relationship between state and civil society, far from having to be adversarial can be collaborative, with both parties having a shared responsibility and vested interest in initiating dialogue and pushing forward change. This can involve a two-way process, with civil society able to voice and present legitimate concerns to state authorities, but equally, state authorities recognising the importance of pro-active collaboration with civil society from the outset.

### *Types of CSOs Contributing to Security Oversight*

Civil society groups often have no inkling that their activities can contribute to democratic oversight and governance of the security sector. Those groups professing to deal with peace and security issues – disarmament groups, academic departments and research or policy institutes dealing with security or criminal justice – constitute the most obvious types of civil society groups likely to become involved in the security sector governance and reform agenda.

However, the spectrum of CSOs that can play a role in security sector governance and reform is actually much broader. Accountability and democratic oversight of the security sector, for example, are often directly linked to questions of human rights, civil liberties and social and transitional justice. Minorities and other marginalised groups may find that their security needs are not being met or, alternatively, that they are victims of excessive use of force, unwarranted monitoring or other types of behaviour on the part of security sector personnel. Police accountability is a primary concern and a subject about which a broad range of community groups and associations can provide information and on which many are already engaged. Additionally, different CSOs have different – but relevant – skills to contribute to the process of public oversight of the security sector.

**Box 5.6 Requisite Skills and Capacities for CSOs Involved in Security Sector Reform Oversight**

- A coherent agenda
- Legitimacy with their constituents
- Advocacy and awareness-raising capacities
- Documentation and research
- Institutional and organisational capacities
- Monitoring
- Networking and alliance-building
- Evaluation and analysis capabilities

*Entry Points for Civil Society Involvement in the Security Sector*

There may also be special opportunities or openings for civil society involvement in SSR, such as addressing specific thematic security concerns such as trafficking or gun crime, or engaging in peace processes following regime change or in post-conflict reconstruction.

Another specialised area where civil society will have a crucial role to play is in engaging in peace processes following regime change or in post-conflict reconstruction and peacebuilding. One example was the role of the Military Research Group in shaping the post-apartheid new African National Congress government's approach to security and the attention it devoted to governance of the security sector. Composed of a coalition of key academics, Congress activists and operatives, the Military Research Group sought to help Congress policy-makers identify voids in their expertise in security governance and to fill those gaps through research and assistance in policy formulation.[6] The activities of this research group were co-ordinated to reflect the needs of the policy-making community, and the close links that developed between them ensured that policy was informed and defined by relevant research.

In societies emerging from armed conflict, SSR programmes are increasingly being put in place to assist in the construction and restructuring of security institutions to make them more effective in serving the public good, transparent and accountable. Civil society not only has a role to play in preventive diplomacy, peacemaking, peacekeeping and post-conflict peacebuilding, but also in providing oversight of the effectiveness of post-conflict security sector governance and reform programmes. In peacebuilding, it has become accepted that local communities must buy into a national peace process if it is to be effective over the long-term. Civil society has also played an important technical role in the resettlement of refugee and internally displaced populations. Channels should be created to tap the expertise and information CSOs have in these areas and feed them back into the peace process. While often over-looked by policy-makers, children, and in particular youth, have a huge potential to contribute to peacebuilding activities, not only because of the energy and fresh perspectives that they can bring to the process but most importantly because of ensuring their engagement in efforts to move away from a past blighted by conflict and towards building a new future.

The effectiveness of disarmament, demobilisation and, in particular, reintegration (DDR) programmes is dependent on the involvement of local authorities and communities. CSOs can provide detailed information on conditions, attitudes and needed skills in local communities that can be used in the planning and implementation of DDR processes. They can also monitor and evaluate these programmes and provide feedback for further improvement of future DDR processes. CSOs can help to ensure that appropriate training is provided to the right people at the right time. Working with local media, CSOs can also raise the awareness of local communities about the need to accept former combatants and re-integrate them into the life of the community.[7] They are also the best placed to provide the essential follow-up that DDR programmes require but that is often lacking.

**Box 5.7 UN Security Council – Monitoring and Reporting**

UN Security Council Resolution 1612 (2005), requests the implementation of a monitoring and reporting mechanism proposed by the Secretary-General in his February 2005 report on children and armed conflict. The aim of the mechanism is to monitor and report on the six grave violations against children in situations of armed conflict, and move towards ending the impunity of violating parties.

An effective monitoring, reporting and compliance regime depends largely on the collaboration of a number of critical stakeholders, particularly Member States, United Nations system partners, NGOs and local civil society in situations of concern. The success of this protection initiative will depend on how effectively collective will, resources and expertise are mobilised and deployed at the multiple levels of the mechanism.

Source: Office of the Special Representative of the Secretary-General for Children and Armed Conflict, http://www.un.org/children/conflict/english/home6.html

### *Restrictions on CSO Activity*

Many states openly repress independent NGOs and seek to intimidate activists. Others may allow CSOs to operate, but only within certain boundaries and with constraints on the right to associate. Some Middle Eastern regimes permit the existence of relatively docile NGOs, while those NGOs that seek to be truly independent or assertive are undermined and their members often harassed, and the NGOs subject to arbitrary dissolution by the state authorities. Legal restrictions on NGO formation, operation and financing are often excessively strict and may be justified in terms of 'national security', 'public order' or 'national unity'.

Certain regimes link civil society activity with political opposition, subversion, and even intervention in domestic affairs, particularly when NGOs receive funding from abroad in support of their capacity-development and involvement in governance issues. This may also extend to NGO efforts to practice 'linkage' between the domestic sphere and the state's relations with other states and international organisations, as in the case of a recent law in Belarus that introduced prison sentences for those training people to take part in demonstrations or protests, discrediting the country's image abroad, and appealing to other states and international organisations to 'act to the detriment of the country's security, sovereignty and territorial integrity'.[8]

**Box 5.8 Zimbabwe – The Closing of Amani Trust**

The Amani Trust was formed in 1993 to treat and rehabilitate victims of torture and organised violence. In 2000-2001, Amani set up safe houses in urban centres to house the many who were internally displaced due to violence. It also released several reports documenting abuses and reporting the names of perpetrators. Around this time, stories in the state press reported that Amani was funded by the British government, that it was publishing false reports, and that it was allowing the safe houses to be used as bases for Movement of Democratic Change 'terrorist' operations. Following the release of Amani documentation on rapes at national youth training facilities and by war veterans, police and youth militia, attacks against Amani in the government-owned press increased. At the beginning of September 2002, the government gave Amani notice that it should cease operations until it was formally registered under the Private Voluntary Organisations Act, legislation to which it should be exempt due to its registration as a trust. The organisation closed its offices in mid-November after threats of arrests in the state-owned press and in Parliament.

Source: Human Rights Watch, 'Under a Shadow: Civil and Political Rights in Zimbabwe'.

The current 'fight against terrorism' has significant implications for civil society. Restrictions on civil liberties taken, or said to be taken, to combat terrorism may impede the legitimate actions NGOs undertake. CSOs that oppose this 'fight', or aspects thereof, or that provide legal assistance to terrorist suspects, may face social stigmatisation or marginalisation by their partner organisations, both serving to obstruct their work. Authoritarian rulers and political leaders have also abused the term 'terrorist' to crackdown on civil society and political opposition who are seeking to establish pluralism within their polity.

In addition, governments that attempt to influence NGO policy by placing restrictions on the use of funds risk undermining the fundamental notion of their independence and neutrality that could have grave consequences for future efforts to bring humanitarian assistance to some of the most vulnerable populations. Such attempts to restrict NGOs in their practices are not only found in the war on terror, but also in other domains including reproductive health programmes.

## The Media's Role in Public Oversight

The media has a hugely influential role to play in transmitting key security, safety and protection information particularly in relation to and on behalf of children. Children need access to the media for obtaining information, but this access should also provide for their voices and opinions to be given space to be heard. And while the media has many positives to contribute, children need to be protected from its harmful influences and potential threats. It must also be recognised that the media is at times culpable of passing misguided, sensational and fundamentally distorted interpretations of issues affecting society, with youth being an easy and regular target.

Free and independent news media are a key element in democracies, where they play a vital political role in keeping governments and citizens aware of and in contact with one another. One of the basic assumptions of democracy is that power rests with the people, and that those who are entrusted with public governance must remain closely in tune with the views and preferences of ordinary citizens.[9]

In a democracy, the media functions as a bridge between society and those who govern. Whilst sections of it may be appropriated by different vested interests in the executive, government and business spheres, the capacity of the media to raise vital questions about the legitimacy of government policy and its implementation at national and international levels remains undiminished in comparison to other platforms.

Countries in which the media is monopolised by executive agencies often develop alternative outlets for relaying information via multi-faceted but usually informal platforms. Here, advances in information technology are providing civil society with accessible and cheap alternatives for transmitting information and generating dialogue around issues of interest or concern – the internet being the obvious case in point.

**Box 5.9 Youth Media and Communication Initiative, Nigeria**

The Youth Media and Communication Initiative is a non-governmental development organisation that equips children and youth from the ages of 10 to 18 with communication skills on child rights, environment, leadership and development to cope with living in a multi-ethnic and multicultural society, thus laying the basis for social justice for future generations of Nigerians. Facilitating the expansion of communication infrastructure for children and youths; increasing their access to comprehensive information about their rights; building the capacity of children and youths to utilise communication resources, and articulate as well as critically analyse issues that impact on their lives; increasing the participation of children and youths in the promotion of child rights and preparing them to participate in such activities through the use of the media.

Source: Youth Media and Communication Initiative, http://www.ymci.info/

Because mass media is closely linked to the political system and the public sphere, it plays a dual role of representing and forming political opinion. On the one hand, mass media communicate information that individuals use to make informed decisions and political choices. On the other hand, politicians rely on the media to present their positions, take stock of public opinion and interact with the public. In its varying forms – public, private, voluntary, charitable – the media ultimately constitute a fundamental inter-connective tissue between society and the government, communicating information, intentions, concerns, priorities and reactions to policies.[10]

Along with other civil society actors, such as NGOs, research institutes and interest groups, the media may help to inform and educate citizens on specialised topics such as national security and public security, enabling deeper policy debates and informed discussion of policy alternatives. The media consequently are both an actor and mechanism in holding governments to account.

More than just observing and reporting facts, however, journalists have the opportunity to contribute to developing critical debate and dialogue in their societies, and thereby to shape public and political agendas. This derives from the view that the news media are institutions central to democratic life, and as such are expected to function not only in the pursuit of profit, but also in the public interest.

**Box 5.10 Excerpt from Principles and Guidelines for Ethical Reporting on Children and Young People**

Children and young people have all the rights of adults. In addition, they have the right to be protected from harm.

Reporting on children and young people carries this added dimension and restriction, especially in the current era when it is nearly-impossible to limit a story's reach. This document is meant to support the best intentions of ethical reporters – serving the public's interest for truth without compromising the rights of children.

In some instances the act of reporting on children places them or other children at risk of retribution or stigmatisation. When in doubt, the reporter must err on the side of caution and the right of the child to be protected from harm. Because these situations are not always clear-cut, reporters are encouraged to consult with UNICEF staff or others in determining the best interests of the child

Source: http://www.unicef.org/malaysia/Guidelines_for_Reporting_on_Children1.pdf

In the context of security policy, this means not only monitoring government policies and their implementation, but also examining alternatives to existing security policy. Yet while the media may help to identify policy options, they tend to be more influential once a policy is in place than before it is decided upon. The media excels at holding political actors, governments and international organisations accountable 'by being eyewitnesses to events, by communicating what they see and hear to their audiences, (and) by publicly juxtaposing a statement made previously with a comment made today'.[11]

Effective oversight by civil society is a product of their expertise and capacity to independently evaluate, challenge, or endorse governmental decisions concerning defence and public security affairs. The media may help to hold political and state actors accountable by showing their audience what is actually happening, which may be quite different from what policy-makers, politicians or diplomats claim to be happening. However, harassment of the media is not limited to transition or authoritarian states. Even in established democracies one finds examples of harassment of journalists.

Investigative journalism – the active and sustained examination by a journalist of possible abuse of power – is viewed as one of the more effective means of exposing wrongdoing in government. The role of investigative journalists can be especially important due to their ability to expose corruption, wrongdoing and misuse of public office in government. For example, in the United States of America, investigative journalism was given a huge boost after the Washington Post's revelations about the Watergate scandal.

In order for there to be a supportive environment for investigative journalism, however, three conditions must be met. First, a good regulatory structure must exist, enabling the development and existence of independent and pluralistic media. This includes entrenching the right of freedom of expression in the constitution. Second, journalists require access to information from a variety of sources. A key means of achieving this is through an access-to-information regime, which would help to legally ensure that journalists and the public enjoy a right to access information held by the state about government and its operations. Finally, the media must be free to publish the findings of investigative journalists, free from censorship or the fear of reprisals, including legal remedies such as libel, insult or slander lawsuits, but also threats and harassment. In other words, what restrictions exist regarding what can be published must be narrowly defined and tightly circumscribed.[12]

**Box 5.11 Investigative Journalism**

GSL, which deals with by far the majority of deportees in Britain, recently won a 10-year Home Office contract to run Bicester Accommodation Centre for asylum seekers. The firm was criticised last month after the broadcast of the BBC documentary Asylum Undercover, which contained claims of abuse by GSL guards. Most of the alleged assaults analysed involve incidents on the way to or at airports. Most concern incidents resulting in cuts, bruises and swelling, although deportees have complained of head injuries, damaged nerves, and sexual assault.

Source: The Guardian newspaper, UK, April 9, 2005.

## Conclusion

The ultimate responsibility for guaranteeing the security of all citizens lies with the state and its various institutions. However, the reality is that they can only succeed in fulfilling their obligations through close collaboration and co-operation with a range of civil society actors. Effective and informed decision-making requires the involvement of the eventual beneficiaries of security, and hence the need for open debate in a range of policy discussions and in priority setting.

Nowhere is the need for dialogue more important than in relation to children and youth who have no political voice of their own. NGOs in particular have been highly active (and are particularly important) in promoting and ensuring political visibility for child protection issues. While young children tend to receive attention because of their apparent vulnerability and dependence, youth, who are already able to have a significant influence on security, do not receive the same attention or support at a political level.

Youth are caught in the classic dilemma of 'damned if you do, damned if you don't'. They are viewed as children, but expected to behave like adults, and expected to take on adult responsibilities, while being treated like children. Acknowledging youth as active participants in society and providing them with purpose and opportunities to contribute constructively on social issues will result in a major contribution to preventive security actions.

Public involvement in the democratic oversight of the security sector can ensure responsiveness and transparency not only across a state's security agencies but also across the policies of the executive and government managing and defining security policy. Moreover, the engagement of CSOs in the security policy domain contributes to accountability and the maintenance of good governance by their acting as a watchdog and providing an index of public satisfaction with security sector activity.

Actions such as monitoring government performance, policy, compliance with laws and upholding of human rights all contribute to this process. Moreover, advocacy by civil society groups representing the interests of local communities and groups of like-minded individuals helps to empower marginalised actors and opens up policy development to a wider set of perspectives and increases the legitimacy of policy. States can facilitate the process by seeking a constructive and dynamic interaction with CSOs on security matters: ensuring freedom of assembly and freedom of speech; institutionalising consultation mechanisms from local to national levels; creating CSO registration legislation which is unrestrictive; and guaranteeing protection for whistle blowers.

**Box 5.12 Investigative Journalism – from Mothers of Prevention**

At the crown court in Preston (UK) on August 10, a trial involving two Asian men caused unusual interest across a number of cities in the north of England. The defendants, Zulfqar Hussain and Qaiser Naveed, were each sentenced to five years and eight months for abduction, sexual activity with a child, and the supply of a controlled drug. They had both pleaded guilty, and they were placed on the sex offenders' register for life.

It seemed a shabby, seedy episode, probably typical of many cases down the years that have involved exploitative men and naive women. Yet, until these convictions, the police in over a dozen towns and cities, including Leeds, Sheffield, Blackburn and Huddersfield, had appeared reluctant to address what many local people had perceived as a growing problem – the groups of men who had been preying on young, vulnerable girls and ensnaring them into prostitution.

Anni, along with other affected mothers, has put pressure on the police to respond by using the local press to back their campaign for justice.

Blackburn is Jack Straw's constituency, and both Anni and Maureen have visited him to beg for help. (N.B. Jack Straw is Member of Parliament for Blackburn, and current Lord High Chancellor of Great Britain and Secretary of State for Justice). 'I have had two cases at my constituency surgery over the past two years,' Straw said, 'and have discussed this with the police, council, community leaders and the Lancashire Telegraph.' The paper launched the Keep Them Safe campaign last year, following an investigation of several cases of Asian pimping gangs.

Under the control of the pimps, the girls develop something akin to Stockholm syndrome, where they begin to have empathy and sympathy for their abusers. Shirley Gorek, a former social worker employed by Blackburn with Darwen Borough Council to advise on child sexual exploitation, has run support groups for girls caught up with pimps. She found the girls can get completely brainwashed by their abusers. 'It is almost as if they are programmed into a cult,' she says.

Where there is pimping, there are other forms of serious and organised crime. Some Asian pimps in Rotherham are also involved in drug dealing and gun crime. Although shootings in the town are rare, the girls caught up with the pimps have disclosed that many of them carry guns. Pimps traffic the girls between towns and cities.

One of the many tragedies resulting from this phenomenon is how it is fuelling racism and mistrust of whites towards Pakistanis where little existed previously.

Source: The Sunday Times, UK, September 30, 2007. Investigation by Julie Bindel

## Endnotes

1 This paper draws extensively on the draft version of Chapter 2 of Eden Cole, 'Strategies for Public Oversight' in *Handbook for Civil Society on Democratic Oversight of the Security Sector*, eds. Marina Caparini, Eden Cole and Katrin Kinzelbach (Bratislava: Renesans, forthcoming November 2008).

2 Organisation for Economic Co-operation and Development (OECD), Policy Brief: 'Security System Reform and Governance: Policy and Good Practice', Recommendation VIII (May 2004).

3 OECD, Policy Brief: 'Security System Reform and Governance: Policy and Good Practice', 4.

4 Marina Caparini, 'Civil Society and Democratic Oversight of the Security Sector: A Preliminary Investigation', paper presented at Fifth International Security Forum (Zurich, 14-16 October 2002), 8.

5 OECD-Development Assistance Committee (OECD DAC), *DAC Guidelines and Reference Series: Security System Reform and Governance* (OECD Publishing, 2005), 39, http://www. oecd.org/dac/conflict/ssr (accessed October 2008).

6 Kai Michael Kenkel, 'Civil Society Participation in Defence Policy Formulation: Academic Experts and South Africa's Post-Apartheid Defence White Paper' *Journal of Security Sector Management* 4, No. 1 (January 2006): 15.

7 Comments of Mark Malan, 'Kofi Annan International Peacekeeping Training Centre (KAIPTC)' in *The report of the AU-Civil Society Consultative Workshop on Enhancing AU-Civil Society Relationships*, organised by the African Security Dialogue and Research (ASDR) and the African Union Commission with support from the Danish Ministry of Foreign Affairs, Kofi Annan International Peacekeeping Training Centre (KAIPTC), Teshie, Ghana, 29-31 August 2005, 39-40.

8 Cited in Carl Gershman and Michael Allen, 'The Assault on Democracy Assistance' *Journal of Democracy* 17, No. 2 (April 2006): 43.

9 Larry Diamond, 'Rethinking Civil Society: Toward Democratic Consolidation' *Journal of Democracy* 5, No. 3 (July 1994).

10 Richard Gunther and Anthony Mughan, *Democracy and the Media: A Comparative Perspective* (Cambridge: Cambridge University Press, 2000), 1.

11 Susan D. Moeller, 'Locating accountability: the media and peacekeeping' *Journal of International Affairs* 55, No. 2 (March 2002).

12 Statement for the World Summit on the Information Society on the 'Right to Communicate', Article 19 (February 2003), http://www.article19.org/pdfs/publications/ right-to-communicate.pdf (accessed October 2008).

# Chapter 6

# The Juvenile Justice System, a Key to Human Security Policy Reform[1]

*Bernard Boëton*

> Today, development, security and human rights go hand in hand; no one of them can advance very far without the other two. Indeed, anyone who speaks forcefully for human rights but does nothing about human security and human development – or vice versa – undermines both his credibility and his cause. So let us speak with one voice on all three issues, and let us work to ensure that freedom from want, freedom from fear and freedom to live in dignity carry real meaning for those most in need.[2]

## From Simplistic Representations to Realities

In a context of globalisation, and in particular with the liberalisation of global economies, there has been a trend towards a reduced role for the public sector as the primary vehicle for the delivery of national policy. At the same time, states' emphasis on providing 'human security' is being interpreted from a strictly security-based perspective, which risks criminalising parts of society already living in exclusion. Often driven by public opinion, such an approach risks ignoring the vital role of the juvenile justice system (functioning based on international norms and standards), not only for children's security, but also for the security of the population as a whole.

Many countries adopt short-sighted policies that are aimed at achieving immediate political gain, rather than investing over the long-term in preventive approaches. In other words, 'punish quickly rather than educate slowly'. To varying degrees, the marginalisation of the juvenile justice system is a universal phenomenon and, even in countries with the economic means to support alternative approaches to prison sentencing, we see 'curfews' imposed in urban areas, or the announcement of measures (ultimately cancelled) for the detection of children 'predisposed to delinquency' from nursery school age (France). In the 1960s, marginal and anti-establishment behaviour was seen as an inevitable, indeed worthwhile, symptom of generational change: today's rhetoric revolves around the 'anti-social' behaviour of minors (United Kingdom). This has gone as far as the Swiss government's approval of the sale of 'Mosquito' devices to home-owners: these devices emit ultrasound waves which can only be heard by animals and youths under the age of 25, and are used to deter the latter.

Associated with urbanisation, an increase in juvenile delinquency tends to be a symptom of social exclusion: for many families life is about survival and as such their children are expected to contribute (if the family link has been maintained), or to take care of themselves (if the family link has been broken). More than half of the world's population now lives in cities, with the majority of economic migrants having moved away from rural areas because of their livelihoods no longer being guaranteed in rural environments where traditional forms of community solidarity have broken down. This psychology of survival can blur the perception that juveniles have of the line between legality and illegality, especially where these youth are physically or psychologically restricted and stressed.

Efforts to combat juvenile delinquency will often be reflected by authorities introducing repressive legislation and in a hardening of attitudes among law enforcement and judicial officers. Resulting actions may include: reduction of the age of criminal responsibility; increase in the length of custodial sentences for minors (who are sometimes detained with adults – prison being acknowledged as 'the school of crime'; dramatic 'round-up' actions or crackdown operations; the criminalisation of vagrancy and begging; and the creation of educational detention centres (presented as alternatives to prison, but whose conditions of detention are often equivalent to those of prison).

In some particularly underprivileged countries, the judicial system is administered in a both hasty and lax manner: for a simple case of cattle rustling, juveniles are remanded in custody for lengthy periods without speedy trial, decision or sentence, and even forgotten about. Holding public office does not allow police or judicial officers to act – or not to act – in total impunity and illegality, or in ways that are an abuse of their power and position. Good governance pre-supposes that public actors can be monitored, held accountable and, if necessary, sanctioned.

In every country of the world, regardless of its level of economic development, policy-makers come up against the problem of juvenile delinquency. The idea of dealing with the problem through a hard-line or repressive approach is often deemed as being the most expeditive and effective in satisfying the immediate demands and concerns of public opinion. Such demands are often dictated by the media, who at times seem quite willing to deal in statistics that can be easily manipulated and that the public is unlikely to fully understand.

The distinction between the delinquency of youths in rich countries that are testing limits, and the delinquency of survival of youths in poor countries is no longer always relevant. Family break-up is no less common in rich countries than in poor countries, although the reasons and cultural and traditional contexts may differ greatly. The psychological abandonment of children in some rich families is indeed equal to the physical and material abandonment experienced by children of poor families.

Differences between rich and poor countries lie not only in the resources available to the state to implement alternatives to detention but also in the influence and capacity of civil society stakeholders (associations, non-governmental organisations, etc.) to influence policy. However, there are also significant risks in the state progressively offloading parts of its responsibility to private welfare and charitable associations – often operating with private funding – particularly in relation to entrusting them with the education and rehabilitation of juvenile offenders and their reintegration into the community.

The frequently cited argument of budgetary constraints is both true and false. True, because juvenile justice is always the poor relation when it comes to government spending in the justice system; but false, because the implementation of sound co-operation between trained professionals can yield results even with small budgets. Added to this is the fact that, in many countries, the economic insecurity of a significant part of the population, sometimes the majority, can be linked to issues such as state withdrawal and the privatisation of public services, sometimes under pressure from international financial institutions, but which can ultimately result in increases in juvenile delinquency.

Aside from the legal requirement to comply with international norms and standards, states must realise that for the overwhelming majority of first-time minor offenders the cost effectiveness of social work and education in an open environment is far more favourable than investing in costly penitentiary institutions, despite the latter having a higher profile and as such a more appealing aspect concerning public opinion. In some countries, it would be worthwhile comparing the price of one day of juvenile detention with the cost of a day in an average hotel in the same city.

In addition, the construction and maintenance of correctional facilities may have the opposite effect of the desired outcome. While detention conditions may improve momentarily, there is a risk of an increase in custodial sentencing and of this punishment being applied for more minor crimes. Indeed, where the private sector is involved, if new facilities are 'put on the market', they will have to be filled to make them profitable.

It should also be noted that in a 'globalised' world, the growth of the migratory phenomenon, internal or international, legal or illegal, places juveniles at extreme risk, sometimes encouraged by their own families, sometimes coerced by traffickers in order to commit illegal or criminal activities. Delinquency among foreign juveniles often leads to the application of marginal, even unlawful, methods in the host country, in a 'two weights, two measures' approach in breach of international standards (including the United Nations Convention on the Rights of the Child). The primary obligation of protecting these children, cut-off from their families, is often neglected in favour of arbitrary proceedings, the meanings of which are often not understood by the minors involved.

Finally, major changes affecting the way in which internal and international armed conflicts are conducted have exacerbated the phenomenon of children recruited into armed forces, militia, guerrilla movements, or other, more or less spontaneously constituted, armed groups. The administration of juvenile justice can become all the more problematic as states, faced with internal strife, impose exceptional legal regimes (as is the case for Palestinian children in Israel), or a sort of 'military law', which waives the requirement to handle juveniles according to the standard criminal code. However, what is clear is that the actual recruitment itself is a form of exploitation and an abuse of power – more often than not under duress – which requires that the child be treated first and foremost as a victim before being considered as a criminal, regardless of the acts committed in combat.

## Promoting State Sovereignty and Security

Generally, a state's responsibility for human security within the territories under its jurisdiction must be perceived as extending to the security of all persons within those territories, and not simply to the security of the state and its institutions. A state's sovereignty cannot be considered as referring exclusively to the security of its own existence and its own governance. Equally, a state that is not in a position to ensure a minimum of security and respect for the human rights of its children, including those responsible for misdemeanours and petty crime, is not deserving of recognition as sovereign on its soil. Given that every year 120 to 130 million children are born into the world (and as an aside, it should be noted that a third have no civil registration at birth), and in light of the relative drop in the birth rate, including in some poor countries, we can estimate that between three and four billion children will be born in the next 50 years. Forty-five percent of today's global population is under 18. The issue of childhood does in fact concern the rights of almost half of humanity – those who will be the humanity of tomorrow.

As such, justice is the very expression of state sovereignty. Neither cultural forces nor foreign interference justify the systematic detention of juvenile offenders through the practice of preventive detention for long durations and under inhumane living conditions which would not even be tolerated for adults.

Juvenile delinquents are also juveniles at risk, and the juvenile justice system must be as much about justice based on protection as it is about justice based on sanctions. Juvenile justice is not a marginal justice: it does not consist of applying 'preferential' measures or making 'humanitarian exceptions' on the pretext that juvenile delinquency is a social, not a legal, problem, or that it is simply a noble principle serving only to conceal arbitrary procedures and practices. The administration of juvenile justice has for decades been subject to international standards, with the requirement that they be applied to national laws and procedures, and which as such require the police, judiciary and correction services to adopt a primarily educational approach to juvenile justice rather than a repressive approach.

The protection of the rights of the child is easily and widely accepted when dealing with child victims (of traffickers, or violence in any form), but it is much more difficult when dealing with child offenders.

The Copenhagen Declaration on Social Development from the 1995 World Summit for Social Development[3] (in which 115 countries participated) provided a vision for social development based on the promotion of social progress, justice and the betterment of the human condition, based on full participation by all. As such, children should be considered as participants and beneficiaries of an approach designed in the higher interest of their future and that of the society in which they live. Social action is not simply concerned with managing the needs of a population deemed to be marginal, abandoned, and left reliant on the initiative of private social and humanitarian associations. While the state cannot be expected to be all-providing, and private stakeholders have their place, the state must, as a minimum, guarantee the conditions of equality of opportunity and access to justice for all. Fairness in the implementation of human rights is one of the foundations of human security.

The United Nations Convention on the Rights of the Child (the 'Convention') defines a child as any human being below the age of 18 years. We should add in respect of this age-based definition that the child is a human being in his or her own right (and not in the 'ante-chamber' of humanity). The child's dignity is equal to that of every other human being, but the child has relative capacities of perception (in relation to the consequences of his or her actions), expression (limited language proficiency), and defence (both physical and psychological). This definition, which underpins the existence of the juvenile justice system and the international norms and standards in this field, also underscores the priority of a restorative approach over a punitive approach. Educational work with the juvenile, and social work with his/her family and community, may perhaps only obtain a 50 percent success rate, but a purely repressive approach (namely via the deprivation of liberty) guarantees almost 100 percent failure.

Even in cases of deprivation of liberty, this does abrogate responsibility for the protection of the juvenile's rights. There is no such thing as human security without legal and ethical references to international human rights instruments: family contact, respect of physical and psychological integrity, respect for privacy at all stages of the proceedings, the right to information, the right to practice a religion, etc.

Debates over juvenile justice have forever focussed on the choice between 'retributive' or 'restorative justice' (repression or education). Each individual develops his or her own opinion, inclination and argument according to their perception, experience or role. Ministries of the interior, justice and defence, as well as legislators, may tend to take a 'repressive' stance, while the Ministries of health, social affairs and family, and many representatives of civil society promote the 'educational' approach. Advocates of retributive justice are persuaded by the effectiveness of punishments that deprive people of their liberty – although the more sceptical take refuge in the argument of 'a shortage of resources' to justify custodial sentencing – while claiming to regret it. Advocates of restorative justice believe in the importance of removing the juvenile offender from judicial proceedings – although in the absence of real means for an education-based policy, juveniles are faced with police and judicial practices of which they understand little and during which they are subject to arbitrary decisions by untrained personnel, without the means to defend themselves or exercise their rights (with which they themselves are often not familiar).

Under these circumstances, it becomes apparent that the most serious breaches of the rights of juvenile offenders do not necessarily stem from malicious actions of any kind but more often than not from widespread ignorance over basic standards and procedures, and a lack of training on the part of the parties concerned.

The very concept of human security alludes to a restorative-based approach. Good governance, with a view to securing democratic progress, implies that the state, which is at once the source and the guarantor of human rights, must strive to inform public opinion on child rights, and deal with children in line with international norms and standards, including using deprivation of liberty only as a measure of last resort. Any decision, or punitive measure, that compounds the child's exclusion from the community is unlikely to succeed.

> In what way is being deprived of liberty a lesson in liberty?
> (J. P. Rosenczweig).

Restorative-based approaches are all the more valid in that, in almost all countries and cultures, tradition and custom have at some stage been based on mediation and reconciliation when faced with breaches of its rules by minors. When launching a project in a country, it is important to use the national laws in force, provided they do not conflict with international principles. It is important to first work with what is in place before trying to change things – but, gaps in the law should not be used as a pretext or reason for failing to innovate in terms of alternatives to the imprisonment of minors. Indeed, national law invariably offers the possibility of developing alternative measures to detention, even if only through a word or a phrase, and can also be inspired by existing, relevant local practices or customs. This does not mean that all traditional punishments, notably corporal punishment, are still acceptable today. The pressure of public opinion is all too often given as a pretext for immediate recourse to a repressive approach, in particular for minor offences committed by first-time offenders. However, the Ministry of Justice always has the option of putting in place pilot projects on a test basis in order to first demonstrate the benefits of pursuing alternatives before proposing amendments to the law governing juvenile delinquency.

## Tried and Tested Good Practices

The Convention excludes the imposition of capital punishment or life imprisonment without the possibility of release for offences committed by persons under 18 years (Article 37.a), yet such sentences persist in some states that have ratified the Convention.

At all stages of the juvenile justice process, children who are alleged to have committed offences are entitled to be treated 'in a manner consistent with the promotion of the child's sense of dignity and worth, which reinforces the child's respect for the human rights and fundamental freedoms of others and which takes into account the child's age and the desirability of promoting the child's reintegration and the child's assuming a constructive role in society' (Article 40.1). Children have the right to be protected from all forms of torture and cruel, inhuman or degrading treatment or punishment (Article 37.a) and any other form of abuse (Article 19).

Street children are among the most vulnerable victims of the most extreme forms of violence, including extrajudicial or summary execution, in many countries. Homeless children are particularly vulnerable to such violence, though children working in the streets are also at great risk even if they are still living with their families. Violence against this group of children represents a particularly egregious violation of their rights (Articles 6 and 37, among others), as it follows upon the failure of the state to offer protection and care to children whose rights are already under attack.[4]

Juvenile justice is not 'compassionate' justice because it concerns children. Being a child does not preclude one's entitlement to benefit from the rule of law and the safeguards it provides: a child has the right of defence, the right to the presumption of innocence, the right of appeal, etc. The juvenile justice system also needs to recognise its responsibilities, not just towards the child offender, but also to the child witness and child victim. A distinction must be made between:

- A child in conflict with the law, who will be dealt with by the criminal justice system.
- A child at risk, who will be of concern for welfare services and not the courts.
- A child victim or witness, who must benefit from protection measures

Good administration of the juvenile justice system implies the specialisation of police, judiciary, educational and welfare staff at every stage of proceedings, trained in the rules regarding children's rights, as well as the implementation of basic rules concerning their protection against any arbitrary exercise of power and violence. The notion of juvenile justice being restorative pre-supposes the application of some fundamental principles.

- Capital punishment and life imprisonment must be permanently and universally abolished for offenders who were minors at the time of events.
- The child must be heard in an appropriate manner, i.e. in accordance with his or her age and maturity, and this includes the presumption of innocence.
- From the initial questioning stage, the approach must be instructional, based on the juvenile's understanding of the consequences of his or her actions and the sanctions applied to him or her.
- The idea of conflict resolution should guide all proceedings, where possible via the use of reparations to compensate the victim. A balance must be sought between the victim's claims and the juvenile offender's situation as, in practice, one is often more compassionate towards the person having suffered the wrongdoing than towards the person who committed it.
- In all cases, educational, non-custodial sanctions must be the rule, and detention must remain the exception: preventive detention is a procedural act only and must on no account be selected as an immediate sanction.
- In the case of misdemeanours or crimes committed by juveniles with a group of adults, the separation of proceedings is a compulsory legal obligation, from the beginning of proceedings until the conclusion of the measures or sanctions.

Experience shows that the training of public actors in juvenile justice must be multi-disciplinary: juvenile justice can only progress if the respective professions involved know their respective legal responsibilities, limitations and possibilities. This approach also avoids inopportune interference in the other party's actions: the lawyer must not be expected to play the role of the social worker and vice versa, etc.

Among the parties, the judge is one of the key persons for the smooth running of the juvenile justice system. All of the other actors are subject to his or her decisions and supervision from the start of proceedings (where there was no possibility of out-of-court settlement) until the point at which the sanction has been fully enforced. Actors in the juvenile justice system cannot therefore receive training without the active presence of judges. However, judges are notoriously reluctant to undertake training programmes alongside other professionals such as police officers, educators and social workers, but an alternative approach can be to invite them as trainers. Experience shows that once the various professions have gained mutual recognition and respect, they are better placed to identify appropriate solutions, even if temporary, which offer more effective and less costly alternatives to the routine recourse to strictly repressive measures.

Judicial proceedings must be conducted in such a way as to avoid victimisation, trauma or discrimination of the offender (and equally victims and witnesses). As such, any juvenile questioned by the authorities must be provided the following opportunities and guarantees, among others:

- To be judged for offences committed, and not according to the demands of, or under pressure from, victims or public opinion.
- Contact with his or her family, where possible.
- Rapid recourse to free legal aid and a lawyer.
- To be informed of the complaints mechanisms available in case of violation of his/her integrity during detention.
- To be briefed and guided throughout proceedings with respect, benevolence and sensitivity, in a language which he/she understands (from questioning during the investigation, to hearings and counsel's address during the trial, and during disciplinary proceedings during detention, etc.).
- To be monitored by a social worker able to establish a background check that the judge can use to determine appropriate educational or punitive measures (or combination thereof) in accordance with both the personal situation of the juvenile and the seriousness of the offence.
- That legal periods of custody and preventive detention are respected.

Alternatives to detention may be applied at any stage of proceedings, from initial questioning, until the end of the application of punitive measures. Furthermore, any decision and any punitive measure applied to a minor must be considered reversible at any given moment, under the supervision of the juvenile judge, according to the child's development, his or her behaviour, and according to the outcome of the educational follow-up he or she receives.

Alternatives are at once a means of conflict resolution, restoring social harmony, repairing the harm suffered, improving public safety and promoting respect for child rights. Alternatives may be introduced in some of the following ways.

- Pre-trial: diversion by means of out-of-court settlement. Depending on the country, police officers may be empowered to settle the problem without initiating legal proceedings.
- Pre-sentencing: legal proceedings are suspended while an alternative is sought, and if this is successful the judge dismisses the case.
- Post-trial: either the convicted youth is not sentenced, or the youth is sentenced but the sentence is not applied, in order to find alternatives.

The applicable alternatives must be appropriate for the age and maturity of the juvenile, and match the seriousness of the offences committed. In the case of minor offences committed by first-time offenders, some alternatives avoid the case being referred to the legal authorities, allowing the child to recognise the consequences of his or her actions and make the parents aware of their responsibilities, but without a criminal record being created. The principle of diversion pre-supposes the consent of the minor and his/her parents or legal guardians, and a restorative approach to justice based on relationships (not the offence), reparation (not the sanction), restoration of social ties (not deterrence), consideration of the victim, and a sense of personal responsibility.

Diversion aims to break the vicious circle of stigmatisation, violence, humiliation and the breakdown of social bonds. It circumvents the 'school of crime' (i.e. detention facilities), reduces the risk of recidivism, avoids legal expenses, and fosters integration rather than exclusion from the social context. Contrary to popular opinion, a large majority of first-time offenders who benefit from these alternatives do not re-offend. Measures include admonition, reprimand or warning (for the juvenile and the parents), conciliation or informal mediation, community service, probation, or supervision by welfare or education services. All these procedures suppose that the actors involved are trained in these practices and that the two parties are in agreement (recognition of the deed by the juvenile and the victim's consent).

Other diversionary approaches exist, even once a case has been referred to the prosecutor.

- Release on probation and re-evaluation by the social worker in association with the family – this procedure being subject to a social report submitted to the judge within a period set by the latter.
- Placement in a non-custodial institution with a socio-educational function, when the age, circumstances or the safety of the juvenile demand or permit it.
- Criminal mediation, initiated by the judge – this can only take place if the victim and the perpetrator of the criminal offence are in agreement. It respects the rights of complainants and alleged perpetrators who may be advised or assisted by a lawyer or other appropriate person of their choosing. It provides a solution to the criminal dispute in a way that is flexible, rapid and simple, by seeking amicable solutions. It enables communication to be restored between the disputing parties and thus moves towards social appeasement.

Community service – performing work to benefit the community, the village or district – is a feature of many customs and traditions. Its use must not be an occasion to exploit the work capacity of a child but, to the contrary, should give him or her an opportunity to realise his or her potential within the community while benefiting from a learning opportunity.

## The Need for National and Local Indicators

In many countries, the statistical recording of the number and conditions of juveniles who are detained or placed in an institution is gravely lacking. Indeed at times, juveniles are subject to judicial proceedings without a case file, or their files are mislaid. In some countries, statistics only exist for the capital city, and perhaps a handful of major towns, and ignore locally applied procedures and methods, about which no-one really knows the extent of arbitrary practices used against juvenile offenders.

The United Nations Office on Drugs and Crime/United Nations Children's Fund Manual for the Measurement of Juvenile Justice Indicators[5] introduces fifteen juvenile justice indicators to assist local and national officials in establishing sustainable information systems to monitor the situation of children in conflict with the law. The indicators are grouped and presented as follows.

*Quantitative Indicators:*

1) Number of children arrested during a 12-month period
2) Number of children in detention
3) Number of children in pre-sentence detention
4) Time spent by children in detention before sentencing
5) Time spent by children in detention after sentencing
6) Number of child deaths in detention during a 12-month period
7) Percentage of children in detention not wholly separated from adults
8) Percentage of children in detention who have been visited by, or visited, parents, guardian or an adult family member
9) Percentage of children sentenced receiving a custodial sentence
10) Percentage of children diverted or sentenced who enter a pre-sentence diversion scheme
11) Percentage of children released from detention receiving aftercare

*Policy Indicators:*

12) Existence of a system guaranteeing regular independent inspection of places of detention
13) Existence of a complaints system for children in detention
14) Existence of a specialised juvenile justice system
15) Existence of a national plan for the prevention of child involvement in crime

A combined analysis of the fifteen indicators is considered necessary for the assessment of the situation of children in conflict with the law. However, in situations where it may not be possible to measure all fifteen, a number of 'core' indicators are identified as priority, namely: indicator one – children in detention; indicator three – children in pre-sentence detention; indicator nine – custodial sentencing; indicator ten – pre-sentence diversion; and indicator fourteen – specialised juvenile justice system.

## Armed Conflict Cannot Be a Pretext for Marginalising Juvenile Justice

Outside the context of armed conflict, some countries lawfully recruit children into government armed forces, others joining military schools with a view to enlisting into the armed forces at a future date. As these children are subject to the military legal system, the Committee on the Rights of the

Child has raised a number of questions about the nature of the criminal procedure, and applicable sanctions, in terms of safeguards and compliance with Articles 37 and 40 of the Convention. Questions must also be raised about the technical and ethical content of training given in these schools.

However, other children also find themselves directly and actively involved in conflict through their recruitment by armed state or non-state actors. In cases of 'child soldiers' tried for crimes committed during an armed conflict, a complex question is whether the fact of being under the age of criminal responsibility can, or should, be systematically used to exempt them from judicial proceedings. What is clear is that applying blanket impunity to transitional justice processes may risk, in the event of a resumption of hostilities, encouraging warlords to recruit children to commit atrocities, in the belief that these minors will evade prosecution. However, what needs to be clearly and rigorously acknowledged is that the warlords themselves, in engaging in under-age recruitment in the first place, have committed war crimes for which they should be held accountable.

Regarding the involvement of child soldiers in post-conflict proceedings forming part of a national reconciliation process, they must benefit from measures designed for the protection of child witnesses or victims, as provided for under international law, regardless of whether their recruitment was voluntary or forced.

> Child victims and witnesses denotes children and adolescents, under the age of 18, who are victims of crime or witnesses to crime regardless of their role in the offence or in the prosecution of the alleged offender or groups of offenders.[6]

It should be noted here that in Articles 37 and 40 of the Convention, concerning the deprivation of liberty and the administration of juvenile justice, it is at no point specified that a conflict or post-conflict situation authorises any derogation from the strict application of the principles of juvenile justice on the grounds of a legal exception. Furthermore, a study by the United Nations Sub-Commission on the Promotion and Protection of Human Rights concluded that military tribunals should not have, as a matter of principle, the jurisdiction to judge anyone under the age of 18.[7]

In post-conflict situations, the restoration of the rule of law should be used as an 'opportunity' to reform the juvenile justice system in compliance with international standards, and integrate it into the establishment of a broader human security policy. The chaotic nature of the post-conflict environment requires that re-establishing a functioning juvenile justice system, including prevention, be set as a priority, at the risk of seeing countless minors turn into habitual offenders. At the same time, the prevention of maltreatment and sexual abuse in institutions or places of detention for the civilian population should be dealt with as an issue of the utmost seriousness.

When an international force intervenes during or after a conflict to oversee an end to hostilities, or for peacekeeping purposes, safeguards to judicial procedure must also be secured in accordance with international standards. Local personnel must be trained to this end, in particular, in countries where relevant national laws are incompatible with international standards or, worse still, are non-existent. Also, in the face of criminal behaviour by members of foreign military and humanitarian forces intervening in situations where the civilian population is especially vulnerable, in particular children, it should be noted that the legal immunity of these military or UN forces does not necessarily extend to covering crimes committed in relation to the civilian population: for example, in cases of child prostitution, or extortion of sexual favours for humanitarian assistance, as has been reported in Africa or Asia in recent years.

Finally, in the context of the 'war on terror', some governments have enacted exceptional laws and procedures that make no distinction between juveniles and adults 'suspected' of acts of terror. Incarcerated with adults from their apprehension, or in preventive detention, their fate is sometimes determined in total non-compliance with basic legal procedures and guarantees of due process such as the presumption of innocence, the right of defence or the right of appeal against the deprivation of liberty. This is not to mention the total absence of social or psychological support. The 'war on terror', having resulted in an extension of preventive and surveillance measures for the civilian population, also means that even during simple public demonstrations (distribution of tracts, etc.), juveniles are increasingly vulnerable to arbitrary arrest and detention, or to being handled 'in secret' along with adults.

> The concept underpinning why under-18s need special protection when they come into conflict with the law does not become invalid merely because they are members of the armed forces or because additional or exceptional legal powers apply. The reasons why children and juveniles are recognised as needing and deserving different treatment remain applicable – so should the requisite standards.[8]

## Conclusions

The experience of one non-governmental organisation, active in the promotion of juvenile justice, reveals a strange paradox: it is the most underprivileged countries that have traditional methods of punishment for juvenile offenders, that are geared towards education and the re-integration of the minor into the community, and never to exclusion (this does not however mean that all forms of traditional punishment can be condoned). In the most developed countries, with their technology-based security approaches, and the available resources to pursue alternatives for children in conflict with the law, they often fail entirely to resolve the issue of the long-term rehabilitation of the minor. While the concept of restorative justice may not be the panacea for resolving all of the problems of juvenile delinquency, the technological approach also has its limitations. Does having cameras on every street corner make us more secure (Switzerland)? Is there any pedagogical value in using a 'Taser' and other electrical stun guns in a teenage street brawl (France)? And, do metal detectors in schools prevent youth delinquency (United Kingdom)? Perhaps! But only as short-term deterrents that divert attention from the more pressing need for long-term preventive strategies that help young people avoid lives of crime and violence.

Who takes the necessary time to hear a child out; to establish or restore relationships built on trust; to teach them that a human right is first and foremost about their interaction with others – 'others' who share the same rights – and, as such, respecting one person's rights means respecting those of others? And so on, and so forth.

The individual future of adolescents is often unpredictable, but in every case of the successful rehabilitation of juvenile offenders, they state that one person or one group proved to be crucial for mending broken bridges – people who acted as role models or mentors, people who gave them a second chance.

Since the dawn of human existence, societies have gradually refined their educational practices to promote inclusion (each society being aware that the next generation is the key to its own survival): so in what way does a society's security justify exclusion?

Human security can only exist through the rule of law, as the law is the instrument that governs – and restores – relationships between individuals once they have been broken. Any regime that establishes a security-focussed society at the expense of human rights develops totalitarian tendencies and, as the last century demonstrated, totalitarian states have a tendency to become criminal.

Human security is, perhaps above all else, a system of representation that is both political (on the part of the authorities) and social (in terms of public opinion), hence the vital importance of the existence of a credible media enabling the viable and accurate sharing of information, an independent assessment of the criteria for establishing data collection, and a real debate on policies adopted to deal with the most serious breaches of human rights.

Any security policy that is built at the expense of the observance of human rights is doomed to failure.

## Endnotes

1 Translation from French by Intonation, Lyon. Interpretation: David Nosworthy.

2 Speech by the United Nations Secretary-General during a speech marking the end of his mandate, given on the occasion of the International Human Rights Day in Geneva, 10 December 2006, http://www.un.org/democracyfund/XNewsHumanRightsDay.htm (accessed October 2008).

3 UN, *Report of the World Summit for Social Development* (including the Copenhagen Declaration and Programme of Action), UN doc. A/CONF.166/9 (New York: April 1995), http://www.un.org/documents/ga/conf166/aconf166-9.htm (accessed October 2008).

4 Extracts from 'State Violence against Children', theme for the day of general discussion during the 25th Session of the Committee on the Rights of the Child (22 September 2000), http://www.unhchr.ch/html/menu2/6/crc/doc/days/violence.pdf (accessed November 2008).

5 UN Office on Drugs and Crime and UNICEF, *Manual for the Measurement of Juvenile Justice Indicators* (New York: UN, 2006).

6 UN Economic and Social Council, Resolution 2005/20, *Guidelines on Justice in Matters involving Child Victims and Witnesses of Crime* (New York: 2005), http://www.un.org/docs/ecosoc/documents/2005/resolutions/Resolution%202005-20.pdf (accessed October 2008).

7 United Nations ECOSOC, Commission on Human Rights, *Administration of Justice, Rule of law and democracy*, UN doc. E/CN.4/Sub.2/2003/NGO/23 (15 July 2003), http://www.quno.org/geneva/pdf/Juveniles-under-milit200307.pdf (accessed October 2008).

8 Rachel Brett, 'Juvenile justice, counter-terrorism and children', UN Institute for Disarmament Research, *Disarmament Forum* (March 2002): 29-36, 38.

# Chapter 7

# Independent Oversight and the Security of Children

*Brent Parfitt*

## Introduction[1]

The protection of human rights requires a network of complementary norms and mechanisms. These include state adherence to human rights treaties; implementation of international human rights obligations in domestic law; a domestic legal system that provides comprehensive substantive and procedural human rights laws; effective and accessible state institutions where individuals can obtain redress for human rights breaches, such as independent courts and national human rights institutions; a lively human rights community, involving non-governmental organisations; and a population that has developed a strong human rights culture.[2]

Oversight mechanisms are designed to provide checks and balances that prevent human rights abuses, including against children, and ensure that institutions operate efficiently and effectively while respecting the rule of law.[3] Democratic oversight and accountability of the security sector refers to a system of control that incorporates civil society involvement. It provides for a transparent, accountable, responsive, efficient, participatory and inclusive political system that delivers security and justice according to people's needs, based on a comprehensive legal framework.[4] Representatives of security and justice institutions must be liable for their actions, and inactions, towards children and should be called to account for maladministration.

For most children many oversight instruments such as the justice system are not accessible and may not provide the remedies they are seeking such as access to housing, education and medical care. There is a pressing need at the international and domestic levels to ensure that children, including those affected by armed conflict, have an accessible and effective mechanism to ensure that their rights are enforced and realised.

Independent oversight institutions have an important role to play in ensuring that children receive fair treatment by governments and that they receive substantive help to which they are entitled under both international and domestic law. The institution of the ombudsman, in particular, has proven to be a useful instrument in stabilising democracies and in allowing for public protection in respect of governmental and bureaucratic processes that are often alienated from the citizens they are supposed to serve.[5]

This chapter first reviews some of the range of oversight mechanisms that exist, before looking more specifically at the potential of the ombudsman as a mechanism for establishing and enhancing children's security by promoting and protecting their rights. Drawing on general literature about the nature of the ombudsman in democratic systems, this contribution canvasses examples of military, police and children's ombudsmen, and concludes by exploring how specialised ombudsmen at the domestic level can play an important role in the oversight of the security sector – a key duty-bearer in relation to the United Nations Convention on the Rights of the Child (the 'Convention') and its two Optional Protocols.

## Children's Security

Security is defined broadly here to include the physical and psychological well-being and safety of people. That there is a role for governments in ensuring such security has been universally established and reflected within international documents. In a general sense, children's rights will be secured by a multi-layered governance system that includes the executive, legislature, judiciary, security services, independent oversight bodies such as ombudsmen and human rights institutions, and civil society actors.

The ability to fulfil children's entitlements, and establish accountability, will be largely influenced by the nature and context of their situation. Such environments may range from states operating functioning democratic systems to fragile states. Moreover, for children who may have perpetrated wrongs on others, there may be a social and cultural need for accountability and an individual need for atonement. In turn, this difference may affect the kind of institution that will best serve such children and highlights above all the need for a flexible system of accountability to assist children whose rights have been violated, particularly in states emerging from armed conflict.

## Oversight Functions – Promoting and Protecting the Rights of Children

The Convention sets out the civil, political, economic, social and cultural rights of children. These standards and obligations are laid out in fifty-four articles, and two Optional Protocols. The Optional Protocols were adopted by the United Nations General Assembly in 2000 to increase the protection of children from sexual exploitation and involvement in armed conflicts. The Optional Protocol on the sale of children, child prostitution and child pornography draws special attention to the criminalisation of these serious violations of children's rights and emphasises the importance of fostering increased public awareness and international co-operation in efforts to combat them. The Optional Protocol on the involvement of children in armed conflict establishes 18 as the minimum age for compulsory recruitment and requires states to do everything they can to prevent individuals under the age of 18 from taking a direct part in hostilities.[6]

However, ratification of an international instrument by a country does not mean that the Protocol automatically becomes 'the law of the land'. In some countries, the constitution provides that, once ratified, an international instrument is law and, as such, is justiciable. Most however require that to become law a ratified instrument must be adopted by Parliament or similar legislative body in order to become domestic law or national law. This is particularly difficult in a federal state where powers (including legislative powers) may be divided between federal and state (provincial) authorities, and the federal government has no authority over subject matter of the instrument. In Canada for instance, the federal government does have control over military matters (including recruitment) and can make it a criminal offence to recruit children into the military.[7] However, it could do little in the area of education and health services as these are matters of provincial competency.[8] Domesticating the Convention and Optional Protocols, once ratified, can require Herculean efforts in such systems. Many countries choose not to address such difficult issues and attempt as best they can to implement the provisions of the Convention and Optional Protocols without the necessary legal authority to satisfy the judicial arm of government.

To realise the rights enshrined in these instruments, oversight of state institutions at all levels needs to operate efficiently and effectively. Local oversight mechanisms are particularly important for institutions such as the police and child protection services, as these can increase their accountability to the children and communities they serve. Institutions within societies emerging from conflict will be in a state of flux and will have differential means and inclinations to provide this security. Such institutions will need support as well as oversight.

Oversight takes many forms such as monitoring, investigating and reporting, as well as pressuring for or ordering change. Oversight could also mean advocating for rights protection in general, or in specific instances. It also implies that there will be methods of seeking rights protection, such as through a right of petition or complaint.

Oversight by definition comprises supervision, inspection, responsibility and control. There are six main, interdependent pillars of oversight and control.[9]

1) *Internal control* includes supervision, review and monitoring among the security services and justice providers.
2) *Executive control* comprises government ministries and advisory bodies and their investigative and decision-making procedures.
3) *Parliamentary oversight* ensures control over budgeting procedures, investigations, law-making and -enacting as well as the visiting and inspecting of state-owned facilities, including juvenile prisons and orphanages.
4) *Judicial review* includes civilian and military courts and legal procedures, adjudicating cases brought against security services and individuals, protecting human rights and upholding the rule of law.
5) *Independent oversight bodies* such as human rights institutions or ombudsmen investigate complaints from the public, raise awareness of human rights violations and ensure compliance with policy and the rule of law.
6) *Civil society oversight* may provide expertise and analyse security and justice policy as well as investigate and monitor violations against children's rights.[10]

The right of complaint or petition is critical in liberal democracy, as is the right to go before the courts.[11] The ability to confront authorities through a medium such as a court, tribunal or ombudsman helps give effect to laws. On the international level, oversight is often anticipated in many laws and legal instruments. United Nations instruments, for example, often anticipate monitoring, as well as the publicising of problems.

The ability of oversight agencies to monitor governmental institutions and to initiate investigations on their own, without advocates necessarily pressing for such investigation, is also a critical practice for ensuring protection of rights and for reforming governmental agencies and actions, particularly in regard to the rights of vulnerable populations.[12]

Monitoring general situations and investigating particular cases, as well as systemic cases, are important because they allow for the marshalling of the facts of events and practices which gave rise to grievances, and for the fair appraisal of problem situations. In turn this allows for the formulation of meaningful recommendations for change.

Advocacy in the form of publicity and public reporting is a critical vehicle for promoting change and helping others to see the need for change. This may also include ordering change, as opposed to relying on persuasion, publicity and advocacy in particular circumstances.

Each of the functions outlined above has its place in helping to ensure child rights promotion and protection. Countries emerging from conflict will, in particular, have to ensure appropriate institution-building to make sure children's rights are recognised, safeguarded and promoted. A variety of institutions may be involved including courts, human rights commissions, truth and reconciliation commissions, mediators, public inquiries and ombudsmen, and one of the key challenges will be to identify the institutions and mechanisms most suited and appropriate to the specific context and situation. Each has its strengths and weaknesses, and an appropriate balance needs to be found between these institutions for the country in question.

The two following sections look at some of the range of oversight mechanisms that could be adopted or promoted at the international and domestic levels. As will be explored further in this chapter, of these mechanisms, the ombudsman represents perhaps a unique, and under-utilised, tool through which to protect and promote the rights of children.

*International Oversight Mechanisms*

*Treaty bodies and international agencies:* Several UN conventions and treaties create entities to monitor progress in certain areas, to see if there has been adherence to agreed standards within the conventions or treaties. The Convention contains such a provision. The Committee on the Rights of the Child created under the Convention monitors states' adherence to the Convention and provides reports and commentary on the situation in countries throughout the world. It has an important role as an oversight institution and through persuasion and publicity can effect change at international and domestic levels.

Currently, four of the treaty bodies may under certain circumstances consider complaints or communications from individuals – the Human

Rights Committee, the Committee Against Torture, the Committee on the Elimination of Discrimination against Women, and the Committee on the Elimination of Racial Discrimination.[13] Recently a number of respected non-governmental organisations active in the children's rights movement have organised a campaign to expand the mandate of the Committee on the Rights of the Child (the 'Committee') to provide it with the authority to investigate allegations of rights violations, under the Convention and Optional Protocols, by ratifying States Parties.

In 2005, the UN Security Council set up a monitoring mechanism to gather information and to report to the Security Council Working Group on children and armed conflict.[14] This mechanism is co-ordinated by the United Nations Children's Fund (UNICEF) working with the office of the Special Representative of the UN Secretary-General for Children and Armed Conflict.

UN Agencies such as UNICEF have had a critical role in promoting children's issues and in providing support for children worldwide. They too provide reports and aid mechanisms in various contexts that provide an important function of informal oversight.

*a) International courts*

Both the International Court of Justice and the International Criminal Court (ICC) can play a significant role in ensuring the security of children through their adjudication. While the jurisdiction of the former is limited in that only a State Party may appear before it, it has the mandate to deal with a number of specific multi-lateral treaties that relate directly to children such as the Protocol to prevent, suppress, and punish the trafficking in persons, especially women and children, the Convention on consent to marriage, minimum age for marriage and registration of marriages, and the Convention against discrimination in education.

Unlike the International Court of Justice, the ICC is legally and functionally independent from the United Nations, although the Rome Statute grants certain powers to the United Nations Security Council. It was established in 2002 as a permanent tribunal to prosecute individuals for genocide, crimes against humanity and war crimes. On 17 March 2006, Thomas Lubanga, former leader of a militia group in the Democratic Republic of the Congo, became the first person to be arrested under a warrant issued by the Court for allegedly 'conscripting and enlisting children under the age of fifteen years and using them to participate actively in hostilities', defined as a war crime under the Rome Statute.

*b) International criminal tribunals and special courts*

In response to acts of genocide, crimes against humanity and serious violations of humanitarian law committed during the conflicts in Rwanda and the former Yugoslavia in the 1990s, the United Nations Security Council established special international criminal tribunals to prosecute those responsible. More recently a series of so-called hybrid courts have been developed that are based in the country where the atrocities were committed, and apply a combination of domestic and international law. An example is the Special Court for Sierra Leone, established jointly by the Government of Sierra Leone and the United Nations in January 2002. One of the often cited advantages of this type of approach is the opportunity that it provides for re-building the capacity of the domestic justice system that may have been significantly weakened by preceding events.

*c) Non-governmental Organisations (NGOs)*

International NGOs such as Save the Children, War Child and the Coalition to Stop the Use of Child Soldiers have played a crucial role in both drawing attention to problems regarding children generally and children affected by armed conflict in particular, as well as in promoting and participating in the drafting of standards of international law respecting children.[15] NGOs have also had a very important role on the ground in various situations as they have provided and facilitated the provision of aid. NGOs have in some instances become the de facto service providers for children in their local communities. They therefore provide an informal oversight role at the domestic level, and are usually extremely active in advocacy both locally and internationally.

*Domestic Oversight Mechanisms*

> … the real litmus test of accountability will lie in the quality of domestic institutional arrangements for ensuring that the national and local levels of government, as well as other key actors, are accountable for any failures which might have been avoided to ensure respect for the rights of the child.[16]

*a) Courts*

In liberal democracies, courts are often seen as the ultimate expression of legal process and the rule of law. Rights protection, although historically often focussed on property as opposed to personal rights, is a critical function of courts in modern democracies. Day-to-day dispensation of justice takes places at the domestic level, whether that be in national, provincial/state or municipal arenas. Judges mete out justice according to the laws and precedents of the territories in which they have jurisdiction. They do so in a formalised fashion in a very formal setting. Depending on the culture, their method may be inquisitorial or adversarial.[17]

However, court systems are expensive to create and costly to run. Courts are often clogged, and court procedures increasingly beyond the means of average citizens.[18] Also, in post-conflict settings, setting up a viable court system will take time, compromising the perceived delivery of justice.

Informal traditional justice mechanisms, including traditional courts, can have an important role to play. In many contexts, 80 to 90 percent of disputes may be dealt with through such informal mechanisms, as opposed to the hard-to-access formal justice system. However, to be able to fully promote such mechanisms it is vital that they be based on approaches that promote restorative justice and reconciliation, and that their actions respect and are in compliance with international human rights standards.

*b) Human rights commissions*

Human rights commissions are useful instruments in ensuring rights protection.[19] They are less formal than courts, with less formalised rules of evidence and procedure. Mandates vary from jurisdiction to jurisdiction. In Canada for instance human rights commissions and tribunals focus on ending discrimination either as decision-makers or educators, or both. International human rights commissions often have broader, more positive roles in enforcing and promoting rights.

As mandates and functions vary so do procedures. In some countries human rights promoters are human rights ombudsmen and in others human rights enforcers are tribunals. Where they are tribunals, they operate on an adversarial basis that, although less formal and expensive than courts, may be problematic for effective problem resolution.

*c) Truth and reconciliation commissions*

Truth and reconciliation commissions vary in form and function. However, most have the task of discovering and exposing past wrongdoing by a government in the hope of resolving the matter. In exposing past wrongdoings they point the way to a better future for the state and its relationship with citizens. Truth and reconciliation commissions have become an important means of addressing human rights violations that have had devastating effects on countries, societies and peoples emerging from armed conflict. They may help people overcome the traumatic effects of such practices and events.[20] Conducted in the form of inquiries, they have the purpose of healing deep social wounds.

Such commissions may be part of the process of reconstruction of post-conflict societies but they cannot be the sole response to individual and societal needs. They are simply not designed for on the ground problem solving, for resolving rights issues and entitlements at an individual level.

*d) Public inquiries*

Inquiry bodies cloaked with legislative authority can perform a crucial role in the protection of children's rights. In the United Kingdom, for example, an independent report (the Blake Inquiry) was commissioned by the Defence Minister to look into the deaths of four young soldiers in barracks at Deepcut, Surrey.[21] Recommendation One states that, 'Young people with suitable qualities for a military career should continue to be able to enlist at 16, with a view to fully participating in all aspects of military duties from the age of 18, so long as their training takes place in a suitable environment dedicated to the needs of such young people, and particular care is taken for their welfare.'[22]

Following the release of the report and in response to the recommendations, the Defence Minister, Adam Ingram, indicated in the media that the Independent Services Complaints Commissioner 'would be able to accept complaints from service personnel or family members'.[23]

*e) Mediators*

In North America alternate dispute resolution in the form of mediation has become very popular.[24] Based on a philosophy of reasonableness and equality of relationships, it focusses on finding fair, and even amicable, resolutions between parties to disputes. Made fashionable by business scholars, it offers a method for resolving seemingly intractable problems through an appreciation of the diverse interests of parties in disputes. It is informal and flexible.

While inequalities of bargaining power may be resolved in part through watchful and careful mediation, it is difficult to truly overcome them completely. Mediation relies on the parties and the information and skill they bring to the process. While mediation may minimise conflict and provide a forum for disputes to be heard, it may not be able to affect just solutions for the mediating parties.[25]

*f) Civil society*

Civil society programmes that work to address children's issues such as human trafficking, gender equity and violence against children may provide oversight of child rights and security sector activities and practices. Programmes that track violence against children can be encouraged to lobby for reform and to build public awareness of the problems and constituencies for change.[26]

*g) The ombudsman*

The modern ombudsman came into being as a means to resolve problems where the state was growing rapidly.[27] The ombudsman, as public protector, emerged as a vehicle to overcome the alienation of people from the state, and also as a link of the state to the public. The ombudsman is an investigator, and the ombudsman plan is an inquisitorial system.

The ombudsman is able to gather and analyse facts of particular situations in relation to standards of justice in order to effect meaningful resolutions of problems. The Committee has attached considerable importance to the ombudsman, and other similar human rights institutions, in the protection of children's rights. Thus, for example, its guidelines for the drafting of periodic reports, requests states to 'provide information on … any independent body established to promote and protect the rights of the child such as an ombudsperson or commissioner'. The concluding observations adopted by the Committee have also commended those states that have established child-specific institutions and have regularly called for their creation in states that have yet to do so.

The Council of Europe has recommended the appointment of a commissioner or ombudsman for children to promote children's rights, and the European Parliament has called on its member states to appoint a children's ombudsman. Finally, regional bodies such as the European Network of Ombudspersons for Children have also sought to give impetus to this approach.[28]

While the ombudsman may also encounter problems of instability and lack of funding, its easy establishment and its utility as a mechanism for securing children's rights make it a potentially interesting model within post-conflict settings. The ombudsman plan bears more in-depth analysis, and it is that to which we now turn.

## The Ombudsman as an Oversight Mechanism

The ombudsman movement has grown tremendously since the Second World War. Ombudsmen abound in the public and private sectors in many countries around the world. Their powers, forms and functions are varied.[29] The ombudsman form has become in some senses ambiguous but it may also be seen as flexible and adaptable.[30] Minimally, it could be said that ombudsmen are concerned with resolving administrative and institutional problems, and more often than not they do so through investigation of the facts of situations followed by reports, recommendations and use of various techniques, including mediation, through which practical resolutions are effected. It typically provides a non-adversarial method of problem resolution.

There are various ombudsmen models including parliamentary, executive and organisational ombudsmen. There are ombudsmen in the public and in the private sectors with general or with specialised, restricted jurisdictions. One of the primary divisions, which is instructive to consider here, is the division between parliamentary and executive ombudsmen. The parliamentary or legislative model is often referred to as the classical model, which is based on the New Zealand ombudsman plan that was brought into existence in the 1960s. The classical ombudsman is said to operate with, and reflect, four major characteristics: independence, impartiality and fairness, credible review processes, and a penumbra of confidentiality.[31] Independence is a necessary characteristic of an effective ombudsman. The ombudsman must be able to make judgments on the merits of cases, free from pressure. Related to this, the ombudsman ought not to be involved in matters in which he or she has self-interest and in relation to which he or she can be biased or seen to be biased. In this model, the ombudsman must have the capability of reviewing matters that come before him or her – and must be able to investigate. Finally the ombudsman must be able to operate in a private and confidential atmosphere, which facilitates information gathering and frankness without compromising the credibility of the ombudsman process.

The classical parliamentary model has been established in many commonwealth jurisdictions. For example, the model has been adopted in most Canadian provinces. These provincial ombudsmen investigate complaints about public administration, form opinions as to what has gone wrong (or right!) and make recommendations as appropriate. In those provinces the independence of ombudsmen is secured through making them officers of the legislature and giving them fixed terms of office. The selection process for ombudsmen ensures all party involvement. In both provinces, confidentiality of the process is statutorily ensured, and the ombudsmen are given extensive powers of investigation including subpoena and summons powers. These ombudsmen also have general jurisdiction, that is, they have the ability to investigate complaints about public administration over a broad range of public institutions. These ombudsmen are given powerful administrative justice codes embedded in their statutes, which guide their investigative processes and their formulation of opinions and recommendations.[32] Finally, these ombudsmen have the ability to investigate administrative problems on their own initiative and not solely in response to complaints from individuals. This latter power carries important obligations and implies that ombudsmen will be engaged and committed watchers of public administration, and will as well be engaged in systemic investigations.[33]

The classical parliamentary ombudsman is a powerful tool and in the right hands it can work effectively to attain individual justice and to promote improvement of and even reform in public administration. This is not to say that it cannot be challenged even in well established democracies. In times of funding shortfalls the ombudsman can be constrained and their jurisdiction curtailed. Finances and ideological attacks on government that lead to privatisation can limit people's right of complaint about service provision.[34] Moreover, even under favourable circumstances, the ombudsman can be of little use if the ombudsman process is treated as little more than a mail drop for complaints or as a technical rather than humane project.[35] Notwithstanding its problems, though, the classical ombudsman model has real potential, particularly in evolving democracies. Its flexibility may be particularly suited to fluid social and political situations.[36]

An executive or organisational ombudsman is different from a parliamentary ombudsman in several respects. This form of ombudsman sits within the institution for which it investigates, mediates or otherwise solves problems. While most such ombudsmen are investigators, they may also be mediators. While they may be established by statute or by-law, more typically they are instruments of policy. The executive ombudsman also typically does not have the investigative powers of the classical ombudsman nor is it able to assure confidentiality in the same way.[37] Executive ombudsmen are often seen as being too tied to their organisations to be truly independent and are often perceived as being controlled by those organisations.[38]

Despite these shortcomings though, executive ombudsmen can be effective complaint handlers and can be promoters of administrative reform.[39] Because they often know their organisations and come to understand the key issues facing those who encounter the organisations, they can often very effectively steer people through problematic situations and help their organisations to treat people fairly.

Ombudsmen may be legislative or executive but have restrictive jurisdiction. In Canada, for example, the information and privacy commissioners at the federal level are ombudsmen. They are information ombudsmen dealing with restricted topics albeit with respect to a variety of institutions. Some university ombudsmen in North America are restricted to only dealing with student complaints while others deal with both employees and students. The potential permutations and combinations are likely endless. The issue ultimately though is whether or not a general or specialised ombudsman can best effect change with respect to a certain set of issues. This will depend on the circumstances of each societal situation.

## Examples of the Ombudsman Institution

There are a variety of ombudsman forms including military, police and children's ombudsmen, as well as human rights ombudsmen. The difficulty faced by most ombudsmen who could effectively deal with the abuse of rights of children whose security is compromised is their lack of jurisdiction over the armed forces, police and other security services. There are few such institutions that have this jurisdiction. If they do, their power could be curtailed if the government holds concerns that an investigation could result in a threat to national security or interfere in the prosecution of an offence. Nonetheless it is instructive to canvass several examples, to see what lessons can be learned, what limitations exist, and to suggest if and how they may be overcome.

### *Military Ombudsmen*

Around the world there are both legislative and executive ombudsmen who deal with the military. The Finnish Parliamentary Commissioner, a legislative ombudsman, for example, has jurisdiction over the military. In Canada, the National Defence and Canadian Forces Ombudsman, an executive position, provides some civilian oversight of the military albeit embedded in a ministry of the Canadian Government.[40]

Their mandates include the ability to ensure respect for the rule of law in the armed forces to promote transparency and accountability in the defence structures and to focus attention on problems in military practice that require correction. Some children of military personnel experience special challenges because of their parent's deployment, work hours and housing issues. For some their educational, social and emotional needs are not met. To deal with this, some defence forces have set up family centres to cope with these needs, sometimes in co-operation with civilian agencies.[41] In some American jurisdictions these organisations have been called 'ombudsmen' but they have little in common with the classical, parliamentary ombudsman model. Their main functions are to connect military families and children with the services they require.[42]

The jurisdiction of most military ombudsmen is restricted to the investigation of complaints from military staff and their families. However, in the Philippines, the ombudsman may also investigate citizens' complaints about military activity and can conduct and initiate prosecutions in cases of abuse or graft.[43]

### *Police Ombudsmen*

Unlike most military ombudsmen, police ombudsmen or police commissioners often have the power to investigate citizens' complaints concerning police conduct. Most are created at the local or provisional levels although some may exercise broader jurisdiction depending on the geographical boundaries of the police force and its organised structure in the country. Governments are reluctant to give generalist civilian ombudsmen the authority to investigate the police. In a case in British Columbia, Canada, the Supreme Court of British Columbia decided that the ombudsman was precluded from investigating a police officer's conduct while investigating a crime, as this was a matter within the jurisdiction of the Parliament of Canada, despite the fact that the ombudsman had jurisdiction over the Police Boards that employ the police.[44]

In New South Wales, Australia, both the Commissioner of Police and Ombudsman respond to complaints against the police and have developed interim guidelines for the handling these complaints, 'to facilitate the sound investigation and appropriate determination of complaints against police whether made to the Commissioner or the Ombudsman'.[45] Governments are more likely to create specialised ombudsmen or commissioners to exercise police oversight responsibility. The Committee, in General Comment No.2 (2002), has recommended that, where there are a number of human rights institutions in a country, they work closely together to ensure that the promotion and protection of children's rights are mainstreamed.[46]

*General Ombudsmen and Children's Ombudsmen*

The Committee has also recognised that ombudsmen and human rights commissions ought to be established for the promotion and protection of human rights.[47] Numerous concluding observations have recommended the establishment of such offices and the improvement of existing institutions. Further, in its guidelines regarding reports to be submitted, the Committee requests States Parties to provide information on independent human right institutions, their mandates, roles and financing.[48] The Committee has also recommended that these types of bodies contribute independently to the reporting process under the Convention and the Optional Protocols.

The two following reports provide examples of how the ombudsman protects the security of children in their countries; one respecting the domestic security of children who may be abused in the family setting, and the other regarding children whose rights are abused by the conscription policies of the government.

a) The Special Report of the **ombudsman for New South Wales** (NSW), Australia, *Domestic Violence: Improving Police Practice*, provides an example of problem identification and the development of practical recommendations to improve governmental response to the issue.[49] The ombudsman of NSW is unique in not only having jurisdiction over the traditional ministries and departments of government, but also having jurisdiction over the state's police, allowing a more holistic approach to be taken. In noting that the police in NSW respond to approximately 120,000 cases of domestic violence each year, the report states that the victims should be entitled to receive a consistent standard of service.

In respect of the domestic security of children, the report notes that approximately 1,400 'children at risk' reports were made by the police each week to the Department of Community Services helpline, of which 800 were referred for further assessment. The Report recommended that the Department and the NSW Police develop a shared risk assessment model to 'assist in alerting either agency about children and young people at risk of harm, particularly in situations of domestic violence'. Regarding inter-agency response, the Report speaks to the need for co-operation between agencies at the local level, but points to two specific challenges being 'sometimes competing ideologies and priorities … and perceived obstacles to sharing information'.

b) In March of 2008 the **ombudsman for Bolivia** declared that unless the Bolivian Government amended its draft laws concerning conscription of young people, he would report the matter to international authorities to 'denounce the government for human rights violations'. The ombudsman observed that the rules in the draft act 'constitute a flagrant violation of human rights and children's rights, making children of 16, 17 and 18 years old fight for the flag in contravention of the UN Convention on the Rights of the Child'. He also raised concern about the legislative process that only gave parliamentarians one hour's notice before debate of the legislation in the Chamber of Deputies.

## Limitations of the Ombudsman Model

The ombudsman model has great potential but it is not without limitation and criticism. As any institution it must have real support and a modicum of stability to survive. If designed improperly it will flounder.

One of the most recent national ombudsman for children offices was established in Ireland in 2002.[50] This office has most of the characteristics of the classical ombudsman including independence from the executive arm of government. The enabling statute indicates that, 'The Ombudsman for Children shall be independent in the performance of his or her functions under this Act.'[51] The enabling legislation goes on to say that the ombudsman shall have regard to the best interests of the child and give due regard to the child's wishes. As with other ombudsman for children offices she or he has the mandate to promote awareness of the rights of the child.[52]

However, a number of problems have been encountered, some of them structural issues in dealing with children associated with armed forces. For example the enabling legislation for the office states that 'persons under the age of 18 who are enlisted as members of the Defence Forces shall not be regarded as children in any case where they are subject to military law under the Defence Forces Act'.[53] A number of other issues have arisen including:

- The lack of a legal ban on the involvement of those under 18 in hostilities
- The liability of children in the Defence Forces to military law
- The lack of support of children who are former soldiers now living in Ireland
- The restrictions of ombudsman investigation of complaints made by young people who are members of the Defence Forces[54]

The ability of the Irish children's ombudsman to investigate breaches of the rights of children are further impeded by the ombudsman's lack of jurisdiction over the police, certain custodial facilities for children, actions in relation to asylum, immigration, naturalisation and citizenship, and where a Minister requests the ombudsman not to investigate. Further, the ombudsman cannot investigate any incidents of complaint that relate to national security or military activity.

These exclusions are by no means unique to the ombudsman for children in Ireland and are duplicated in ombudsman legislation in many jurisdictions.[55] The structure, the legislated mandate, jurisdiction and capabilities of the ombudsman are thus clearly important and if insufficient will hurt the overall effectiveness of this institution.

Beyond the structural, there are on the ground issues of support and implementation that may hinder the effectiveness of an ombudsman. Ombudsmen models in Latin America have sometimes been seen as ineffectual because of lack of support. It has been said for example that El Salvador's Human Rights Ombudsman Office, which includes a Children's Rights Ombudsman, is both under-staffed and under-funded.[56]

In addition, many social and political factors may hinder an ombudsman in being forthright, and may militate against an ombudsman speaking out on issues.[57] To work properly an ombudsman must have institutional, functional and personal independence.[58]

## Modelling an Ombudsman for Children in Post-conflict Societies

Reconstruction in societies emerging from conflict and post-conflict societies requires the establishment of the rule of law and respect for civil and political rights. In order to be effective, it must allow for capacity-building in the development of a range of administrative institutions that provide or will provide services to the public. The ombudsman model has the potential to be a flexible and independent oversight body that can contribute to state capacity-building. Through its recommendations and interaction with state authorities to ensure that the domestic and international rights of citizens are respected, based on principles of fairness, the ombudsman is able to influence the culture and attitudes of these state authorities. Having both a substantive and procedural focus, it can help institutions build processes that truly serve children while acting appropriately in the public interest.

In order to ensure the security of children it is recommended that, firstly, States Parties to the Convention and its Optional Protocols domesticate all provisions, including those of other relevant international instruments, through appropriate legislative measures so that the rights contained therein are justiciable, enforceable by the courts and other tribunals within the State.

It is further recommended that the States Parties create an ombudsman office, or expand the mandate of existing ombudsmen, to accept and investigate complaints concerning violations of children's rights including threats to a child's security. Such an office could be generic or specialised (a Military, Police or Children's Ombudsman) but must have a broad jurisdiction to investigate all government and contracted agencies that are involved, such as ministries of the interior, defence, justice, education, health and social services. In some ombudsman offices a Deputy Ombudsman for Children has been established with a specific mandate to investigate complaints concerning children. Whatever the form, to be effective in ensuring the security of children the ombudsman's office should have:

- Unfettered jurisdiction over all security services including the military, police, border security and immigration authorities.
- Adequate investigative powers including the right to summons and subpoena.
- The ability to take complaints directly from children or their advocates, including any complaint of maltreatment, bullying or harassment
- The ability to commence investigations on the ombudsman's own initiative.
- The ability to report directly to the legislative arm of government and the public generally on her/his findings and recommendations.
- The necessary financial and human resources from the legislative arm of government to effectively discharge the office's mandate.
- The statutory responsibility to review, monitor and report on the implementation of the Convention, its Optional Protocols and other relevant international instruments, including declarations made by the States Parties.
- The ability to resolve complaints either after or during the course of an investigation.
- The ability to visit, unannounced, cadet schools, police academies, military bases, immigration facilities, war or post-war venues,

(juvenile) detention centres, rehabilitation centres and recruitment centres based on a complaint or on the ombudsman's own initiative.

- The duty to promote and create awareness of the domestic and international rights of the child among children, the public at large and government.

## Conclusions

The protection of human rights requires states to adhere to international human rights treaties, firstly by incorporating their provisions into domestic law, but also by providing a domestic legal system through which individuals can obtain redress for human rights violations.

Oversight mechanisms are designed to prevent human rights abuses, including against children, and ensure that institutions operate efficiently and effectively. Guaranteeing human rights may be particularly challenging in post-conflict settings, and the selection of the most appropriate, effective and viable oversight mechanisms a key element of re-establishing rule of law, and as such the protection of children.

As has hopefully been demonstrated here, the ombudsman model offers a perhaps under-utilised option for ensuring children's security in post-conflict settings, including addressing and responding to the specific issues faced by children who have been directly affected by the armed conflict.

The particular strengths of the ombudsman office in protecting the security of children include its independence, accessibility, informality, confidentiality, reporting/transparency and investigative powers. The major challenges that face the institution are structural in that offices may not have the authority to investigate all the agencies that have an impact on the security of children, and lack financial and human resources, which results in an office that is a mere token for oversight.

Nevertheless, the ombudsman office can and does play a significant role in protecting and promoting the security of children in all settings, including the home, the school, the community and society at large.

In regard to children affected by armed conflict, a specific role for which ombudsmen, specialised or generic, have the potential to contribute is in increasing their capacity and effectiveness in ensuring that children are not conscripted into armed forces or used in hostilities. They also have an important role to play in monitoring recruitment techniques in general and, in those states that do permit recruitment under the age of 18, ensuring that appropriate safeguards are respected in the process, and that new recruits are treated in a manor consistent with the state's duty of care obligations. In addition, for those children who have been directly affected by conflict, the ombudsman can have a crucial role in ensuring that the children concerned receive the appropriate and necessary level of care and rehabilitation from the state, required in order that they may resume a constructive role in society.

## Endnotes

1 The author acknowledges the contribution to and comments about this paper made by Greg Levine.
2 Linda C. Rief, 'Building Democratic Institutions: The Role of National Human Rights Institutions in Good Governance and Human Rights Protection' *Harvard Human Rights Journal* 13 (2000).
3 Organisation for Economic Co-operation and Development-Development Assistance Committee (OECD DAC), *Handbook on Security System Reform: Supporting Security and Justice* (Paris: OECD, 2007), 112.
4 Hans Born and Vincenza Scherrer, Democratic Oversight and Accountability of the Security System: Challenges and Lessons Learned (Geneva: DCAF, forthcoming 2009).
5 Rief, 'Building Democratic Institutions'.
6 Optional Protocol to the Convention on the Rights of the Child on the involvement of children in armed conflicts. Adopted and opened for signature, ratification and accession by General Assembly Resolution 263, UN doc. A/RES/54/263 (New York: May 2000).
7 Canada, Constitution Act, 1867, ss. 9.7 and 9.27.
8 Ibid., 92.
9 OCED DAC, *Handbook*, 112.
10 Ibid.
11 For example, the petition of right has been a longstanding right in English law – see for example, John H. Baker, *An Introduction to English Legal History* (London: Butterworths, 1990), 116.
12 Stephen Owen, 'Current Ombudsman Issues: An International Perspective' in *The Ombudsman: Caribbean and International Perspectives*, ed. Patrick Emmanuel (Cave Hill, Barabados: University of the West Indies, 1993), 102-107.
13 Human Rights Committee (in relation to the International Covenant on Civil and Political Rights) may consider individual communications relating to States parties to the First Optional Protocol to the ICCPR. The Committee Against Torture (in relation to the Convention against Torture) may consider individual communications relating to States Parties who have made the necessary declaration under Article 22. The Committee on the Elimination of Racial Discrimination (in relation to the Convention on the Elimination of Racial Discrimination) may consider individual communications relating to States Parties who have made the necessary Declaration under Article 14. The Committee on the Elimination of Discrimination Against Women (in relation to the Convention on the Elimination of Discrimination against Women) may consider individual communications relating to States Parties to the Optional Protocol.

14 UN Security Council, Resolution 1612, UN doc. S/RES/1612 (New York: July 2005).
15 See, for example, the following web sites: http://www.savethechildren.net; http://www.warchild.org.uk; http://www.child-soldiers.org (accessed October 2008). With respect to standard setting and international law, see Claire Breen, 'The Role of NGOs in the Formulation of Compliance with the Optional Protocol to the Convention of the Rights of the Child in Involvement of Children in Armed Conflict' *Human Rights Quarterly* 25 (2003): 453.
16 Philipp Alston and John Tobin, *Laying the Foundation for Children's Rights: An independent Study of Some Key Legal and Institutional Aspects of the Impact of the Convention on the Rights of the Child*, Innocenti Insight (Florence: UNICEF, 2005), 39.
17 Roy Gregory, 'The Ombudsman: An Excellent Form of Alternative Dispute Resolution' *International Ombudsman Yearbook* (2001): 98.
18 In Canada there are ongoing projects in civil justice reform aimed at making the courts more accessible.
19 Rief, 'Building Democratic Institutions'.
20 See for example, Christopher Connolly, 'Living on the Past: The Role of Truth Commissions in Post Conflict Societies and the Case of Northern Ireland' *Cornell International Law Journal* 39, no. 401 (2006).
21 BBC News, 'Commissioner plan after Deepcut', 13 June 2006, http://news.bbc.co.uk/2/hi/uk_news/ politics/5076036.stm (accessed October 2008).
22 Report of Nicholas Blake QC, *The Deepcut Review: A Review of the Circumstances Surrounding the Deaths of Four Soldiers at Princess Royal Barracks, Deepcut between 1995 and 2002* (London: The Stationery Office, March 2006).
23 BBC News, 'Deep Cut Inquiry news report', http://news.bbc.co.uk/1/hi/in_depth/uk/2005/deepcut_inquiry/default.stm (accessed October 2008).
24 See, for example, the description of the role of the Dispute Resolution Office of the Ministry of the Attorney General of British Columbia, available on http://www.ag.gov.bc.ca/dro (accessed October 2008).
25 Shirley A. Wiegand, 'A Just and Lasting Peace: Supplanting Mediation with the Ombuds Model' *Ohio State Journal on Dispute Resolution* 12 (1996): 95, 130.
26 Paraphrased from OECD DAC, *Handbook*, 117.
27 Donald Rowat, *The Ombudsman Plan: Essays on the Worldwide Spread of an Idea* (Toronto: McLelland and Stewart, 1973).
28 Alston and Tobin, 'Laying the Foundation for Children's Rights'.
29 Daniel Jacoby, 'The Future of the Ombudsman' in *The International Ombudsman Anthology*, ed. Linda Reif (The Hague: Kluwer Law International, 1999), 15-18.
30 Richard Gregory, 'The Ombudsman: An Excellent Form of Alternate Dispute Resolution' *International Ombudsman Yearbook* (2001): 98-100.
31 Dean M. Gotterher and Michael Hostina, 'Essential Characteristics of a Classical Ombudsman', http://www.usombudsman.org/documents/PDF/References/Essential.PDF (accessed October 2008).
32 Gregory Levine, 'Administrative Justice and the Ombudsman: Concepts and Codes in British Columbia and Ontario' *Canadian Journal of Administrative Law and Practice* 17 (2004).
33 Gregory Levine, 'The Engaged Ombudsman: Morality and Activism in Attaining Administrative Justice' *International Ombudsman Yearbook* (2004).
34 Brent Parfitt, 'The Effect of Privatisation on Ombudsman Jurisdiction' *International Ombudsman Yearbook* (2000).

35 Gerald Caiden et al., 'The Institution of the Ombudsman' in *International Ombudsman Handbook*, ed. Gerald Caiden (Westport: Greenwood, 1983), 17–19.
36 Donald Rowat, 'Introduction' to his *The Ombudsman: Citizen's Defender* (Toronto: University of Toronto Press, 1968), xxii-xxiii.
37 The idea of ombudsman privilege has emerged in the common law, and it may be that over time executive ombudsmen will be able to protect information more fully. The ombudsman privilege concept though has thus far had a chequered history in the courts of the United States and Canada.
38 Office of the Ombudsman (British Columbia), 'Fair First: An Ombuds Audit of the WCB Ombudsman' *Public Report* no. 37 (Victoria: Office of the Ombudsman, 1999).
39 Irwin Weiss, 'Comparing Legislative and Executive Ombudsman in the United States' *Ombudsman Journal* 7 (1988): 37.
40 National Defence and Canadian Forces Ombudsman, *Overhauling Oversight: Ombudsman White Paper*, Special Report (Ottawa: 2005).
41 Kingston Military Resource Centre (Ontario, Canada), http://www.kmfrc.com (accessed October 2008).
42 See, for example, Military.com, 'Family Liaison Officer or Ombudsman'.
43 See documents on the Canadian military ombudsman and the Philippines ombudsman web site, which can be found at http://www.ombudsmaan.forces.gc.ca and http://www. ombudsman. gov.ph (accessed October 2008).
44 Forum of Canadian Ombudsman, 'British Columbia Supreme Court, Friedmann vs. Attorney General Macdonell J.' (June 7, 1985), http://www.ombudsmanforum.ca/ documents/caselaw/friedmann-v-attorney_general_bc_f.asp (accessed October 2008).
45 See for example the 'Interim Guidelines between Commissioner of Police and Ombudsman for handling of Complaints against Police', http://www.omb-hcscc.nt.gov.au/publications/ app910001.pdf (accessed November 2008). See also Kim Ralston et al., 'Police Corruption: The New South Wales Experience' (New South Wales Young Lawyers Group of the International Society for Criminal Law Reform, 2004).
46 UN Committee on the Rights of the Child, The Role of Independent National Human Rights Institutions in the Protection and Promotion of the Rights of the Child, General Comment no. 2, UN doc. CRC/GC/2002/2, Para. 7 (Geneva: June 2002).
47 Ibid.
48 Ibid., para. 2.
49 New South Wales Ombudsman, *Domestic Violence: Improving Police Practice*, a special report to Parliament under s. 31 of the Ombudsman Act 1974 (NSW: December 2006).
50 See Irish Ombudsman website, http://ombudsman.gov.ie/en.
51 Ombudsman for Children Act, Statutes of Ireland, n. 22, s. 61 (2002).
52 Ibid. s. 7.
53 Ibid. s. 7.5.
54 Ombudsman for Children, Ireland, 'Press Release of Emily Logan', 12 October 2007.
55 Ombudsman for Children Act 2002, ss. 11(1)(b) and (e)(i)(iii), 11(4); UN Convention on Rights of the Child.
56 Ilene Cohn, 'The Protection of Children in Peacemaking and Peacekeeping Processes' *Harvard Human Rights Journal* 12 (1999): 129-142.
57 Ibid.
58 Maarten Oosting, 'Protecting the Integrity and Independence of the Ombudsman Institution' *International Ombudsman Yearbook* (2005): 19–21.

# Part IV

# Children, Armed Conflict, and Post-conflict Peacebuilding

## Chapter 8

# Children in Peacebuilding and Security Governance

*David Nosworthy*

When the Human Security Report was published in 2005 it surprised many by concluding that, contrary to even informed opinion, the number of (and extent of) global conflicts worldwide had been decreasing steadily since the early 1990s. Similar findings were presented by the Human Security Brief[1] of 2006. The Brief also challenged the commonly held belief that civilians are increasingly being targeted during conflict and, again, questioned the widely quoted estimate that 90 percent of those killed in today's conflicts are civilians. Acknowledging the lack of authoritative sources on the recording and reporting of civilian deaths due to political violence, it noted that the suggestive trend, based on available data, was of a clear decline since the mid-1990s.

The end of the Cold War introduced a new global security environment, marked by intra-state conflicts and mounting threats to individuals. It also, however, created 'the political space for traditional peacekeeping operations to extend their mandates to a wide range of peacebuilding activities'.[2] Largely accrediting the decline in the number of active conflicts to the peacemaking and peacekeeping efforts of the international community, the difficulty of securing the peace has regularly been highlighted. It is widely stated that countries emerging from conflict face a 50 percent risk of a relapse into violence within five years, some dispute the accuracy of this estimate and indeed suggest that the evidence here also points towards a more positive situation than is widely perceived.[3] The Brief does observe that in relation to wars that end in negotiated settlement, half will restart within five years. The misperception that characterises conventional wisdom in relation to conflict is reminiscent of the distorted reporting associated with youth violence that was mentioned earlier in the publication.

Having said this, nothing should be taken away from the complexity of the challenge that is faced, not only in making the peace following armed conflict, but in building and maintaining a post-conflict environment that offers security, and enables sustainable development that addresses the root causes of the original conflict. For sustainable development to be achieved, consideration must be given to the needs and aspirations of children and youth who will otherwise be unable to realise their full potential and contribution to peacebuilding, development and society as a whole. By overlooking the security and protection needs of young people they will remain vulnerable to abuse, exploitation and recruitment into armed groups.

Security policy has to recognise its complex interaction with outcomes for children as, not only does it have the obligation to protect children as victims, through its failings children and youth can become vulnerable to the approaches of elements intent on recruiting them into armed conflict, terrorism or criminal activity.

## Special Protection of Children During Armed Conflict

The security sector has specific obligations to fulfil in protecting and promoting the rights of children even during armed conflict.

In the context of armed conflict, children are protected under a range of instruments that are found in both international human rights law and international humanitarian law. In terms of these bodies of law, children affected by armed conflict are considered as either civilians or as participants in hostilities. In either case, they are entitled to special protection as children.

International humanitarian law is applicable not only in conflicts between two or more states (international armed conflicts), but also in internal conflicts (non-international armed conflicts). The main treaties of international humanitarian law are the four Geneva Conventions of 1949, and two Additional Protocols adopted in 1977. They oblige all parties to a conflict, including armed non-state actors, to respect certain minimum humanitarian rules with regard to persons who are not, or are no longer, taking part in hostilities.

Children benefit from protection on two levels: first, as members of the civilian population in general and, second, as a vulnerable category deserving of special protection. The Fourth Convention and two Protocols deal specifically with the protection of civilians, Additional Protocol II expanding the common Article 3 of the Geneva Conventions relating to non-international conflicts. Non-combatant civilians are guaranteed humane treatment and are covered by the legal provisions on the conduct of hostilities. Between the Fourth Geneva Convention, Protocol I and Protocol II, there are more than twenty provisions that give special protection to children affected by armed conflict. Children who take direct part in hostilities do not lose this special protection.

> Children shall be the object of special respect and shall be protected against any form of indecent assault. The Parties to the conflict shall provide them with the care and aid they require, whether because of their age or for any other reason.
> (Protocol Additional I to the Geneva Conventions).[4]

Contrary to international humanitarian law that is applicable only during armed conflict, international human rights law is in principle applicable both during peacetime and war. However, the application of some human rights conventions may be limited during armed conflict due to a derogation clause allowing restriction of the exercise of human rights during public emergency.[5] Any such derogations should fulfil basic safeguards and are prohibited with respect to several basic rights such as right to life, and prohibition of torture and slavery. The United Nations Convention on the Rights of the Child (the 'Convention') however does not contain a derogation clause and as such it may be concluded that the Convention remains fully applicable even during armed conflict.[6]

The Additional Protocols to the Geneva Conventions and the Convention with its Optional Protocol, along with other international instruments, also set limits on children's participation in hostilities.

In the simplest terms, international law protects children by banning any recruitment and direct involvement in hostilities of those under 15 years, into any form of armed forces or armed groups, in any type of armed conflict, international or non-international (the Convention, Article 38 and 1977 Additional Protocols to the four Geneva Conventions). In other words, under no circumstances should government armed forces, informal armed forces such as militias, civil defence or local defence forces, or opposing armed groups, have persons below the age of 15 years recruited or amongst their fighters.

However, international law has been developing towards the position that states take measures to ensure that no-one under 18 years of age takes direct part in hostilities, nor be recruited (African Charter on the Rights and Welfare of the Child, Article 22; International Labour Organization Convention No. 182 concerning the Prohibition and Immediate Action for the Elimination of the Worst Forms of Child Labour, Articles 2 and 3; Optional Protocol to the Convention on the Rights of the Child (the 'Convention'), on the involvement of children in armed conflicts, Article 1.[7] On 25 May 2000, the United Nations General Assembly adopted by consensus an Optional Protocol to the Convention on the involvement of children in armed conflict, which raises from 15 to 18 years the age at which direct participation in armed conflict will be permitted and establishes a ban on compulsory recruitment below 18 years.[8]

Both the United Nations Committee on the Rights of the Child and the International Committee of the Red Cross Advisory Service encourage states to adopt national measures to ensure that children enjoy the legal protection to which they are entitled.[9]

## Post-conflict Peacebuilding

In 1992, then UN Secretary-General Boutros Boutros-Ghali defined peacebuilding in his Agenda for Peace as 'action to identify and support structures which tend to strengthen and solidify peace to avoid relapse into conflict'.[10] The Supplement to an Agenda for Peace of 1995 expanded the term, emphasising that peacebuilding applied not only to post-conflict settings but across the whole conflict spectrum – before, during and after conflict.[11] In 1994, Boutros Boutros-Ghali named Graça Machel, who had served as Mozambique's first post-independence Minister for Education, to conduct a study into the impact of armed conflict on children. The report, published in 1996, was ground-breaking in bringing attention to children affected by armed conflict and highlighted among other things the important role of the international community in supporting post-conflict recovery and peacebuilding.[12]

In 2001, the UN Security Council recognised that peacebuilding 'is aimed at preventing the outbreak, the recurrence or continuation of armed conflict', requiring short- and long-term actions that focus on 'fostering sustainable institutions and processes in areas such as sustainable development, the eradication of poverty and inequalities, transparent and accountable governance, the promotion of democracy, respect for human rights and the rule of law and the promotion of a culture of peace and non-violence'.[13]

This broader understanding of peacebuilding involves addressing the root causes of conflict and promoting development and democracy in countries not affected by conflict. Indeed, many of the associated activities are the same as those of development co-operation or democracy promotion. However, peacebuilding is distinct from these in that it is conflict sensitive and an instrument for conflict prevention, conflict management and post-conflict reconstruction. The term 'post-conflict peacebuilding' reflects a narrower concept of peacebuilding.[14]

The United Nations Security Council has acknowledged that protecting child rights and preventing violations are integral to peacebuilding efforts in post-conflict environments. Since 1999, the Security Council has made children a priority, discussing the issue on an annual basis, culminating in Resolution 1612 (2005) that called for the implementation of a monitoring and reporting mechanism – the first time such an initiative has been taken by the Council. While the focus of their deliberation has been the recruitment or use of children by armed forces or groups, their concern is also with a number of other 'grave violations', namely: killing or maiming of children, attacks against schools or hospitals, abduction, rape or other grave sexual violence against children, and denial of humanitarian access for children. Members of both armed forces and armed groups appear in early reports as perpetrators of abuses against children, highlighting the importance of engaging these same actors in safe-guarding the security of children. Not only are these security actors the key players in protecting the rights and physical well-being of children, they are also key to preventing some of the gravest violations against children.

As presented earlier, the security sector has a legal obligation to protect and promote the rights of children. Nowhere is this need more pressing perhaps than in the post-conflict environment where lack of traditional support and protective structures undermine the ability of communities and families to protect their children, and the local authorities and security structures that are ostensibly responsible for providing the necessary security cover are unable or unwilling to do so at a time when they are desperately in need of reform. The challenge is to get children onto this agenda – an agenda that is, in general, blind to their specific security needs and concerns. A focus on security governance is proposed here as the necessary framework for guiding the priorities and actions of the reform process – the ultimate aim being good security governance, that is accountable to the citizens that it is meant to protect.

Children and youth have an active role to play in developing and promoting sustainable post-conflict initiatives. Unfortunately, however, the idea of mobilising this resource is generally overlooked, viewed as an issue that is exclusively the domain of social workers or teachers. What is argued here is that establishing young people's participation is not only essential to fulfilling the obligations that the security sector has for providing for the security of all, but is an imperative if the hard-won peace is to be durable. Children and youth have their own perspectives on their experiences of security and insecurity, and engaging with them will not only allow a better understanding of the issues required for designing and delivering appropriate services, but will also provide valuable insights into potential or evolving security threats.

Beyond developing the notion that the security sector is bound by its obligations to protecting children's rights and preventing wrongs, it is also important to identify the entry points through which opportunities exist for developing a better understanding of the situation of children and youth. This includes exploring ways in which children and youth can provide concrete contributions to the post-conflict peacebuilding process. Particular attention is drawn here to Chapter 12 of this publication, where Save the Children Norway demonstrate just how the views and opinions of children can be captured in a meaningful way and inform public discussion on the expectations for and delivery of security provision.

In recent years the international community has been paying increased attention to peacebuilding, witnessed not least through the decision of the United Nations to reinforce its peacebuilding capacity by creating the Peacebuilding Commission – an intergovernmental advisory body whose main purpose is to improve the co-ordination among relevant actors.[15] While substantial improvements have been made in the international community's peacebuilding capacity, there are still considerable gaps in the development of concepts, policies and practice that would facilitate post-conflict peacebuilding and make it more effective.

At the same time the profile of 'children and armed conflict' on the international stage has increased considerably notably through the deployment of Child Protection Advisers in recent UN missions and the Security Council establishing the monitoring and reporting mechanism[16] on grave violations committed against children during armed conflict. However, the significance of children to the peacebuilding environment, particularly in relation to creating stability and sustainable development, has not been fully recognised or reflected particularly in programming aimed at children and adolescents.

If peace is to be lasting, the security needs of both the state and its population must be addressed equally and in parallel with political and socio-economic aspects of reconstruction. Just as in the political and socio-economic dimensions of post-conflict peacebuilding, security requires due attention to governance, particularly good governance in the security sector.[17] The impact of and implications for children and youth need to be considered in each dimension of the peacebuilding process.

Restoring normality to young lives requires that actions aimed at addressing the legacies of conflict involve young people directly, including their active participation, allowing a better understanding of how they have been affected and how to design and implement appropriate programmes to assist them in dealing with the consequences of conflict.

Breaking the cycle of violence will mean dealing with unaccountable or corrupt security services; where necessary engaging armed non-state actors; demobilising and reintegrating former child soldiers into society; addressing the proliferation of small arms and light weapons; implementing mine action initiatives; reforming the justice system particularly the juvenile justice system; implementing transitional justice mechanisms; re-establishing rule of law; dealing with criminality; addressing past human rights violations; and providing youth with alternatives, and a vision of a constructive and productive future.

One of the challenges in identifying and responding to gaps in children's security is the tendency to categorise issues on a thematic basis. In recent years the categories to have received such special attention have been those of 'child soldiers' and 'trafficking'. While it may be hard to judge whether this phenomenon is generated by international organisations or the demands of donors to see where and how funding is dispersed and its impact, what should be acknowledged is that this compartmentalised approach is not necessarily compatible with addressing the broader security and protection aspects of many of the issues that affect children. Children will not be exclusively the victims of trafficking but rather the victims of a series of causal effects that make them vulnerable to such exploitation. The children recruited to serve in the ranks of fighting forces will have suffered compound violations of their rights that eventually led to them being susceptible to recruitment.

In presenting the issues affecting children in such a packaged way, academic and programming attention tends to be channelled accordingly, including in terms of the allocation of resources. Focussing on such 'high-profile' issues risks diverting attention away form a range of broader concerns that children may face, some of which that may appear relatively minor on the surface, but that are potentially the catalysts that make children susceptible to more serious violations. Restricting our emphasis in this way risks ignoring children's realities, and diverts attention from building more robust protective systems that could offer a safety net to children affected by a broader range of issues, including domestic violence, drug misuse, bullying or perhaps neglect, just to name a few. Also, presenting these thematic issues as technical and complex areas of programme intervention may restrict the range of actors who may be prepared or willing to engage. Multi-sectoral approaches need to recognise the importance of all duty-bearers to the process of building a protective environment, including the vital contribution of security sector actors to providing a secure environment.

## Security Governance and Security Sector Reform

Closely linked to the raised profile of the peacebuilding agenda, security sector reform (SSR) is also receiving increased attention. Notable recent developments include the Commission of the European Union's communication on 'A Concept for European Community Support for Security Sector Reform' (May 2006), the UN Security Council's debate on Security Sector Reform in February 2007 with the call for the Secretary-General to submit a report to outline a UN approach to SSR subsequently presented in May 2008[18], and the release of the Organisation for Economic Co-operation and Development – Development Assistance Committee (OECD DAC) Handbook on Security System Reform also in 2007. The initiatives by the European Union and UN Security Council are particularly interesting as both bodies have also stated commitment, respectively, to the issues of children affected by armed conflict, and children and armed conflict. From a policy perspective, one of the first priorities should be to bring together these two stated policy priorities with the aim of demonstrating that, rather than being entirely distinct areas of interest, linkages can and should be created so that complementary goals can be pursued.

Considering that the objectives of SSR tend to focus on the technical aspects of institutional and procedural reform, it may be easy to lose sight of security's connection to children. This indeed seems to be the case when reviewing the reform discourse – the only apparent connection to children being the demobilisation of child soldiers. It is only when taking a step back and asking 'what is it that security is meant to do for us' that children come into relief. Security provision for the population means that the security needs of all individuals are addressed, including children. However, recognition does need to be given to the fact that children can also be offenders, and therefore the implications that this has for dealing with scenarios where the security threat is from a child. International standards recognise that children in conflict with the law are ultimately victims themselves and should be treated accordingly. There is complex interaction between security and outcomes for children, with the security sector not only having obligations to protect children as victims, but through its failings children and youth can become vulnerable to the approaches of peace-spoilers intent on recruiting them into armed conflict, terrorism or criminal activity. The challenge becomes how to balance and integrate these various security aspects of children and youth into the security agenda without securitising children.

As mentioned earlier, the guiding framework that needs to be adopted is that of good security governance, by which children become legitimate recipients of security provision – where previously they had been invisible.

This also means that SSR must be guided by the principles of good security governance. The risk for SSR otherwise is that it becomes an entirely technical or mechanical exercise along the lines of many of the existing disarmament, demobilisation, and reintegration (DDR) and explosive remnants of war programmes. With security there is an important human component lying behind the reform process and as such it is important to maintain this in view. This can only be done by reaffirming commitment to the overriding goals of good governance, namely the protection of the population as a whole through establishing rule of law, respect for human rights and fundamental freedoms, access to justice, democratic process, accountability and transparency. Governance becomes the framework of principles that guide security actions, and SSR becomes one of the vehicles to achieving them.

Fundamentally, the good governance framework comes back to the premise that there needs to be a focus on encouraging children's positive citizenship. This happens through open and informed society – encouraging young people to engage constructively with their communities and with their surroundings, and providing them with the support networks that can offer options, outlets or alternatives if or when necessary.

'Security governance' is also a means of conceptualising and linking post-war security challenges. The threats to security in post-conflict situations are multi-layered, multi-faceted, and inter-connected – addressing them effectively requires an approach that both acknowledges this reality and generates more systematic and holistic strategies for addressing them. Re-establishing a secure post-conflict environment requires a complex and lengthy process of reconfiguring the roles and responsibilities of a wide range of actors from security, political or civil society spheres.

A significant component of this process will be to address the legacies of conflict, covering a range of security 'realms' including: disarming, demobilising and reintegrating former combatants, including child soldiers; removing/controlling the presence of the explosive remnants of war such as small arms and light weapons, landmines and unexploded ordnance; carrying out reform of the security sector to establish effective security governance mechanisms; disbanding non-statutory armed forces, or integrating them into new statutory ones; establishing rule of law; redressing human rights violations including past crimes and atrocities; and implementing peacebuilding initiatives aimed at promoting reconciliation and avoiding any slide back toward violence.

## Post-conflict Security Governance

In order to understand and develop a security governance analysis of a complex post-conflict situation, four cross-cutting issues emerge as needing consideration:

- The framing conditions, or specific context, of the situation including the security, political and socio-economic factors past and present that lay behind the conflict.
- The role and influence of external actors who have the commitment and resources to assist national players in re-establishing security and kick-starting development.
- The challenges and dilemmas of fostering local ownership.
- The sequencing of a complex range of inter-related security and peacebuilding activities involving multiple actors, and the challenges this entails for co-ordination.

Understanding the complex dynamics of these relations requires effective information gathering and analysis. Establishing such processes must be a priority activity from the outset of any response or intervention. Factoring children and youth into the security agenda requires that the issues affecting them are considered an integral part of this initial planning phase. Currently child soldiers will receive nominal mention, but rarely will consideration be given to the broader threats to children and opportunities that may exist for strengthening child protection systems. Factoring children and youth into the security agenda is a vital part of the post-conflict peacebuilding equation, and represents a major step towards re-establishing normality and breaking the supply lines of disaffected youth so often exploited by 'peace-spoilers'[19] or former combatants using their skills as 'violence entrepreneurs'[20].

As mentioned, it is important that children and youth do not become a securitised issue, but rather that their special security needs are acknowledged and factored into the security governance framework. In order to do this, reflection is needed on the key elements of the security agenda that impact or resonate with the protection needs of children and youth. This involves the security sector responding not only on its obligation to provide for the security of all but also its responsibility to ensure the protection of children's rights.

While it may be inevitable that there will always be a caseload of habitual young offenders, evidence is increasingly showing that programmes working specifically with young people can divert them away from lives of crime or violence. This has significant implications for policy-making in that approaches and actions aimed at providing a stable environment for children and youth ultimately realise the benefit of preventive action by empowering young people to say 'no' to crime and violence. While young offenders are often portrayed as demons and a threat to security, it is more helpful and accurate to consider their presence as evidence of a breakdown or failure of the structures and mechanisms that should be protecting children and guaranteeing their rights.

The situation of children may not currently be reflected in security analysis, but in any given situation there will be a range of agencies involved in child protection activities that will be gathering information on the situation of children that has the potential to be of direct relevance to an accountable security sector. Different agencies (local, national and international) tend to have different mechanisms for monitoring and reporting on the situation of children, but there are some standard tools available, notably the inter-agency Initial Rapid Assessment tool for emergencies that has recently been undergoing field testing. An institutional initiative worthy of specific note is the United Nations High Commissioner for Refugees' Participatory Assessment methodology that engages beneficiaries, including children, from the outset of programme planning and uses the information gathered in developing more effective responses.[21]

One of the challenges in terms of children and their security is to also ensure that there is robust independent monitoring of the performance of security actors in relation to their obligations towards children. While institutions such as human rights commissions and ombudsman spring to mind when thinking of oversight, the ground-breaking initiative of the UN

Security Council to establish a monitoring and reporting mechanism, mentioned earlier, on the children and armed conflict is worthy of note.

Field assessments provide a valuable snapshot of what is happening in a given situation and should feed into a broader situation analysis that will help inform decision-makers in terms of the larger picture. Equally, though, projects and programmes need to ensure that evaluation activities are an integral part of the programme cycle and are used to constructively analysis successes and failures and orient future actions. This includes capturing the experiences of lessons learned and identifying good practices.

Ensuring that the views and opinions of children and youth form an integral part of the assessment and analysis of a situation should be of primary concern. An important aspect of this is having base-line information available that will allow quantitative and qualitative analysis of trends.

### *Framing Conditions*

Understanding the security, political and socio-economic framing conditions of a given situation are essential to identifying opportunities and constraints for post-conflict peacebuilding. From a security perspective, the duration of a conflict, level of violence, factionalism and ethnic or religious dimensions all play an important role. The impact that conflict has had on children and youth will directly affect the way in which they respond to the post-conflict setting. For those who volunteered or were forced to take direct part in hostilities, their only life experience may be of violence. In a void of post-conflict authority, these individuals will be prime targets of peace-spoilers and violence entrepreneurs looking to exploit an unstable situation for political or economic ends.

The level to which communities in general, and children in particular, have experienced trauma will also have a range of recurrent consequences on the overall security situation. By not addressing root causes of the original conflict, such as exclusion, the ingredients for a return to violence remain in place. Youth will have a significant impact on the shape and nature of the post-conflict environment, and overlooking their needs and concerns is done at great risk. Not only will young males be the most likely recruits of criminal elements, they will also be the majority of the victims of violent crime.[22]

The political environment will be a key determinant for the shape of, and expectations for, post-conflict stability and as such the possibility to drive through security reform. Efforts to establish democratic governance will quickly be undermined or derailed in situations that are characterised by corruption, clientism, repression and impunity. A residual lack of trust from citizens may result in them seeking their security elsewhere, such as through support for non-state armed actors. In such cases, civil society itself is likely to be weak, both in relation to mobilising support for change, and in its ability to provide an effective monitoring role. Promoting inclusive, pro-reform political forces within the domestic political sphere will go hand in hand with empowering civil society and re-establishing trust in political process. And, while children themselves do not have access to political recourse through voting rights, they are nevertheless a significant proportion of all societies and, as such, government has a key responsibility in terms of being sensitive to their needs and responding to them. The well-being of children and youth in many ways reflects the aspirations of society and will directly impact the lives and prospects of their families and communities.

Available social and economic capital will influence the potential for post-conflict peacebuilding, with children and youth being a significant resource that can contribute constructively to the peacebuilding process. Excluded and disaffected youth will have a negative impact on the future economic possibilities of a society. Lack of access to education and other opportunities will hinder economic development potential. Children and youth need to be encouraged and assisted to develop to the fullness of their potential, and their energy and creativity as active members of society used for the benefit of all. Lack of economic opportunities will create a void that will likely be filled by organised criminal elements and encourage violence entrepreneurs.

*External Involvement*

A range of external actors will have an important role to play in promoting reform by providing the resources and expertise to encourage and support both the security and development goals of post-conflict peacebuilding process. Key external actors may include a combination of peacekeeping forces, transitional administrations, donor governments, relief and development agencies (UN and inter-governmental organisations), as well as international non-governmental organisations, and commercial enterprises. Regional groupings may be in a position to exercise particular influence not only through knowledge and understanding of the context, but in terms of promoting a regional peace dividend and providing linkages between international organisations and local constituencies. The cross-border security dimension of conflict is also a significant factor requiring regional co-operation in order to address issues such as child recruitment and arms flowing to and from different conflict zones. A key function of external actors will be to encourage and promote the adoption of international human rights standards, including regional treaties, as the benchmarks of transparent and accountable reform.

However, external interventions tend to be characterised by poor co-ordination and misguided approaches not adapted to the given context. There is also a tendency for the concerns of children and youth not to be recognised as 'hard' issues in terms of security and the immediate priorities and actions of post-conflict stabilisation. Children and youth are seen as part of the longer-term development agenda that can be addressed at a later stage when time and space allow, rather than an integral part of the security landscape and something that if not attended to will have implications and consequences on the immediate security situation.

Also, there are likely to be challenges associated with co-ordination due to overlapping mandates and contrasting approaches. The relationships between international organisations are often characterised by competitive rivalry, at times bordering on hostility, hardly conducive to the mission of restoring stability and promoting reform.

Engagement in post-conflict peacebuilding requires a readiness for long-term commitment. For multilateral actors such as the UN, establishing and consolidating a position of authority with regard to security governance requires paying careful attention to questions of legitimacy and accountability. Just as important is the political will to sustain involvement until national actors are in a position to assume responsibility for their national security sector governance. What this requires is not local support for donor programmes, but rather donor support for programmes and projects initiated by local actors.[23]

### *National and Local Ownership*

International involvement in post-conflict situations is generally reflective of an inability of the local political system to resolve differences and move reform forward in a collaborative manner. The purpose of the external intervention will be to provide the space and time for a peaceful resolution of the issues and grievances at the heart of the particular hostilities. An international force may need to be deployed to bridge the security gap that typically persists between the end of active hostilities and the establishment of credible domestic security institutions. As such, the need to clearly define the division of responsibilities and establish mechanisms to build trust between these local institutions and international actors in peacebuilding contexts is of crucial importance. The absence of a credible and transparent approach to the transfer of security functions to local authorities can threaten the peacebuilding process due to the unfulfilled expectations of local actors.

Establishing ownership also requires attention to different levels of ownership. Institutional reform will predominantly be a process initiated and driven by national interests and as such call for the buy-in and support of relevant national bodies. As part of their security role, those same national actors should also be recognised as key duty-bearers in the promotion and protection of child rights. Local ownership, however, is something very different as it infers a broad ownership by very different constituencies spread across the country and often separated not only by geographical distance but political, cultural or religious ideology. At the local level, security and child protection come together as both having particular resonance with affected populations. Being priorities of local communities, they should be empowered to effectively engage with strengthening both. While generating national ownership may be a relatively easy proposition, the process involved in establishing local ownership and long-term stability will be much more complex. The ability of a given situation to avoid a slide back into conflict will be just as much defined by local ownership as it will be by national.

Ultimately, post-conflict peacebuilding tends to be characterised by fragmented political authority. Domestic actors will base their claims to authority on representing key constituencies within the war-torn state, without necessarily having the ability to reasonably verify such claims until post-conflict elections can be conducted. Weak local authorities may be unable to effectively respond to security threats, or in some cases be unwilling to do so for specific constituencies. Regardless of the situation however, civil society will have a key role to play in monitoring the administration's performance and advocating for change where necessary.

Civil society must also be recognised for its capacity to act as a service provider in support of local authorities. Indeed, the private sector may have an important role to play based not only on its ability to raise resources but also for the capacity and expertise that it can provide.

In terms of bringing together the security and child protection agendas, perhaps the most important function that civil society has to play is that of interlocutor between children and youth and the local authorities. Providing youth with the space to express their own security concerns and expectations can provide valuable intelligence to security actors in terms of evolving threats, but equally enables the security sector, particularly the police, to engage constructively in information sharing on issues of concern and about strategies for improving local security.

Too often in peacebuilding contexts, security governance is dominated by the political concerns and priorities of the international community, rather than the realities and interests of the post-conflict state. Local ownership requires commitment to local capacity-building and support for local decision-making, not the implementation an externally defined agenda.

### *Sequencing*

The multidimensional nature of peacebuilding means that linear sequencing of activities is next to impossible. Addressing the security, political and socio-economic aspects of the process requires first and foremost an approach that is rooted in the realities of the given context and that directly responds to the priorities of local constituencies. Any such process will have to tackle the challenge of addressing a range of issues from establishing rule of law, to DDR, and social reconciliation.

The need to address the legacies of conflict must form an integral part of the security debate from the outset of peace negotiations, and include issues of human rights violations and transitional justice mechanisms. Grave violations against children, for which perpetrators must be held accountable, include killing or maiming of children, recruiting or using child soldiers, attacks against schools or hospitals, denial of humanitarian access for children, abduction of children, and rape and other grave sexual abuse of children.[24]

Sequencing of these various security realms will be a highly complex process and in order to address good security governance obligations will require an in-depth understanding of the implications for children and youth. Situation analysis should inform policy responses and prioritise interventions, and be informed by real-time assessments performed by a range of actors operating in the given situation.

A key early response will be the need to address spoilers or violence entrepreneurs. Re-establishing rule of law will in part be facilitated by youth having options and alternatives to such destabilising elements. Information campaigns on political and security reform will be essential to developing an environment in which youth have the sense of being able to actively contribute to a development process. However, mobilising youth does not happen in isolation and capacity-building with local authorities and security providers will be necessary, along with efforts to mobilise local communities around the security issues that concern them.

At the heart of security provision is the protection of social capital, i.e. providing the environment for sustainable development, in which the vast majority of youth will be key players. The fulfilment of this obligation also calls for the security sector to promote respect for human rights. This directly commits them to preventing rights violations and, at the same time, ensuring that they themselves are not guilty of committing such violations.

Establishing a protective environment for children also requires the provision of positive outlets for young people, including support networks. Enabling access to education represents a basic requirement, but this will need to be complimented by a range of other social support mechanisms. Adolescents, in particular, will require special attention as they negotiate one of life's more complex phases, with services needing to be adapted to their needs and realities. The most effective way to guide any interventions for children and youth is to encourage and assist families and communities to take responsibility for providing the necessary support and protection.

The empowerment and mobilisation of civil society is central to promoting both security and child protection agendas. Enabling meaningful two-way dialogue on the development of national policy and its appropriate implementation in the local context is vital.

Particularly in situations where national authorities lack the ability or capacity, service provision is taken on by local authorities. In some contexts there has been a trend towards the sub-contracting of services to private companies. While decentralisation may infer the possibility of civil society playing a more dynamic role in defining local priorities and shaping local services, the state has ultimate responsibility for realising its obligations under international law and should be responsible for ensuring robust and transparent monitoring mechanisms of all service delivery involving children.

## Addressing the Legacies of War

The recognition of a broader security agenda that includes the security of the individual as well as the state, means that not only is it necessary to manage a wide range of security actors at multiple levels in post-conflict contexts, but that there are an equally broad range of security 'realms' to be addressed. The security challenges that generally confront post-conflict societies include: the need to disarm, demobilise and reintegrate large numbers of former combatants, including child soldiers; to curb and remove remnants of war such as small arms and light weapons, landmines and unexploded ordnance; to carry out sweeping reforms in the security sector in order to establish effective security forces and governance mechanisms; to disband non-statutory armed forces, or to integrate them into new statutory ones; to establish the rule of law including under transitional administration; to redress past crimes and atrocities with some urgency; and to promote reconciliation. A number of these 'realms' are associated with specific actions on the part of security sector actors that require special attention to, and consideration of, children.

In general, though, security discourse has not linked children's specific requirements to the elements and actions required of the post-conflict peacebuilding process. However, if we consider the security governance imperatives of the process, and its three over-arching themes, the link between children and their special protection does indeed become apparent and therefore an issue of importance and concern for security sector governance.

- *Disarmament, Demobilisation and Reintegration:* When talking about children and DDR, a distinction needs to be drawn between the very different approach that is required to redress a rights violation in the case of children, and the regular DDR programmes for adults, which form part of the formal peacemaking process. According to the Integrated Disarmament, Demobilisation and Reintegration Standards it is important to distinguish the special requirements of child DDR as an attempt to prevent or redress a violation of children's human rights.[25] Child DDR requires that the demobilisation (or 'release') of children, especially girls, be actively carried out at all times and that action to prevent child recruitment should be continuous.
- *Rule of Law and Transitional Justice:* The rapid reform of national justice mechanisms will be vital to ensuring that accountability is brought to bear for war crimes and human rights violations. Having former combatants who have committed war crimes and/or sexual violence against women and children being released back into their community for 'reintegration' seriously affects community perceptions of safety, and undermines the legitimacy of the justice system. International mechanisms may also have an important role to play. Specifically related to children, justice reform must include the need to have juvenile justice systems in place and functioning properly. The main goal of the juvenile justice system will be rehabilitation rather than punishment.

- *Security Sector Reform and Governance:* Police reform projects should emphasise police-community relations, community policing, human rights, mediation and conflict resolution skills and criminal investigations techniques that respect human rights but are also effective in solving crimes. Community-based policing represents an organisational strategy allowing the police and community to work together to solve problems of crime, disorder and safety.

Professionalising the police and military will mean incorporating robust human rights training into curricula focussed on the role and responsibility that they have as duty-bearers in the protection of individuals, in particular those with special protection needs.

The monitoring of the security sector's performance in relation to child rights implementation should form an integral part of the workings of oversight bodies, including parliamentary committees, ombudsman offices and human rights commissions. Again, empowering non-statutory civil actors, such as the media, NGOs, research institutions and community groups, will reinforce security governance capacities for monitoring and advocacy on behalf of children.

## Conclusions

Conflict significantly disrupts social dynamics and in turn impacts directly on young people's ability to navigate a smooth and constructive transition from childhood to adulthood. Access to education opportunities may have been limited or non-existent during the conflict. Fear, intimidation or force may have led to young people picking up arms for 'protection' or self-preservation. And while the resilience of the majority of young people will have provided them with the necessary coping strategies to mitigate the worst affects of their experiences of armed conflict, efforts that strengthen the protective environment around children and limit the risk factors that they face are essential to assisting them in regaining a sense of normality.

In post-conflict situations, policies that encourage youth employment will not only help to provide livelihoods for young people, but can dissuade them from being re-recruited into armed groups. Special attention needs to be directed towards education, including life-skills and vocational training, to ensure that young people have the necessary skill sets required by the local labour market. In this context, training has to go hand in hand with job creation in both formal and informal labour markets. The success of such policies and programmes will depend on the wider economic and social environment of a country, including the trade situation, the availability of drugs and small arms, the extent of illicit weapons trafficking, and various gender-related factors.[26]

Central to this process will be reform of the security sector aimed at providing a secure environment for the population as a whole, and that will be a necessary step in the process of re-establishing the rule of law, respect for human rights, and the necessary conditions for social and economic development.

Reform of the security sector needs to achieve the combined objectives of ensuring state security and at the same time delivering, as a public good, security services that are receptive to the needs and aspirations of communities and individuals including children and youth.

## Endnotes

1 Human Security Centre, The University of British Columbia, *Canada Human Security Brief 2006* (2006).

2 Richard Ponzio, 'The United Nations Peacebuilding Commission: origins and initial practice', http://www.unidir.org/pdf/articles/pdf-art2627.pdf (accessed May 2008).

3 Astrid Suhrke and Ingrid Samset, 'What's in a Figure? Estimating Recurrence of Civil War' *International Peacekeeping* 14, no. 2 (2007): 195–203. This article examines the process whereby the findings were made, and offers a note of caution about the wholesale adoption of such figures by policymakers and academics.

4 Protocol Additional to the Geneva Conventions (August 1949), and relating to the Protection of Victims of International Armed Conflicts (Protocol I), Article 77, para. 1 (June 1977). The same protection is accorded by Article 4, para. 3 of Protocol II relating to the Protection of Victims of Non-International Armed Conflicts.

5 See for example Article 4 of the International Covenant on Civil and Political Rights, adopted and opened for signature, ratification and accession by General Assembly Resolution 2200A (XXI) of 16 December 1966.

6 Rachel Harvey, *Children and Armed Conflict: a guide to international humanitarian and human rights law* (University of Essex: The Children and Armed Conflict Unit, June 2003).

7 United Nations High Commissioner for Refugees (UNHCR)/International Save the Children Alliance, Action for the Rights of Children (ARC), 'Resource Pack on Child Soldiers' (2002), http://www. savethechildren.net/arc/files/main.html (accessed October 2008).

8 Optional Protocol to the Convention on the Rights of the Child on the involvement of children in armed conflicts. Adopted and opened for signature, ratification and accession by General Assembly Resolution 263, UN doc. A/RES/54/263 (New York: 25 May 2000).

9 International Committee of the Red Cross (ICRC), Advisory Service on International Humanitarian Law, *Fact Sheet: Legal Protection of Children in Armed Conflict* (Geneva: ICRC, 2003).
10 United Nations General Assembly, *An Agenda for Peace: Preventive Diplomacy, Peacemaking and Peacekeeping*, Report of the Secretary-General pursuant to the statement adopted by the Summit Meeting of the Security Council on 31 January 1992, UN doc. A/47/277-S/2411, para. 21 (New York: 17 June 1992).
11 UN General Assembly, *Supplement to An Agenda for Peace*, Position Paper of the Secretary-General on the Occasion of the Fifth Anniversary of the UN, UN doc. A/50/60-S/1995/1, para. 46 (New York: January 1995).
12 United Nations, *Impact of Armed Conflict on Children*, Report of Graça Machel, Expert of the Secretary-General of the United Nations, UN doc. A/51/306 (New York: August 1996).
13 UN Security Council, Statement by the President of the Security Council, UN doc. S/PRST/2001/5 (New York: February 2001).
14 Alan Bryden and Heiner Hänggi, *Security Governance in Post-Conflict Peacebuilding* (Münster: LIT, 2005).
15 UN General Assembly, 2005 *World Summit Outcome*, Final document of the High-level Plenary Meeting of the General Assembly, UN doc. A/60/L.1 (New York: September 2005), 25-26.
16 UN Security Council, Resolution 1612, UN doc. S/RES/1612 (New York: July 2005)
17 Nicole Ball, 'The Challenge of Rebuilding War-Torn Societies' in *Turbulent Peace: the challenges of managing international conflic*t, eds. Chester Crocker, Fen O. Hampson and Pamela Aall, (Washington: United States Institute of Peace Press, 2001), 723-725.
18 UN Security Council, *Securing peace and development: the role of the United Nations in supporting security sector reform*, Report of the Secretary-General, UN doc. A/62/659–S/2008/39 (New York: January 2008).
19 Michael Brzoska, 'Embedding DDR Programmes in Security Sector Reconstruction' in *Security Governance in Post-conflict Peacebuilding*, eds. Alan Bryden and Heiner Hänggi (Münster: LIT Verlag, 2005).
20 Heiner Hänggi, 'Approaching Peacebuilding from a Security Governance Perspective in Security Governance' in *Post-conflict Peacebuilding*, eds. Alan Bryden and Heiner Hänggi (Münster: LIT Verlag, 2005).
21 UNHCR, *Tool for Participatory Assessment in Operations* (Geneva: UNHCR, May 2006).
22 Etienne G. Krug et al., *World report on violence and health* (Geneva: WHO, 2002).
23 Laurie Nathan, 'Participation, Inclusion and Local Ownership of SSR', Workshop on Enhancing Whole-of-Government Approaches to Swiss Support to Security System Reform (SSR), Federal Department of Foreign Affairs and Federal Department of Defence, Civil Protection and Sport (Berne: 29-30 March 2007), 2.
24 UN Security Council, *Children and armed conflict*, Report of the Secretary-General, UN doc. A/59/695–S/2005/72 (New York: February 2005), http://www.unama-afg.org/docs/_UN-Docs/_repots-SG/2005/2005-72.pdf (accessed October 2008).
25 UN, 'Integrated Disarmament, Demobilisation and Reintegration Standards, Module 5.30: Children and DDR' (2006), http://www.unddr.org/iddrs/framework.php (accessed October 2008).
26 UN Department of Economic and Social Affairs, *World Youth Report 2005: Young people today, and in 2015* (New York: October 2005).

# Chapter 9

# Children and DDR

*Irma Specht*

There is growing international consensus that the forced or compulsory recruitment of children – girls and boys under the age of 18, and their use in hostilities by both armed forces and armed groups, is illegal and one of the worst forms of child labour. This consensus is expressed in a comprehensive set of international legal instruments. Under the Rome Statute of the International Criminal Court (2002) it is a war crime to conscript or enlist children under 15 years old into armed forces or groups. The United Nations Convention on the Rights of the Child (1989) and the two Additional Protocols to the Geneva Conventions already prohibit all recruitment and use of those under 15. The International Labour Organization (ILO) Convention 182 prohibits 'forced or compulsory recruitment of children (under 18) for use in hostilities' as one of the worst forms of child labour. The Optional Protocol to the Convention on the Rights of the Child (2000) requires that states bound by it take all feasible measures to prevent those under 18 within their armed forces from fighting, refrain from conscription of those under 18, raise the minimum age of voluntary recruitment from 15 years, ensure that voluntary recruitment of those under 18 is genuinely voluntary based on awareness of duties involved, conducted with parental consent and submission of reliable proof of age, and prevent all recruitment and use of those under 18 by non-state armed groups.

These instruments provide a solid legal basis for the prevention of under-age recruitment, but also for efforts to facilitate the release and reintegration of those children already recruited into armed forces and groups. States' legal obligations in this area also extend to providing an effective framework of standards for governing security provision for the population, and establish the security sector as key duty-bearers in assuring security to all, including children.[1]

Children associated with armed forces and groups (CAAFG) perform a variety of duties including fighting, spying, cooking, washing and sexual services. They are part of formal armies, rebel groups, militia and paramilitary in most conflicts around the world. Generally, the longer an armed conflict lasts, the less adult recruits become available, and more and more boys and girls are enlisted. While children are often forcibly recruited, many choose to join due to lack of alternatives.

In recent years there has been a shift in disarmament, demobilisation and reintegration (DDR) thinking towards a more rigid security rationale. DDR is sometimes even referred to as being part of security sector reform (SSR), with its objective being to re-establish security, and to recreate the monopoly on the use of force in the hands of the government. However, if DDR is planned and implemented exclusively from this security angle, former combatants who are considered not to be a direct security threat tend not to be assisted. This is unacceptable from a social and, in the long term, security perspective.

Specifically in the case of children recruited illegally, and robbed of their childhood, they will need assistance, protection and encouragement to reintegrate – to relearn civilian values and ways of behaviour, to catch up with the missed years in schooling, and to be assisted in earning a viable living. Not only is there a moral obligation towards the child and the communities that receive them, but a failure to do so is a violation of the child's rights. Ultimately, if reintegration fails or proves unsustainable, these children will be more frustrated than before, and risk re-recruitment.

This chapter explores the experiences and impact of past and ongoing DDR programmes for children, in the framework of formal DDR programmes associated with peace agreements and post-conflict SSR initiatives. It also examines opportunities for strengthening such initiatives, in particular recommending approaches that acknowledge local realities, and promote local ownership and sustainability. It will suggest ways to improve the continuum between DDR and SSR on the one hand, and DDR and development on the other.

## Risk Factors of Child Recruitment

> What people believe as a motive for their conduct is at least as important as the actual sequence of events.[2]

An important aspect of developing appropriate reintegration and preventive actions, reflected throughout this chapter, is the need to clearly understand the reasons behind children's involvement in armed conflict, the different ways that children find themselves involved with armed forces or groups, and the motives of recruiters to target them.

*Understanding the Demand for Child Combatants*[3]

Numerous variables, country or region specific, play a role in the complex combination of dynamics that will determine whether children are recruited or not. Some of these factors are demand driven (the reasons recruiters target children), and others supply based (why children choose to join, or are vulnerable to recruitment).

Firstly, as a conflict continues, armed forces or groups may experience shortages of adults to recruit, perhaps due to overall losses incurred, but possibly as a result of shortfalls in the number of adults volunteering due to an erosion of the legitimacy of the belligerent. This may then begin to create gaps within the ranks of the fighting force, not just in terms of direct combatants but also in the available support functions such as porters or cooks – children may be specifically targeted to fill these deficits. As such, the longer a conflict continues, the more likely it may be that children will be recruited, and the new recruits will potentially become younger and younger. Children are more readily used in combat in countries where child labour is part of normal everyday life. In Myanmar, incentives are given to soldiers and commercial recruiting agents to bring in as many recruits as they can – the easiest targets for them are adolescent boys, and 35 to 45 percent of the Burmese army's recruits may be children.[4]

A second determinant is the availability of small arms. The manufacture and spread of inexpensive small arms has made it much easier to turn young children into soldiers.[5] Even a 10-year-old can nowadays strip and reassemble these light and easy-to-use weapons.

Even more complicated is the migration of small-armed groups, light weapons and child soldiers over national boarders. One of the clearest examples of this is found in West Africa where children and young adults move back and forth from Liberia, Sierra Leone, Côte d'Ivoire and more recently Guinea. Children, separated from their families, are more likely to migrate with their leader than adults with families. While in most cases adults have been socialised in the norms of civilian life before participating in warfare, children involved in protracted conflicts may never have had the opportunity to experience full socialisation outside the context of the armed group. The commander-child soldier relation replaces the father/mother-daughter/son relation.

The belief that young people can in fact be 'sculpted' into effective combatants is another reason for armed groups to recruit them. It is no coincidence that some of the most heinous acts of violence during armed conflict are committed by youth. In general, however, commanders do not seem to distinguish between a 17-year-old or an 18-year-old – they simply recruit from the pool of unoccupied youth who are easy targets, and include children and young adults.

Last but not least is the willingness of young people to be recruited. In order to understand this point, we must examine the supply side.

### *The Supply Side: Recognising the Causes of Child Participation in Combat*[6]

A study by the ILO found that 'volunteers' accounted for two thirds of child soldiers interviewed in four Central African countries.[7] While forced recruitment of children receives much attention, focus also needs to be maintained on those who claim to have made a voluntary choice to fight.

Although many children associated with armed forces and armed groups define themselves as having volunteered rather than having been forced to join, analysis of the factors that led to their involvement raise questions about the effective degree of free choice. This issue of voluntarism is especially important because some parts of the current legal framework exclude protection for those who are not recruited by force and who are above 15 years.

It is essential to understand the reasons that young soldiers themselves identify for joining armed forces or armed groups in order to provide assistance that makes their reintegration sustainable. Taking them back to where they ran from, without some significant change in circumstances, will not help. In turn, understanding why they joined also indicates what needs to be done if others are not to follow in their footsteps. As some of these young soldiers themselves recognise, joining not only has the immediate consequences of their participation in the conflict, but also limits other future possibilities even when (or if) the conflict ends.

The support required by the child after release will also depend on their experiences, and be heavily influenced by the local context. What is important is to always challenge assumptions, for example, about the voluntary nature of the decision to join in the first place, or the notion that the experience of those joining the regular army is qualitatively different from that of young people joining armed groups.

Youth is marked by the individual developing an understanding of their own identity and place in the community and society, and a new capacity to make choices and to take on responsibilities. It is also a time of opportunity with greater freedom, but is equally characterised by feelings of opposition and resistance to authority and power structures, and injustice is strongly opposed. Certain things impact more directly on young lives than they do on adults, such as education or the lack of it. Unemployment increases youth vulnerability to recruitment.[8] The reasons why young people join armed forces and armed groups reflect all these aspects of their stage of life, and therefore reintegration assistance should be informed by, and tailored to, the concerns of the children in order to be relevant and sustainable, and ultimately successful.

The most cited reason in Africa for children participating in conflict is 'poverty'. It is indeed true that most child soldiers come from impoverished circumstances, and not only in Africa. However, many poor children do not become child soldiers. Thus it is clear that, although poverty may create a general vulnerability to military recruitment, it cannot be the only factor. Poverty is an environmental factor that sets the context, without which the risk of recruitment would be greatly reduced.

A second level of factors relate to the individual's personal history, which can predispose certain young people to join, while others who share the same general background do not. Indeed, the precise combination of factors that lead to the decision to join is unique in each individual case. In each individual story there is generally a trigger for the specific decision to join. Some young people think about joining for years before actually doing so, others may not have considered it at all until their world disintegrates around them and they see no other option.

The most common risk factors, expanded below, for a child joining an armed group can be divided into the broad areas of the war itself, family, education, unemployment, peer group and other social influences:

*a) War*

Few young people go looking for a war to join; for many, war comes to them and becomes part of their environment. With it, war brings insecurity. It causes schools to close, impoverishes and disrupts families through death, injury and displacement, and leaves few avenues for employment other than military ones. Children join for protection, not only of themselves but often to protect their family members. The presence of war creates military role models and status symbols, and validates violence as a means of protection. Evidently, eliminating armed conflict would be the single most effective means of preventing children's involvement.

Preventing the reoccurrence of war through shoring up fragile states can be a significant contribution to preventing under-age recruitment.

*b) Family*

The absence of family is a crucial predictor of recruitment or embroilment in armed conflict, as well as pressure on single-parent families, sometimes headed by children. However, family itself can also be a risk factor. Where the family is involved in the conflict, or has a military tradition, the involvement of the children is more likely, including through enrolment in cadet programmes that often lead to children joining the military later on. In addition, an abusive or exploitative family could prove to be a significant factor in the individual decision to leave home and join. This is an important cause for girls who face sexual as well as physical abuse and domestic exploitation, although many boys also run away due to physical abuse by a parent. Adolescence is a time when there is likely to be greater vulnerability to such exploitation or abuse because of the inter-generational power struggle, the difficulties of puberty for both the 'child' and the 'parent', its physical and emotional challenges, and the young person's wish for greater autonomy and independence.

*c) Education*

Both the access to and the content of education are significant factors in the lives and decisions of children. In general, access to school should be a strong preventive measure to recruitment – however, the picture is more complex. Even where schooling is free, many children are unable to attend because of the inability to purchase school materials (pens, books, uniforms, etc.). Equally, the family may need the additional earning power of the young person, or may need an older child to stay at home to look after younger siblings – girls often being the first victims of such economic constraints. There is also the issue of safe passage to and from the school, particular during time of active conflict. School itself can be the source of specific personal issues, such as denigration, bullying and corporal punishment, that can impact negatively on young people. For children excluded from education, or who drop-out, belonging to an armed group may not only be an attractive alternative, but may also be a form of self-protection.

*d) Schools*

Schools are often linked to deliberate recruitment strategies by the regular armed forces through offering classes, use of schools for advertising, linkages to cadet or other military training programmes, or through offering further education or training opportunities. It should also be recognised, however, that schools may be used to encourage students to join the 'armed struggle' whether in the name of liberation, religion, ethnicity or other cause. In cases where schooling is segregated on racial, religious, linguistic or other grounds this can be a factor in exacerbating tensions in society through fostering isolation or exclusion. The schooling system may also be a point of focus for what may be seen as an oppressive regime, and may thus in itself become a cause of conflict or fertile breeding ground of resistance.

*e) Unemployment*

Children without adequate and appropriate schooling are limited in their employment opportunities. In many contexts the armed groups are the major source of 'economic' activity and alternative opportunities are scarce. A military life can provide them with access to food, money and luxury items that cannot be obtained elsewhere. The recent publication *Red Shoes: experiences of girl combatants in Liberia* takes its title from the story of a 14-year-old girl whose friend got shiny red shoes from her new commander boyfriend, which led her to join as well.[9] The sadness of these stories is that these girls live in societies where the only way to have access to these (for them) important items is through joining the violence in one way or another. Unemployed parents, and the need for personal or family survival, can also be a risk factor that drives children into armed forces or groups to gain access to food and financial support, often with the consent of parents.

*f) Peer group and other social influences*

The influence of siblings, friends and schoolmates, and the search for status and 'acceptable' role models, is a key factor influencing young people's lives. In many situations adolescents encourage or push each other into doing things, including seeking adventure, risk-taking or defining their own role models. Often a group of friends join an armed force or group together. Where having a gun or being in uniform is perceived as desirable, these will be significant factors in recruitment, particularly where the opportunity is readily available. Culture, tradition and the media may portray these elements as positive or something to aspire to, and where these images and role models are filtered and reinforced by school and family their influence is magnified.

## Demobilisation and Release

> Taking a child rights-based approach to the problem of children associated with armed forces or armed groups, the Principles underscore the humanitarian imperative to seek the unconditional release of children from armed forces or armed groups at all times, even in the midst of conflict and for the duration of the conflict.[10]

While the international community has developed guidelines based on lessons learned from formal DDR programmes in post-conflict contexts[11], the scenario of informal release of children during conflict is less well covered and presents additional challenges related to security, protection and the risk of re-recruitment. A question that arose during an assessment mission for a reintegration programme of child combatants in the Democratic Republic of the Congo in 1999 was 'Reintegration into what'? The conflict was ongoing and recruitment of children a top priority of warlords. An average mother could feed her children once every three days, businesses were selling their assets, factories were closing, and salaries to the police and the army had not been paid for five months. Was this a situation to demobilise thousands of child combatants? What could the government, the communities, the private sector or international organisations offer to these children in terms of human security? Who would pay their medical bills, clothes, food and school fees? What level of local security could be guaranteed if policemen were hungry and in a survival mode?

While there may be agreement with the principle that children should not be members of armed forces and groups, a question remains as to whether CAAFG should be demobilised on the basis of international morals and standards if their only option is then to join street children in robbery and prostitution?[12] A central consideration in any action affecting a child must be the child's best interests. Where that decision favours the release of the child, this should go hand-in-hand with a commitment to ensure that all is done to provide the necessary support for the child to have a realistic chance of being able to successfully reintegrate into their community. In a similar vein, the right of the child to demobilise at any time should be respected and mirrored by the availability of support and care programmes, as and when required. The Integrated Disarmament, Demobilisation and Reintegration Standards (IDDRS) state that: 'Efforts should be made to ensure that child DDR is not contingent on adult DDR or the conclusion of broader SSR and power-sharing negotiations.'[13]

If it is realistically possible to offer sufficient assistance, another challenge is how to ensure that children in armed forces or groups can be made aware that dedicated programmes are available for them, in order to encourage formal and even informal release during and after conflict.

Where conflict has actually ended, the demobilisation of children normally has highest priority. Children are demobilised separately from adults and are normally transferred to Interim Care Centres. This is where they receive appropriate assistance such as food, health services, counselling and sometimes basic education. From the Interim Care Centres, the large majority of the demobilised children are placed back into their communities as a result of family tracing programmes and receive follow-up from social workers in their communities. A good DDR programme will then put in place reintegration services such as access to school, psycho-social support, vocational training and business set-up, or employment for the older children, and income generating support for the parents of younger children.

**Box 9.1 Components of a Typical Child DDR Programme**

**Disarmament:**

- Disarmament
- Removal and decommissioning of arms including landmines, etc.

**Demobilisation:**

- Interim Care Centre (separate from adults)
- Family tracing
- Health check-ups and care. Note: No cash payments are made to children!

**Reintegration:**

- Psychological support and special care
- Community structures such as welfare committees, children's clubs, etc.
- Education and catch-up education
- Vocational training
- Business training

To aid durable reintegration, services need to be in place to assist older children with:

- Referral and placements in jobs (including in the new security forces)
- Support to start-up businesses
- Business Development Services to mentor and assist the new entrepreneurs
- Targeted investments in infrastructure that will boost local economies
- Scholarships and referral services to higher education

Another important factor in programme decision is to try to avoid the exclusive targeting of demobilised children or their families, but to be aware of and respond to wider community considerations at the same time. First of all, singling out former CAAFG will further separate them from the community's other children and will thus have an adverse effect on their reintegration. Also, providing priority or even exclusive benefits to demobilised children will spread the wrong message that joining armed groups or forces and violence pays. This is very dangerous as it will potentially create a bigger supply of both willing children, and commanders prepared to recruit them in the hope of benefiting themselves. Of course, this is even more an issue if the war is ongoing. On the other hand, these children often do need tailored support in order to become 'normal' children again. The balance is important, and hard to find. In the recent Liberia child DDR programme, children were overly singled out in the skills training component, where the ratio of demobilised children to other children was nine-to-one. In the same DDR programme, those children who went to school received no priority benefits but the school was assisted in terms of training of teachers, books and sports materials that benefited all children.

It is clear that less-exclusive targeting, such as a 50-50 balance between CAAFG and community children, would be a better reintegration approach, but the reality is that costs will double as well. Equally, if the definition of who is a CAAFG is too broad, those resources that are available will be spread too thinly. Strategic decisions may have to be taken, but in such a way that donors are engaged and involved in the process. Context-specific approaches will need to be designed based on thorough assessments of the potential impact of targeting. The financial costs and social benefits need to be carefully balanced.

Finally, for children who miss out on the formal DDR process, either because of being overlooked or because of spontaneous release outside of formal programmes, there are no special back-up mechanisms in place to assist these children other than the regular child protection programmes, which are non-targeted and therefore have no specific means to identify or assist the self-demobilised children.

## Gender Considerations in Child DDR Programming

Based upon experiences in Liberia and elsewhere, it is clear that DDR programmes fail to effectively identify and reach girls associated with armed groups and armed forces. If women associated with armed groups and armed forces have received scarce attention in DDR processes, girls hardly ever figure as a target group in their own right in most programmes, although they do form a substantial and increasing share of armed groups.[14] The problem starts at the assessment period, where little or no effort is made to find the girls and to solicit their views on their needs, concerns and ambitions. Gender and DDR expert Vanessa Farr stresses that 'mainstreaming a gender perspective involves changing how situations are analysed. A brief profile of how and why women's needs are different from those of men's should be the starting point of the analysis. These basic insights should influence the understanding of the contents and raise issues to be explored in each project component.'[15]

A report on the Assessment of Women Associated with the Sudan People's Liberation Army in Southern Sudan[16] stresses that reintegration support to girls and women must focus on addressing some of the most basic needs – food, shelter, health care and access to sustainable livelihoods – in addition to prioritising social reintegration needs. A particular challenge is addressing issues that have a high level of stigma attached, including sexual and gender-based violence, survival prostitution, and non-legal marriages.[17] The issues around bush marriages (relationships established within the armed groups) are complex and rarely addressed in the current reintegration processes. In Liberia, former bush husbands attacked an Interim Care Centre in order to get back their 'wives'. In Sudan, women associated with armed groups and armed forces reported being rejected completely by their families or by the man's family as a result of non-payment of dowry, and that it represented a serious barrier to their reintegration.[18]

Another dilemma is the fact that some girl combatants have occupied leadership roles in military structures but are rarely included in peace negotiations. While political positions are bestowed on their male colleagues, these female military leaders are generally neglected and security-related matters such as DDR left to men.[19] Gender-based power relationships are thereby reinforced. At the same time, an opportunity is missed to reassess gender relations and find ways to make them more conducive to a peaceful society. In fact, many revolutionary movements have listed gender equality as one of their initial goals to mobilise women but have not followed through on their promises in actual peace negotiations. Also, because male leaders of armed groups almost always negotiate the terms of ceasefires, peacekeeping and DDR efforts, including justice and amnesty provisions, there is a tendency to perpetuate impunity for crimes committed during violent conflict, particularly sexual violence, against women.[20]

The devastating impact of inter-personal violence and the need to respond to it is only just being recognised, including the need to address the situation and treatment of girls within the family. Although children of both sexes are liable to physical abuse, girls are more likely to be sexually abused than boys, and are also more likely to be expected to stay at home to undertake domestic chores, or to be sent to extended family for this purpose. This links with the need to address more generally the status and treatment of girls (and women) in society. Perversely, the broader challenge may be easier in one sense because it falls within the public rather than the private domain and so is more accessible to public policy responses such as linking it to girls' access to education, employment, skills and leadership positions. An important measure that would contribute to reducing adolescent re-recruitment would be to address the issue of violent masculinities: the gender stereotyping that proposes that boys become popular through being violent.

Research conducted among girls in Liberia[21] highlighted that many decided not to join the formal DDR process and therefore received no assistance. Considering that girls constituted an integral part of the fighting forces, whether as combatants, wives or supporters, the failure of disarmament and demobilisation to reach them is not only regrettable from a social perspective, but may also undermine longer-term peace prospects. Girls who are not formally demobilised automatically become ineligible for reintegration assistance. This seriously damages their prospects of acquiring education, skills training and, ultimately, new jobs and other assistance that DDR programmes offer, such as family tracing, psycho-social counselling, health and child-care, life skills training and so on. The reasons for non-participation given by girls interviewed in Liberia provide important insights that could be helpful in understanding how to better reach girls in future DDR or release programmes. Some of their concerns are developed below, along with their own perspectives.

### *Lack of trust in the cease-fire and the DDR process*

Many girls cited their reason for non-registration as lack of trust in the cease-fire, which made them keen to retain their weapons. One social worker was also told that girl combatants felt that the DDR programme was 'sweet talking them', but would not follow up on its promises. For some girls, the reason was lack of trust in the process. In a few cases, girls had had bad experiences with DDR in the first war; older girls especially gave this as a reason for non-participation in the process this time. A girl who was a child soldier in the first war explained her disappointment as follows:

> I was involved in the first DDR. But it didn't help me. It was of no use. The people eat the money. And there was also no good reintegration. And then I went fighting again. So now I'm not doing the DDR any more.

## *Fear of Repercussions*

Some girl ex-combatants did not want to reveal their past because they were afraid of repercussions. They did not want to be registered and photographed (a pre-condition at the DDR camps), as they feared that they might later be prosecuted in a criminal court for their involvement in the war. Information that some of the girls received through formal and informal channels regarding the DDR process also discouraged some from participating. One of the rumours was that ex-combatants would never be able to travel to the United States because their picture and name, registered at the DDR, would be forwarded to relevant offices denouncing them as criminals or even terrorists.

> If you do the Disarmament and Demobilisation then they take your name and your picture and put them in the computer. If you want to travel in the future to the US or Europe then they can see in the computer that you are an ex-rebel and then they not allow you. So I didn't want to go through the DDR. I gave my weapon to somebody else who took it to the DDR.

While extensive information on the DDR was disseminated, it did not reach these girls, or was outweighed by information received from other sources, including their peers. The importance of getting good information to children in a way that they can understand remains problematic.

## *Fear of Social Exclusion*

Other girls did not want to reveal their past as ex-combatants because they were afraid they would suffer consequences of social exclusion. Many people remembered, and told them, of the reactions of the civilian population to the proposed targeted DDR programme in the 1990s when 'the general perception was that ex-combatants should not be further rewarded for having been fighters. Many atrocities were committed by soldiers even against their own tribal groups, so that reintegration of fighters or those known to have been involved in such acts is difficult.'[22] It was common practice then for combatants to burn their ID cards and claim to have been refugees, as the benefits offered by the reintegration programme did not counterbalance the problems they would encounter if people knew they had been combatants. Many girls and women preferred to hide their history rather than benefit from assistance programmes.[23] The fear is not simply that the population will resent 'rewards' being offered to combatants, whom they view as having caused suffering, but that their character will remain stained in the future.

> Most of my friends don't know that I was fighting. I like to keep it that way. People don't like ex-fighters. After the war I went living with my aunt, only she knows, but for the rest I don't want them to know. If they know and something bad happens they will point at me, saying I did it.

*Wish to Escape the Past*

Some girls said that they just wanted to forget as quickly as possible that they had been part of a fighting force. They thus avoided formal demobilisation in order not to be confronted with their past and their former colleagues. A related reason was that they were unwilling to enter a camp again as they believed the DDR camps would be too similar to the circumstances they encountered in the bush camps that they stayed in during the war.

> I don't want to go to the Disarmament and Demobilisation and talk with a counsellor what happened to me, I don't think that that is good for me. I just want to forget.

*Avoiding Separation from Their Commanders*

Many girls, especially younger ones, did not want to be separated from their former commanders.

> After the war we lived with many of us in an empty building in Monrovia. Me, some other girls, the boys and our commander. He didn't do the Disarmament and Demobilisation so we didn't do it as well – we wanted to stay with him.

Most girls remained strongly dependent on and committed to their commanders after the conflict ended, and often wished to continue staying with them. Some girls did not go to the Interim Care Centres to avoid separation from their commanders. Others, who did go, lied about their age when they arrived at the cantonment sites, claiming to be 18 years or older in order to stay at the cantonment site where their commanders also stayed, rather than going to separate Interim Care Centres for children after which they would be reunified with their parents. In other cases, girls ran away from Interim Care Centres to rejoin their former commanders. Social workers confirmed that the large number of girls who claimed to have been born in 1986 (i.e. just turning 18 at the time of the DDR) was striking.

Another consequence of the girls' continuing wish to be with their commanders was that some girls lied about their origin and the identity of their parents, giving the names of their former commanders or his/her relatives, in the hope of being reunited with him or her after the Interim Care Centre. Others said that they did not want to go to a camp because they did not want to listen to anyone other than their commanders, nor live by the rules of DDR personnel.

> I don't want to go in a camp because I'm not used to the people there. I don't want them to tell me what to do. I don't know these people. I rather stay with my friends.

*Teen Mothers*

Information gathered from the interviews in Liberia appeared to indicate that teen mothers were less likely to participate in the formal DDR process than other girls. From the 583 girls who had stayed in one Interim Care Centres, 34 girls brought a baby with them, a few were pregnant, and two of them gave birth in the Interim Care Centres. However, considering the prevalence of rape and sexual activity reported amongst girl combatants in Liberia, it appears that many teen mothers were not participating in the formal Disarmament and Demobilisation because they did not want to take their children to encampment sites (even if there were child-care facilities).

> They asked me whether I wanted to go in the camp. Because at that time my family was in town here. My two younger ones, my daughter and the grandmother. So everybody was here. So I cannot leave them and then go lay in the camp for two to three weeks.

*Access Denied*

Besides girls who chose not to go for various reasons, there were also girls who wanted to go but were denied access for one reason or another. Often this had to do with commanders wanting to keep girls to compensate for their loss of power, or to use them for household and family tasks. This occurred most often in the case of young non-fighting girls in male units. In most cases, however, the girls said they voluntarily stayed with their 'bush husbands' or commanders.

The first criterion for entering the formal DDR programme in Liberia was handing in of a weapon or ammunition. Although there was a policy that girls associated with armed groups and armed forces could also enter without handing over a gun, a number of girls stated that they were unable to register because their commanders had taken away their weapons. Before the official DDR had started, girls had been ordered to leave their guns with their commanders, and to go to town or their homes. One girl explained that her commander told her that it 'would look bad on you to walk around with a gun now we are no longer fighting'.

People arriving at disarmament sites with their weapons or ammunition would be given a ticket allowing them access to demobilisation. After a few days in a demobilisation camp, they would receive a cash instalment of 150 USD, to be followed up by a second instalment of 150 USD a few months later. In the case of children, Transitional Safety Allowances were paid to parents. Although not designed as a 'weapons buy-back' programme, the system was perceived as such by the combatants.

At the time, an AK47 could be found on the local black market for 23 USD, and this would guarantee access to the Disarmament and Demobilisation programme. After a few days' shelter, food and health assistance, the gun would lead to a return of 150 USD. Local business people were implicated in providing guns to boys and demanding 75 USD after their return from the camps. As such, many of the ticket holders were not ex-combatants, while many ex-combatants remained outside of the process – a disproportionate number of girls among them.

> … he made a deal with me that I could only get my ticket if I agreed in giving my commander 100 USD from my first payment and 50 USD from my second payment. I agreed and this is what we did.

### *Commanders' Lists*

In DDR programmes implemented around the world the target group has been defined by lists of unit members supplied by commanders. Access to the DDR and assistance then depends upon being on one of these lists. This method was developed in the context of relatively 'organised' conflicts (e.g.

Mozambique) where it was more or less clear who was and who was not a member of the armed groups. However, it presents difficulties in contexts such as Liberia in which armed groups are less organised and the distinction between civilians and combatants is difficult to define.[24] A recurrent problem is that commanders abuse their power to identify beneficiaries. This system is generally discriminatory against children, and girls in particular, as in many cases commanders put family members, relatives or friends on the list instead of CAAFG. In other cases, commanders simply took girls' ID cards and sold them to somebody else.

Much depended on the sincerity of individual commanders. In some cases, without the encouragement of a commander, girls would not have registered for Disarmament and Demobilisation. Commanders also helped in finding and accessing some of the girls.

The United Nations Children's Fund (UNICEF) has expressed concern about the reluctance of commanders to put children on demobilisation lists for fear of harming their reputation and facing social, political and legal repercussions. One general did indeed cite fear for his reputation as his main reason for not listing the children in his unit. However, some of the social workers interviewed suggested that it was not a question of commanders being ashamed but rather that they were simply motivated by the amount of Transitional Safety Allowance they could squeeze from the process (adults were given cash, while children were not).

### *Concluding Observations on Gender Considerations*

The examples discussed above demonstrate a variety of reasons that led girls not to participate in the formal DDR process, many of which were experienced in combination by girls. Various considerations affected lower-ranked girls differently to higher-ranked girls, as well as younger girls compared to older girls. Although gender was stated as an express consideration in Liberia's DDR programme, cases where girls missed out on assistance were all too common.

Future DDR processes should carry out extensive assessments of the concerns of girl combatants, so that the DDR programme can be better designed to encourage the inclusion of more girl combatants. It is essential that differences experienced by girls during conflict are understood according to their age and maturity, their rank, whether they were active combatants, whether they were part of a women's or mixed unit, whether they had a female or male commander, whether their association with the armed group forced them to leave home, and the length of their association.

These factors tend to directly link to the degree by which girls were exposed to sexual and other forms of violence, their relationship with men, their self-confidence, their level of gender equality, the nature of their relation to their commanders, the welcome they encounter within receiving communities and ultimately their reintegration into civilian life.[25]

The main challenges faced by girls associated with fighting forces in the immediate aftermath of war are:

- Finding income for themselves and their dependants
- Gaining access to and supporting themselves during education
- Feeling dependent on/loyal to former units/commanders
- Relating to their war-time partner ('bush marriages')
- Adjusting to a new social status
- Returning to dependence on male providers
- The negative perception of the receiving community
- The negative perception of employers

## Sustainability

A peace agreement followed by a DDR process is not sufficient to assure a durable peace if the socio-economic situation is not improved, and youth are unable to find a constructive place in society. In the peace process, the voices of the young are generally neglected, and their needs are rarely taken into account by DDR and the reconstruction of the economy and society.

As a result, the post-conflict period tends to remain highly unsatisfactory for these young people, pushing many of them into re-recruitment, criminality or prostitution, and all of them into insecurity. Young combatants are particularly vulnerable in this context: they are perpetrators and victims of conflict at the same time. Their situation is often manipulated and used by spoilers for the benefit of power claims or other ambitions (political or economic).[26]

The need for capacity-building of national actors to support demobilised and other children after a formal DDR process must be stressed. Also, programmes require sufficient resources and solid understanding of local realities to ensure sustainable rehabilitation and reintegration so as to avoid re-recruitment. The need for robust monitoring and follow-up of child DDR programmes requires long-term commitment on the part of the agencies and donors involved.

**Box 9.2 Impact of Child DDR Programme in Liberia**

The reintegration programme has shown significant success in terms of the social reintegration of CAAFG both at individual and community levels. The behaviour of former CAAFG has improved and therefore former CAAFG are not identified as hard-core problematic groups, in fact they are rarely identified as security threats or as a special group. Community-based child protection mechanisms have been put in place to safe-guard the protection of children, and also ensure their participation.

The combination of vocational training/apprenticeships with education seems to be among the biggest successes of the programme, increasing the chance of a better future for children, while addressing the immediate needs for income. This positive impact on this new approach deserves replication in other DDR contexts.

The provision of Transitional Safety Allowances (cash), first to the children and later in the programme to the parent, gave the wrong signal that child soldiering pays, hence fostering feelings of unfairness among other war-affected children and their parents.

Skills training often did not respond to real demands in the labour market and the quality of the training varied greatly. No efforts have been made to create an enabling environment for economic reintegration such as boosting local economies. Follow-up of new businesses was too weak while the young inexperienced entrepreneurs are operating in highly competitive markets and need intense follow-up and mentoring in order to succeed.

Therefore, there is a need to make reintegration programmes longer, or to come up with bridging programmes that can build upon the positive dynamics initiated through the DDR programme for children. If this cannot be assured, there are serious risks that the results of the reintegration programme will not be sustainable with children becoming vulnerable to re-recruitment again, also in neighbouring countries.

The Paris Principles[27] set out bold objectives for long-term engagement and adequate resources, but questions remain as to how these are realised in practice. A mid-term impact evaluation completed by UNICEF Liberia in April 2007 highlights some of the core issues that are worthy of consideration in other contexts.

## Children and Youth

The international community has repeatedly condemned the recruitment of children into armed forces and stressed the importance of protecting them. The age categories established under the current legal framework should, however, not lead to the neglect of those over 18 years of age. Definitions of 'youth' overlap with those of 'child' and 'adult', but they form a distinct group on the ground that needs more explicit attention, and specific programmes that are appealing to and tailored for them. IDDRS acknowledges youth as a separate group and includes a module on Youth and DDR.[28]

Most combatants are youth (15-24 years). Their experiences of combat, and the complexity of the transition from war to peace, require (re)integration programmes that respond to their diverse needs and aspirations, and address their specific vulnerabilities.

Currently, DDR approaches do not cater for them. Those under 18 are regarded as child soldiers and are protected and assisted as children.[29] Those above the age of 17 years, including so-called 'aged-out' child combatants of perhaps 18 and 19, are treated as adults in programmes with a 'livelihood focus', which may overlook their need for protection, catch-up education, life skills training and career development. DDR programmes for children and adults need to effectively co-ordinate with each other in order to deal with the particular needs of this 'in-between' group and make sure that people who started out as child soldiers but are now over 18 receive proper support. A smooth transition is also required from DDR programmes to national youth policies and action plans that recognise youth as an asset in the reconstruction period.

This involves analysing and dealing with the causes of youth participation in armed conflict; understanding the youth labour market, increasing the employability of youth; addressing the health needs of youth, particularly reproductive health, and providing long-term care for those with HIV/AIDS; assisting youth who have child-care responsibilities; and opening up opportunities for further education and training.[30]

Emphasis is needed on the demand side of the labour market – the creation of jobs, boosting local economies and increasing the absorption capacities of communities. Without investing in this, reintegration will not be sustainable and the new youth-led businesses will fail.

While DDR practitioners will say that it is not the role of a DDR programme to boost local economies, and that their role is simply to provide links to other programmes, the reality is that few such programmes exist or are operational at the time of DDR or release of children, which seriously compromises the prospects of these young people, and as such the sustainability of the peace.

A key question is, to what extent child DDR programmes should be distinct from, and operate independently of, adult DDR programmes? In

Afghanistan, Liberia and Sudan, the United Nations Development Programme's adult programmes and the UNICEF-led children's programmes are implemented in relative isolation. This however, could have negative consequences for youth who find themselves on either side of the divide. The imperatives and priorities of DDR for adults and DDR for children are quite different, and as the IDDRS notes '... child DDR is not the same as that for adults ... rather, it is a specific process with its own requirements, several of which are fundamentally different from adult demobilisation programmes.'[31] This should not however mean that they function in complete isolation from each other. Although there may be co-ordination through working groups on DDR, too often agency competition, funding problems and personality clashes have led to an absence of collaboration.

Key reasons for providing special attention to youth, whether in adult or child DDR programmes, include:

- The majority of combatants are youth
- Young people have a huge contribution to make to reconstruction – youth are the biggest asset a country has
- Armed conflict has a severe impact on the physical and psychological development of youth
- Youth unemployment is a major contributory factor to conflict
- Disaffected youth could represent a threat to security

## Community-based Reintegration

While disarmament and demobilisation are largely centralised processes, there is growing recognition of the need for community-based programmes to support successful reintegration. This approach, with communities having ownership and a lead role in the process, is of particular relevance to the rehabilitation and reintegration of children and youth.

As addressed in earlier chapters of this publication, investing in and strengthening civil society has a critical role to play in monitoring and advocacy at the community level. Both are essential to establishing a protective environment, which will be a major factor in reducing the risk of re-recruitment. A key element of ensuring the success of reintegration is the need to actively promote the re-forging of community links and bonds, which will generate a sense of belonging and give a renewed sense of purpose to the individuals involved.

In earlier DDR programmes, such as those of Mozambique and Angola, combatants were disarmed and demobilised in encampment sites far away from their communities. Once this 'military' process was completed, they were transported to their villages of origin. Before their discharge from the centres, demobilised combatants were provided with relief food, basic non-food items and assistance packages including, for example, tools for agricultural activities. However, problems often arose related to access to land, social tensions and feelings of unfairness as the ex-combatants were coming back with goods, cash and identity cards that would prioritise them to access other assistance projects. Some of the better programmes included components for the 'receiving communities', such as awareness-raising and trauma healing.

One complexity related to current DDR activities is the difficulty associated with differentiating between armed groups and armed civilians, with examples around the world from Kashmir to Côte d'Ivoire. The nature of warfare has changed and the dichotomy between combatants and civilians has become increasingly blurred, with many combatants remaining part of their communities but ready to pick-up arms as or when required. The chronological model of first disarming, then demobilising, and then reintegrating is often not appropriate to these more complex conflict situations. This 'grey' area is a particular challenge when considering the legal obligations that exist for the immediate release of children from armed groups and forces, whether or not conflict is still on-going.

While children will have changed as a result of their experiences of combat, communities too will not have remained static, and re-establishing a stable and harmonious relationship will be dependent on communities and ex-combatants working together. Programmes for the release of children need to find ways to facilitate their acceptance in their villages of origin, and recognise that many of them will not be willing to go back to farming or to live under the authority of elders.

In looking at alternatives to the conventional targeted DDR programmes, consideration should be given to other models that may be more appropriate to children's release such as 'collective', 'area-based' or 'community-centred' approaches. Community-based services, however, need to be linked to centralised bodies such as the ministries of health and education. For example, education and vocational training needs to ensure quality and certification that is meaningful beyond the borders of the communities.

## Children and Transitional Justice

Children associated with armed forces and groups are by definition first and foremost victims, as their recruitment and participation in hostilities resulted from an illegal act. However, some of them may have been perpetrators of violence, possibly even against their own communities. Obviously, for effective and sustainable reintegration to be possible, these issues need to be aired and addressed.

In general it is acknowledged that children should be made aware of the wrongs that they have done and be held responsible for these deeds, in a child-appropriate manner that would focus on restorative justice rather than punitive justice.

Due to their flexible structure and inclusiveness, Truth and Reconciliation Commissions could be an appropriate mechanism by which to provide accountability for past crimes against children, offer a safe space for children to recount their experiences, and contribute to community healing.

It is extremely important to have clarity on the relationship between the Commissions and the formal judicial system, and its impact on children, and this needs to be communicated publicly. While academically we can distinguish between courts and Commissions, many children cannot. If they fear that they might be prosecuted, this could seriously disrupt the success of DDR.

The other dimension of transitional justice, and perhaps the most important issue for child reintegration, is to stop the culture of impunity that is often associated with conflict and make children responsible for their actions. Communities often complain about ongoing harassment and continuing atrocities by demobilised children and youth, and this is one of the most important reasons for rejection of former CAAFG. Addressing impunity also applies to holding recruiters accountable, many of whom may still be present in the receiving communities.

## Linking Child DDR to SSR and Development

Rebuilding war-affected societies must include an element of change in which the underlying frustrations and insecurities of the people are understood and addressed. This is certainly true of child DDR programmes that, if implemented in a sustainable manner, contribute to the human security of the population as a whole. DDR is a tool in the process of achieving stability in a broader security and development sense.

The roles and responsibilities of a range of security sector actors in guaranteeing the protection of children are not always well defined at the country level. And while military and civilian co-operation in DDR is generally improving, attention is still needed, especially concerning the release and treatment of children. One approach that would certainly be beneficial would be appropriate training for more senior military staff. One of the difficulties often encountered is that the military and civilian organisations have different planning processes and cycles, use different language, and criteria for intervention. Misunderstanding and frustration on both sides is a common feature and hampers co-ordination and collaboration. An area of civil-military co-operation calling for improved co-ordination is the handling of information on children and the way that it is dealt with. If it was perceived that militarily sensitive information is being shared, this could compromise humanitarian assistance, endanger children's safety and be an obstacle to release.

One of the challenges on the ground is sequencing. Not only do SSR processes move more slowly than DDR, but their aims are qualitatively different. Previously, DDR processes were taking six to ten months but currently, demobilisation is as short as three days to five weeks, within which time SSR processes will only be starting up. DDR programmes sometimes operate alongside, but are not connected with, security forces' vetting processes. Without co-ordinated policies of reintegration and vetting, not only could children be reinserted into the transformed forces, but human rights abusers including those previously responsible for recruiting or using children could also be re-recruited, thereby simultaneously undermining one of the aims of vetting as a transitional justice measure.

In order for reintegration to be successful and sustainable a minimum level of security is required at the local level. In the first place it is crucial that the physical security of children and their carers can be assured – this should include consideration of their food and economic security. During the first release in the Congo, some of the demobilised children resorted to prostitution in a search for income. In other locations, Interim Care Centres were attacked and demobilised children forcibly re-recruited (abducted/kidnapped) by opposing groups, and cholera outbreaks in certain centres caused the death of many.

Overall, closer collaboration between the DDR and SSR processes can play an important role in preventing the re-recruitment and abuse of children. This can be accomplished through establishing appropriate procedures and oversight mechanisms, and by sensitising and training local authorities, including the police and armed forces, on international law relating to child rights and child soldiers; and strengthening the state's capacity to enforce such procedures.[32] The reform of the security sector is best achieved if it is part of an overall institutional reform process in a post-conflict setting.[33]

Finally, it is essential that demobilised children be encouraged to engage with local youth in tackling the challenges of creating local security. Whatever the situation, the participation of children and youth in the identification of security problems and in finding solutions is of great importance. 'The notion of 'local ownership', central to security sector governance, means encouraging pro-active engagement and dialogue, including with youth, in the identification and resolution of local security problems. Such a process is also likely to result in young people sensing a more meaningful role for themselves within community life as a whole. This engagement in local security agendas between young people, civil society and the local authorities can subsequently be directed and used in informing and influencing national security agendas in a meaningful way.'[34]

## Conclusions

Understanding why young people become involved in armed forces or groups is essential to devising and implementing appropriate and effective prevention and release strategies. Time and resources need to be invested in early assessments that determine the demand and supply factors of recruitment and that are capable of informing relevant interventions that assist released children towards successful reintegration and prevent their re-recruitment.

Furthermore, it is important to acknowledge that underage combatants are not a homogeneous group – they include older and younger girls and boys, higher and lower ranks, disabled children, orphans, drug addicts, as well as educated and illiterate children. These differences must inform the individual reintegration assistance needed for each child.

Addressing the issue of youth should be a crucial aspect of future DDR programmes, requiring increased flexibility and a degree of latitude over age criteria. Child DDR programmes have a tendency to focus on protection and less on empowerment. However, many children are expected to contribute to the family economy or even cater for themselves and, as such, are in need of economic reintegration assistance. By contrast, aged-out children may need more protection than is currently available from adult or formal DDR programmes. An important issue for this group could be 'catch-up' education. In addition, teaching young people life skills, such as how to resolve interpersonal conflicts non-violently, would not only help them in staying out of trouble but also reinforce basic human rights values.

Developing linkages between DDR and SSR processes is an essential step in assuring the security that is a pre-requisite of successful reintegration. Transitional justice mechanisms and interim security measures need to be co-ordinated. Community policing and the establishment of basic juridical structures are essential for re-establishing rule of law. Controlling access to small arms and light weapons will impact positively in reducing child recruitment and children's potential involvement in criminal activity.

Issues of social equity and decent work need to be defining features of efforts to reconstruct societies. To ensure the effective and lasting reintegration of demobilised children, and to prevent their re-recruitment, all dimensions of the human security agenda need to be addressed, especially the contextual factors that led to children's involvement in the first place. One thing that is certain is that young ex-combatants without promising alternatives, including decent jobs, healthy bodies and minds, and a certain pride in what they are doing, remain vulnerable for re-recruitment.[35]

The international community should assist national governments and civil society in fulfilling their responsibilities to ensure that child rights are respected and their well-being guaranteed. As such, the responsibility of security sector actors to respect and promote child rights should be an important element of SSR, and of any interim security and justice measure. Training of national security sector actors has great priority, but also the training of international peacekeeping forces and DDR actors. Unfortunately, child rights is still regarded as a specialised occupation of UNICEF and its friends, while in truth it should be the concern of every adult on the planet.

## Endnotes

1 Excerpts from David Nosworthy, *Children's Security in Post-conflict Peacebuilding* (Geneva: DCAF, 2007).

2 Stephen Ellis, *The Masks of Anarchy* (London: Hurst, 1999).

3 Based on Irma Specht, 'Jobs for Rebels and Soldiers' in *Jobs after war: A critical challenge in the peace and reconstruction puzzle*, ed. Eugenia Date-Bah, (Geneva: ILO, InFocus Programme on Crisis Response and Reconstruction, 2003).

4 Human Rights Watch, *My Gun was as tall as me: Child Soldiers in Burma* (New York: Human Rights Watch, 2002), http://hrw.org/reports/2002/burma (accessed October 2008).
5 Rachel Brett and Margaret McCallin, *Children: the invisible soldiers* (Stockholm: Radda Barnen, Save the Children Sweden, 1996).
6 This section presents the key-findings of Rachel Brett and Irma Specht, *Young soldiers: why they choose to fight* (Boulder: Lynne Rienner, 2004).
7 International Labour Organisation (ILO), *Wounded childhood: The use of children in armed conflict in Central Africa* (Washington D.C.: ILO, 2003).
8 See the United Nations Office for West Africa, *Youth Unemployment and Regional Insecurity in West Africa*, Report on the linkages between youth unemployment and conflict, UNOWA Issue Papers (2005).
9 Irma Specht, *Red Shoes: Experiences Of Girl-combatants in Liberia* (Geneva: ILO, 2006).
10 French Ministry of Foreign Affairs (MFA) and UNICEF, 'The Paris Principles: Principles and Guidelines on Children Associated with Armed Forces or Armed Groups' (MFA, UNICEF, February 2007), http://www.un.org/children/conflict/_documents/paris principles/ParisPrinciples_EN.pdf (accessed October 2008).
11 United Nations Inter-agency Working Group on DDR, 'Integrated Disarmament, Demobilisation and Reintegration Standards (IDDRS)' (UN, 2006), http://www.unddr.org/iddrs/ framework.php (accessed October 2008).
12 Specht, 'Jobs for Rebels and Soldiers'.
13 IDDRS, 'Module 5.30: Children and DDR'.
14 Translated from Irma Specht, Fundacion Ideas para la Paz, *Juventud y reinsercion*, Working paper FID (Bogata: August 2006).
15 United Nations Development Programme (UNDP), 'Gender Approaches in Conflict and Post-Conflict Situations: BCPR Gender Manual', http://www.undp.org/women/docs/gendermanualfinalBCPR.pdf (accessed October 2008).
16 UNDDR Southern Sudan, 'Assessment of Women Associated with the SPLA and Female Combatants in the SPLA' (October 2005).
17 These refer to marriages where the dowry has not been paid, the blessing has not been given by the families, and/or it is part of an adulterous relationship on the part of the woman.
18 UNDDR, 'Assessment of Women'.
19 Vanessa Farr, 'The importance of a gender perspective to successful disarmament, demobilisation and reintegration processes' *Disarmament Forum* (April 2003).
20 Nicola Johnston and William Godnick, *Putting a Human Face to the Problem of Small Arms Proliferation: Gender Implications for the Effective Implementation of the UN Programme of Action to Prevent, Combat and Eradicate the Illicit Trade in Small Arms and Light Weapons* (London: International Alert, 2005), http://www.international-alert.org/pdfs/gender_and_ programme_of_action.pdf (accessed October 2008).
21 Specht, *Red Shoes*.
22 Irma Specht and Carlien van Empel, *A Challenge for Social and Economic Reintegration: Targeting Ex-Combatants or All War-affected People? The Liberian Experience* (Geneva: ILO, 1998).
23 Elise F. Barth, *Peace as Disappointment: The Reintegration of Female Soldiers in Post-Conflict Societies. A Comparative Study from Africa* (Oslo: PRIO, 2002).
24 Specht, 'Jobs for Rebels and Soldiers'.

25 Larry Attree and Irma Specht, 'The reintegration of teenage girls and young women' *Intervention: International Journal of mental health* 4, Psychosocial work and counselling in areas of armed conflict, no. 3 (November 2006).
26 Francoise Achio and Irma Specht, 'Youth in Conflict' *in Jobs after war: a critical challenge in the peace and reconstruction puzzle*, ed. Eugenia Date-Bah, (Geneva: ILO, InFocus Programme on Crisis Response and Reconstruction, 2003), 153-166.
27 'The Paris Principles'.
28 IDDRS, 'Module 5.30: Children and DDR'.
29 Most organisations working with children use the legal definition of children in accordance with the UN Convention on the Rights of the Child. A child is therefore every human being below the age of 18.
30 IDDRS, 'Module 5.30: Children and DDR'.
31 Ibid.
32 UK Department of International Development (DFID), 'Understanding and Supporting Security Sector Reform' (June, 2002), 35, www.dfid.gov.uk/pubs/files/supporting security.pdf (accessed October 2008).
33 International Center for Transitional Justice and UNICEF, Children and Truth Commissions, Basic Considerations, Draft (March 2007).
34 Nosworthy, *Children's Security in Post-conflict Peacebuilding.*
35 Specht, 'Jobs for Rebels and Soldiers'.

# Chapter 10

# Children Affected by Armed Conflict: Engaging a New Constituency of Actors

*'Funmi Olonisakin*

## Introduction

This chapter proposes some new approaches and policy options for more effective interventions on behalf of war-affected children. The impact of armed conflict on children has been all too apparent and systematically documented in various works since the Report of Graça Machel, Expert of the Secretary-General of the United Nations (referred to as the 'Machel Study') first drew global attention to this issue in 1996.[1] Despite increased attention to the issue of war-affected children in the last decade, generations of young people across regions affected by armed conflict remain condemned to bleak futures. Opportunities for self-development among these young people are limited as many war-affected countries are confronted by the reality of the surging youth population, particularly in Africa. This rising youth population will potentially place enormous pressure on social and other services in the absence of adequate plans for translating their energy and talent into meaningful support of the state. Thus, failure to effectively address the plight of war-affected children invariably compounds the crisis faced by youth as they are joined by cohorts of young functional illiterates, excluded from mainstream life and of limited use to themselves and society. The continuing suffering of children in situations of armed conflict is not only a reflection of the gaps in responses to their plight, but also of the dearth of new thinking in terms of approaches to this problem.

In this chapter, I argue that there is a need for 'outside the box thinking' and new approaches to addressing some of the pressing challenges faced by children affected by armed conflict through more systematic engagement with particular sectors. While responses in the past decade have no doubt included active engagement with a cross-section of actors, there has been relatively limited use of cross-learning in ways that might help broaden approaches to the issue of war-affected children. The regional dimensions of the impact of war on children, and the lessons of disarmament, demobilisation and reintegration (DDR) efforts, for example, have thrown up glaring gaps and inadequacies, which the application of new thinking and more innovative collaboration with critical actors and sectors can help address. Two of such actors and sectors examined in this chapter are the security sector and regional organisations and networks. In order to creatively engage these actors in the protection of war-affected children, this chapter argues that some degree of adaptability among traditional child protection actors is required. Much of the illustration in this chapter, of the challenges and responses to the issue of war-affected children, is taken from the African region, which has been the theatre of much armed conflict in the last decade.

This chapter benefits from my experience in the office of the United Nations Special Representative of the Secretary-General for Children and Armed Conflict (SRSG) between 1999 and 2003, and a survey that I conducted on behalf of the UN Department of Peacekeeping Operations Best Practices Section as part of its study of the impact of Child Protection Advisers in 2006[2], including field visits to the UN Missions in the Congo and Sudan.[3]

## Children Affected by Armed Conflict: The Origins of International Attention and the Normative Framework

The impact of armed conflict on children began to receive global attention at the end of the Cold War with the outbreak of armed conflict across several regions, particularly in Africa, where the end of superpower rivalry created space at times for the violent expression of many long-standing conflicts. In these largely intra-state conflicts, civilians have been the focus of the violence as witnessed, for example, in the conflicts in Liberia, Sierra Leone, Democratic Republic of the Congo, Sudan and Northern Uganda. In many instances, children have been targeted in multiple ways. The civil war in Liberia set the scene with the recruitment of children as young as eight years by the National Patriotic Front of Liberia to fight as soldiers in its war against the Samuel Doe regime. The voluntary and forced recruitment of children as soldiers in war has since become a pattern in the many armed conflicts in Africa since 1990.[4] The phenomenon of child soldiering has become the best known feature of the problem of children affected by armed conflict given the vivid images in the media of children bearing arms. There has nonetheless been increasing attention to other dimensions of this problem including, for example, internal displacement, refugee and unaccompanied children, and gender-based violence among others. From the initial media reports in the early 1990s, studies of the phenomenon of child soldering have increasingly gained recognition.[5]

The Machel Study marked the first time that the UN brought the problem of war-affected children to a global audience. The concerns of children in contexts of armed conflict were marginal to the consideration of the UN prior to the Machel Study, which outlined comprehensively the multidimensional ways in which violent conflict alters the course of children's lives for the worse. The Machel Study examined the victimisation of children in wars raging around the world, emphasising the following eight key issues:

- Recruitment of children as soldiers
- Refugees fleeing the consequences of armed conflict
- Displaced within their countries
- 'Unaccompanied children' separated from their families
- Gender-based violence
- Exposure to landmines and unexploded ordinances
- Increased child mortality due to poor health conditions
- Lack of access to education which further exposes children to other risks

Among the ten recommendations outlined in the Machel Study two are particularly relevant for the purposes of this chapter. [6] One is that UN personnel in the field and relevant organisations must treat the issues of children in situations of armed conflict as a distinct concern in all their monitoring and reporting activities. The other is Machel's recommendation on the appointment of an SRSG to monitor the report's implementation and to ensure that the concerns of children in situations of war are brought to the fore of international human rights, peace and security, and development agendas.

In response to the Machel Study, the General Assembly recommended the appointment of an SRSG. Olara Otunnu was appointed SRSG in September 1997 and, at the end of Otunnu's tenure in 2005, Radhika Coomaraswamy was appointed to the role, following an interim period.[7] The creation of this office and the appointment of the SRSG was a critical step in ensuring sustained advocacy for the protection of war-affected children and in support of the work of operational agencies on the ground, not least the United Nations Children's Fund (UNICEF), which had been at the forefront of drawing attention to the challenges posed by armed conflict. Additionally, the office of the SRSG was also particularly relevant in clarifying a normative framework for the protection of children affected by armed conflict and the application of these norms.

Field visits were not the only methods through which this part of the UN sought to mobilise action for the protection of war-affected children. Various initiatives were undertaken, targeting not only other parts of the UN system, but other global, regional and local actors, including, for example, regional organisations, communities of faith, non-governmental organisations and other civil society actors. In this regard, the office of the SRSG has played a crucial role in raising international awareness on the issue of children and armed conflict. But the outreach to all parts of the UN system was a necessary basis for the global outreach.

This global outreach was underpinned by the effort to strengthen the normative framework, particularly within the UN. The UN Security Council became a critical player on the issue of children for the first time in 1999 with the adoption of Resolution 1261. After that, other Security Council Resolutions were adopted on this issue: resolutions 1314 (2000), 1379 (2001), 1460 (2003), 1539 (2004) and 1612 (2005). Collectively, these resolutions have sought to ensure that the concerns of children affected by armed conflict are reflected in the responses of critical actors during armed conflict, throughout peace processes, and in post-conflict contexts. All of these resolutions also call for a systematic response by a broad constituency of actors before, during and after conflict.

A close examination of these resolutions will indicate an evolutionary pattern in the discourse on war-affected children in which incremental progress was realised each year. The Security Council has set the standards through the establishment of norms and values for the protection of children in situations of war by a range of actors, through articulating mechanisms for monitoring and reporting violations against children, and through strengthening enforcement mechanisms by naming perpetrators. Indeed, with Resolution 1612, the development of a normative framework came full circle. Resolution 1612 has allowed for more specific reporting including the 'naming and shaming' of parties to armed conflict who continue to perpetrate the abuse of children. It is now possible to focus on individual conflict environments on the basis of the standards set by the Security Council. The UN Secretary-General's report on Sudan in 2006 was the first attempt to undertake such specific reporting. It is still too soon to read the longer-term impact of resolution 1612 and its application on the protection of children in situations of armed conflict.

Having made children affected by armed conflict a UN peace and security concern, an attempt was made to embed this agenda throughout the UN's peace and security work. Peace operations provided a very important platform for translating Security Council resolutions into concrete action on the ground and so they represented (and still do) an important platform for implementing the agenda of war-affected children. The Security Council explicitly incorporated the protection of children into peace operation mandates beginning with the UN Mission in Sierra Leone (UNAMSIL) in 1999, and subsequently deployed Child Protection Advisers (CPAs) where it was considered relevant to do so.

The office of the SRSG, the Department of Peacekeeping Operations and UNICEF jointly drafted the generic terms of reference to guide the work of CPAs in 2000. Through the terms of reference, they sought to ensure that Child Protection Advisers would maximise their comparative advantage as a component of a peace mission while also complementing the work of UNICEF and other partners engaged in the protection of children's rights in conflict and post-conflict settings (notably the Office of the High Commissioner for Human Rights and the human rights components of peace missions). The first Child Protection Adviser was deployed to UNAMSIL in 2000. Since 2000, CPAs have been deployed in seven other peace operations: MONUC (Democratic Republic of the Congo), UNMA (Angola), ONUCI (Côte d'Ivoire), UNMIL (Liberia), ONUB (Burundi), UNMIS (Sudan) and MINUSTAH (Haiti).[8] There are currently about 60 CPAs deployed in six missions, with the largest number of CPAs concentrated in UNMIS and MONUC.[9]

The attempt here is not to assess the performance of CPAs or the extent to which these objectives were met. A separate study by the UN already deals with these issues.[10] The focus here is on the extent to which the UN system's leadership (CPAs included), has managed to change the lives of war-affected children for the better through their actions – including policy and programmatic interventions.

Despite obvious gaps in approach (discussed in the next session), the UN system's response and the engagement by other actors outside the UN system have no doubt achieved significant results for the protection of children affected by armed conflict. The placement of the concerns of children and armed conflict on the Security Council agenda and the corresponding adoption of ground-breaking resolutions and the creation of the child protection role in peacekeeping missions, has contributed in no small measure to two significant developments.

First is the strengthening of the normative framework for the protection of children affected by armed conflict. It should be noted that the Security Council's increased role coincided with other processes – the adoption of the Optional Protocol to the Convention on the Rights of the Child on the involvement of children in armed conflict, which provided a rallying point; the Rome Statute on the International Criminal Court; and the Statute of the Sierra Leone Special Court. The last two have made the recruitment of children as soldiers a crime of war. The Security Council resolutions, not least 1612, provide the ideal accompaniment, giving credibility to enforcement regimes. It has been possible to use these frameworks to bring pressure to bear on major perpetrators. The recruitment of children as soldiers was one of the 11 counts on which the former President of Liberia, Charles Taylor, was indicted by the Sierra Leone Special Court. Similarly, Thomas Lubanga, a former militia leader in the Democratic Republic of the Congo, was indicted for the recruitment of children by the International Criminal Court.

Apart from the precedent set by these cases, the deterrent effect of the new norms was made all too clear in Côte d'Ivoire, where the armed group Forces Nouvelles became increasingly nervous after Lubanga's indictment, and the imposition of sanctions against one of its commanders, for child recruitment. Many child protection practitioners believe these events made it possible for the ONUCI, through its Child Protection Adviser, to extract a commitment from the leadership of Forces Nouvelles to release children within its ranks and to set a time table for doing so in 2006.

Second, the increased role of the Security Council has also served to expand the constituency of actors working for the protection of war-affected children. And this expansion of actors has in turn yielded a number of positive results, some of which are highlighted here. Among other things, Security Council resolutions have made it possible to extend the task of monitoring the situation of war-affected children within the UN system beyond those traditionally responsible for child protection issues. The existence of UN resolutions on this issue has compelled those who would not ordinarily consider this a part of their work to devote more attention to the concerns of war-affected children. Although the process is a long one, converts are gradually being made out of those sectors, which either paid lip service to child protection issues because UN resolutions demanded periodic reporting, or those who resisted engagement with the issue. Some examples are provided below.

We are witnessing an emerging institutionalisation of child protection within the police and military components of peace operations – a constituency that traditionally tends to shun 'soft security issues', particularly those regarding women and children. One result of CPA activism and efforts to mainstream a child-sensitive approach throughout peace missions has been the inclusion of a child-conscious approach in the work of police and military personnel. Child protection has been systematised into the programmes of most UN missions, including regular induction training as well as training of trainers, all of which are repeated with newly deployed police staff and with the rotation of military personnel in every contingent, particularly in missions with a child protection mandate.

In UNMIS, for example, there is an integrated training centre and integrated induction training for the military and the police in addition to police-specific training that includes a briefing on child protection. As a result of the continuous inflow of newly deployed staff into the mission, such briefings take place weekly in Khartoum and they are provided by CPAs. Military observers and civilian police are especially relied upon by CPAs to not only adopt a child-conscious approach but to monitor and bring to the attention of CPAs issues concerning children in the field. All missions with CPAs have come to internalise this approach.

Although the degree to which a major attitudinal shift has occurred among mission military personnel across the board is debatable, child protection training helps to develop an understanding of the key issues and focusses their attention on these issues in the field. In MONUC, the Child Protection Focal Point in the military demonstrated a good grasp of issues of children and armed conflict. Similarly, in UNMIS, the Chief of Staff, operating in Juba as of June 2006, clearly articulated a child-conscious approach while confronted by the practical challenges of implementing the provisions of the Optional Protocol. The Deputy Police Commissioner in UNMIS, also operating in Juba at the same time, and who had previously served in Liberia, seemed keen to apply lessons learned in the field of child protection in other contexts.

Additionally, the child protection training and the resultant development of a child-sensitive approach among the police and military personnel have had knock-on effects on the community in the mission area. In Sierra Leone, for example, the efforts of UNAMSIL and its International Civilian Police were crucial in the creation of Child Protection Units in key police stations across the country. In Liberia, collaboration between several parts of the mission was evident not least between the International Civilian

Police and the Gender Adviser's Office in the proposal for the establishment of Women and Children's Units in Police Stations in Liberia.

A movement-like response has gradually evolved since the late 1990s consisting of active advocacy and engagement on the issue of children affected by armed conflict by international and local civil society groups, including communities of faith, non-governmental organisation networks and regional organisations, among others. The various Security Council resolutions on children and armed conflict have provided a legitimate basis for a cross-section of actors to place the protection of war-affected children on their agendas, while advancing the work of governmental and inter-governmental organisations. In particular, increased civil society engagement produced active collaboration with the UN. Organisations such as Save the Children, Human Rights Watch, the Coalition to Stop the Use of Child Soldiers, and the International Rescue Committee, among others, formed the bedrock of several Arria Formula meetings at the UN Headquarters from 2000.

Beyond this contribution, civil society collaboration with UNICEF and field missions has also been evident in the formation of in-country Child Protection Networks (often supported and facilitated by UNICEF) to support the national government (through the relevant line ministries in charge of children's affairs) and/or the UN to advance the cause of war-affected children. In places such as Sierra Leone and Sudan, members of national Child Protection Networks supported UNAMSIL and UNMIS CPAs to undertake child protection training for mission personnel. In 2000, Save the Children (Sweden) facilitated child protection training for senior military personnel from a number of Economic Community of West African States (ECOWAS) member states. It is noteworthy that active, if not systematic, engagement by select parts of the UN system (UNICEF, Office of the Special Representative, CPAs and Office of the High Commissioner for Human Rights and field missions) helped galvanise action among this group of actors.

## Continuing Challenges and Gaps in Responses

Despite the obvious progress realised in the past decade, much remains to be done. More than ten years after the situation of children in armed conflict caught the imagination of the UN General Assembly, and seven years after the deployment of the first Child Protection Adviser in a UN mission, questions remain about the effectiveness of efforts to protect war-affected children, for example, as to how to more creatively develop cross-sectoral engagement in ways that will generate new approaches for responding more effectively to the needs of these children.

Gaps remain in both our understanding and in the responses to the challenge of war-affected children. These gaps are reflected in the continuing and sometimes worsening plight of children in some contexts. The focus here is on only certain aspects of this challenge. The policy and programmatic interventions of the past decade have not always managed to transform the lives of the majority of war-affected children. While it is difficult to accurately measure the magnitude of these gaps, the noticeable trends in the situation of war-affected children can tell us something about the impact (or lack thereof) of the policies and programmes of the last decade. In discussing these trends, attention is focussed on developments in the African region over the past decade.

*Specific Gaps in the Reintegration of War-affected Children*

In the area of disarmament, demobilisation and reintegration of children, for example, some categories of children regularly fall through the cracks. Many war-affected communities have been victims of unimaginative demobilisation programmes with no consideration for the reality of the terrain. The net effect is that thousands of cheaply demobilised children are released into communities. It is not uncommon for a large number of young people to receive similar vocational training – as carpenters, blacksmiths, cloth dyers – all competing for the same non-existent markets in ghost towns and villages. There is a glaring lack of opportunity structures across these communities whether or not they have suffered the direct impact of armed conflict.

One issue that deserves greater attention and concerted action is the 'growing' challenge, whereby 15- to 17-year-olds pass through demobilisation programmes and become a bigger challenge for the community shortly after leaving the programmes. This is largely because little consideration is given in many instances to the need for more creative initiatives to prepare for their proper re-socialisation into adult societies. This age group might not always have, or accept, the option (if it were available to them) of returning to formal education, particularly when they have been out of school for too long. Given the limited opportunity structures in the communities, this group of youth is particularly vulnerable – the only option often available to them is to compete for subsistence on the margins of the state alongside other excluded youth, who already effectively occupy this space.

In this terrain, both war-affected and non-war-affected children subsist on the margins of the state through a combination of illegal and non-illegal (even if socially unacceptable) activities. These include, for example, trafficking for use in varied labour markets, transactional sex, sports, involvement in the informal security sector including ethnic militia, vigilante groups and private security companies, street hawking, cross-border activities including re-recruitment for participation in armed conflicts in neighbouring states and absorption into religious groups. The group of young people mentioned above is particularly vulnerable once released into this environment.

This situation is further complicated by the fact that some of these activities are sometimes perpetrated by employees of the UN and international relief agencies – the very actors that are entrusted with the protection of the populations (not least children) in the affected countries. Since the cases of sexual abuse and exploitation by international relief agencies hit the headlines, the UN has found it difficult to make this a thing of the past. This is despite the 'zero tolerance' policy adopted by the UN.

### *The Need for Better Understanding of the Strategic Environment*

There is a glaring gap in the way child protection actors engage with the strategic environment. The overall environment in which all the multiplicity of actors undertake child protection cannot be discounted. Child protection programmes, not least DDR, are being implemented in environments where other strategic activities that can impact on child protection for good or bad are often not taken into account. At best, such programmes will have limited impact and, at worst, they can negate the effect of work being done on the ground. There are noticeable some trends in the neighbourhoods (largely in Africa) in which war-affected policies and programmes are being implemented, which invariably determine the fate of these children and their communities.

One trend, which poses an enormous challenge for the protection of war-affected children, is the surging youth population, mentioned earlier in this chapter. Another is the sheer volume of activity relating to children in neighbouring countries or regions, which are not necessarily undergoing large-scale armed conflict. These include, for example, the use of children as labourers in plantations and domestic labour. In a socio-economic context that is largely dominated by poverty, dire shortage of social amenities and lack of access to good education and healthcare, the available options for young people are predatory activities that provide alternative sources of livelihood. Among these are a plethora of private security and community security actors, waiting to prey on children and young people that have been cheaply demobilised into society. The trafficking of children across African borders is already well documented.

Unless the protection of children in armed conflict takes this strategic environment into account, the impact of contiguous issues will gradually chip away at the incremental progress being made in the protection of war-affected children. There is a need to more systematically engage with sectors not often considered as primary child protection actors, including the military and other private, non-state actors who are inevitably present in this strategic environment.

## The Case for New Actors and New Approaches

There is a need for new approaches and methods that can add value to existing ones and new resources for the protection of war-affected children. This section focusses on two areas for action and engagement in order to advance the agenda of children affected by armed conflict. One is the need to bring on board all the range of security institutions and actors operating in war-affected regions. The second concerns the use of regional institutional frameworks for addressing the regional dimensions of the challenge of children and armed conflict.

There is a dearth of new ideas at the strategic level even if they exist in some local settings in the form of small projects and initiatives. The security sector, as well as regional organisations, could be more creatively involved in the protection of war-affected children. The lack of innovation is due in part to the cautious (and necessarily so) approach of traditional child protection actors. It is understandable, for example, that it is difficult to engage, even if in a post-war environment, with the same military and security personnel who preyed on children during war time.

There can be no doubt that the method of work of key child protection actors has added to the already heavy burden of the strategic environment. Typically, child protection actors (not excluding UN agencies), like parts of the humanitarian community, adopt, perhaps correctly so, a puritanical approach to the business of child protection, failing to collaborate with actors that come from traditional military and security settings. Security institutions within war-affected countries are often not considered potential partners in child protection even when they are undergoing reforms. The net effect of this is that the role that a well-trained and well-governed security sector can play in child protection is hardly ever explored.

*The Security Sector Has a Role to Play*

If UN peacekeeping security personnel can be seen as potential child protection actors, the same allowance could be made for national security institutions undergoing reform, often with the support of the international community. Indeed, envisaging a child protection function as part of the security sector reform process offers a chance to institutionalise good practice and achieve sustainability of good initiatives that began during the life of a peace mission.

While collaboration with the military within peacekeeping missions has no doubt yielded important results, this does not often extend beyond peace missions. The security establishments in the target environments are often condemned as unprofessional, untouchable, and a place not suited for children and young people who had been previously traumatised by these actors. Yet the harsh reality on the ground is that in many places, these security agencies will be left behind to 'protect' the populations when the UN leaves. It is with these institutions that the wider international community continuously engages, making them targets of reform and transformation programmes – although the results of such programmes are chequered. The challenge that faces those seeking to bring lasting peace to those environments is how to re-build a professional security establishment that is democratically accountable to civil authority. The reform of the security sector has become a priority concern of peacebuilding efforts in war-affected countries. Examples include Sierra Leone, Liberia, the Democratic Republic of the Congo and South Sudan. It should be possible to find a framework for the protection of children within these arrangements.

*How Can Security Sector Reform Provide a Framework for Addressing the Challenge of War-affected Children?*

The introductory part of this volume already discusses the essence and essentials of security sector reform and governance and the relevance to children. This section highlights aspects of this process that can be triggered for the protection of war-affected children.

In post-conflict environments, there are different points of engagement during peacebuilding and security reforms in general. The first obvious point of engagement is the DDR process, which is seen as the first stage of security sector reform. The way in which former combatants and people associated with fighting forces (not least children and youth) are demobilised invariably affects the efforts to consolidate peace and ensure longer-term security. Disrupted demobilisation programmes in Sierra Leone (due to reignited violence) and short-term demobilisation initiatives in Liberia have shown how disarmed but poorly integrated former combatants become ready agents for continuing conflict in neighbouring Côte d'Ivoire or simmering conflict in Guinea. Indeed, had a creative approach being taken to demobilisation, it might have been possible to control the spill-over effects. Indeed, even when young people do not move across borders into neighbouring countries, in many cases they fall prey to unscrupulous actors operating on the margins of the state. Leveraging available resources for longer-term education and training of older children offer the best chance to prevent these fallouts from DDR processes.

Another approach is to treat DDR and SSR as intertwined components when it comes to the reintegration of older children in ways that offer longer-term protection. The first is by addressing the 'growing challenge' described earlier by targeting older children, including 16- and 17-year-olds, for inclusion in the security sector once they reach the age of 18. A staggered arrangement in which special programmes are spread out over a period of time for children that will soon reach the age of 18, but unlikely or unwilling to return to formal education, can offer viable alternatives that keep them out of harm's way. The engineering and signals corps of armed forces can offer attractive opportunities when they reach the age of 18. The police service, in particular, offers perhaps a readily acceptable alternative for reintegrating young people eventually. Keeping these options open offers a better chance to combine the reintegration of young people with the reform of the security establishment.

By retaining them as 'professional men and women in waiting' and offering opportunities to keep them in separate schemes as part of official, often externally supported, SSR programmes, these young people can get another chance at structured re-education and professional training, which is often unavailable in the armed groups that they rejoin after demobilisation. There is a greater chance of reintegrating through formal education 10- to 12-year-olds that have lost out on several years of education, than a 17-year-old who has been out of the loop for many years and who does not want to consider the option of returning for formal education. Yet these older children are the most attractive to armed and other groups operating on the margins of the state. By including them as parts of a reform army or police service, not only are they kept out of harm's way in the immediate aftermath of conflict, they benefit from professional training that offers stability and career development, and society is ultimately the better for it. In this regard, programmatic interventions must seek to include advocacy to private security actors as potential partners in observing agreed practices or codes of conduct.

Additionally, in post-conflict environments, building child protection norms and values into policy and practice of security institutions from the start offers perhaps the best hope for reversing the trends of abuse from the era of conflict. This requires multiple levels of engagement, beginning with active involvement in the design and implementation of security sector reform programmes. For example, the role and inclusion of older children in non-combat activities across the security sector can perhaps form part of the dialogue in the development of a security policy framework and in any sectoral reviews. This way, a normative framework can be established by including and defining the responsibilities of the different parts of the security establishment in the national security policy and consequently in defence acts, police acts and other legal frameworks.

By securing the commitment of the security establishment to particular standards in the treatment of young people entrusted to them for training and professional development, it then becomes possible for legislators to conduct requisite oversight through public hearings, periodic questions and reviews. Similarly, training institutions can structure curricula along the priorities identified in the policy process, including those particular to children.

All of these are possible in reconstructing societies, particularly in post-conflict contexts, but they require a major commitment and collaboration across the board among traditional child protection actors as well as those working to promote security and sustainable development in general. The rebuilding that occurs as a consequence of armed conflict offers an opportunity to include the protection of children in the rebuilding plan. In Sierra Leone, the office of the SRSG was able to obtain President Kabbah's consent to establish a National Commission for War-Affected Children in 1999.[11] At the time of the Commission's establishment, the link between children and SSR was not well defined beyond seeking the release of children from the ranks of rebels, armed forces and militia.

It is more difficult, however, to pursue this type of agenda in other fragile states that are not experiencing large-scale conflict. In those contexts, much depends on the goodwill of leaders. Indeed, in all cases, leaders play an important role in determining how permissive that terrain is to innovative ideas and programmes. The best hope is to look for targets of opportunity in different contexts. Sometimes, it will take reformists and champions of change in different institutions to break new ground by advancing the discourse on child protection and creating a new framework for addressing the challenges. The role of Parliaments can be crucial in this regard – they can be makers (or breakers) of new agendas.

Whereas the constraints described above can be encountered within states, regional organisations provide another viable framework for advancing the agendas of war-affected children. The ECOWAS experience forms the focus of the next section.

## Strengthening Regional Approaches: The West African Case

The apparently narrow focus of child protection activists and indeed UN agencies is also reflected in the lack of engagement along regional lines beyond the immediate conflict or operational setting. As such, the much needed cross-connection to other child protection issues is often not achieved. There have been notable exceptions, such as Save the Children's (Sweden) engagement with ECOWAS on child protection training, which was not sustained, and office of the SRSG and UNICEF engagement with the Child Protection Unit of ECOWAS, which was also not sustained. A great deal of cross-learning and engagement with regional actors is necessary in order to achieve comprehensive action, and a holistic approach.

It is important to look outside of existing mainstream agendas and ideas. In regions where the human misery generated by war and poverty alike has made common victims of war-affected and non-war-affected communities, policies must seek cross-cutting solutions and avoid situations where the children's agenda is held hostage by a desire to engage only with the familiar. Here, we examine the West African experience and how regional institutions can be used to generate a multiplier effect.

The problem of war-affected children is not just a national problem within countries undergoing civil strife. Rather, it raises a plethora of interrelated issues for West Africa as a whole. Among these are the influx of small arms and light weapons; violence, and illicit trafficking of resources and drugs; population displacement and resettlement; the outbreak and spread of diseases; and child labour and exploitation.[12] All of these problems have major security implications and necessitate regional approaches to resolving them. The continuing threat of high- and low-intensity conflicts in West Africa, from Casamance to Nigeria's oil-rich Niger Delta, means that arms will continue to flow into this sub-region and compound the already high level of insecurity. And children will remain an attractive constituency to agents of insecurity operating in these environments.

To be certain, the problems affecting children in war-affected countries are present in nearly all of the other countries in West Africa. Huge numbers of street children exist throughout the sub-region, many of them victims of the recent decade of political turmoil, economic decline and social conflicts. It is clear that the challenge of how to engage the time and talents of young people will intensify as more children and young adults are disarmed and demobilised along the corridors of armed conflict. Without long-term programmes and adequate resources, the situation of young people will remain volatile.[13] Young people in the sub-region's war zones feel alienated, abused, discouraged and abandoned. Often illiterate and unemployed with little hope of gainful employment, millions of young people invariably succumb to the lure of life on the margins of the state, where legal and illegal alternatives abound.

Regional organisations thus provide an important umbrella for addressing the cross-cutting regional impact of armed conflict on children as the ECOWAS experience has indicated. A formula for a regional approach emerged in April 2000 at the Accra Conference on War-Affected Children, which was co-sponsored by the governments of Ghana, Canada and the office of the SRSG. Its purpose was to facilitate a dialogue among West African states on the problems of war-affected children in order to develop a regional framework for the protection of children affected by armed conflict. At this conference, ECOWAS member states and their representatives adopted the Accra Declaration and Plan of Action. Both of these documents built on the Declaration of ECOWAS foreign ministers on Child Soldiers, signed in Bamako in March 1999, as well as the African Charter on the Rights and Welfare of Children.

The Accra Declaration and the Plan of Action of 2000 urged ECOWAS member states, civil society representatives and international organisations to take steps to address the multidimensional problems of children affected by conflict. The Accra conference set broad principles for the protection of war-affected children in West Africa. The Plan of Action contains a number of elements aimed at addressing the challenges highlighted earlier.[14] These include the following, among others:

- Implementing international conventions and legal instruments for the protection of children including, for example, UN Security Council resolutions 1261 (1999); 1265 (1999); the four Geneva Conventions and their Additional Protocols; the African Charter on the Rights and Welfare of the Child; the Convention on the Rights of the Child and the Optional Protocol on the involvement of children in armed conflict, among others.

- Working closely with civil society groups and other actors to ensure the successful DDR of child combatants and the rehabilitation of all war-affected children.
- Taking political, social and economic measures to address the factors that contribute to the occurrence or recurrence of armed conflicts – including good governance and democratic practice.
- Incorporating child rights and the protection of children into training programmes for the military and other security services.
- Implementing early warning systems to forestall armed conflicts and the victimisation of children, as well as their involvement in armed conflicts.
- Integrating child protection into ECOWAS' peacemaking and peacekeeping initiatives and its security mechanism.
- Promoting sub-regional cross-border activities to reduce the flow of arms.
- Implementing the ECOWAS Moratorium of 1998 in order to halt the proliferation of small arms and light weapons in the sub-region.
- Institutionalising child protection within ECOWAS and establishing an office within the ECOWAS secretariat in Abuja for the protection of war-affected children.
- Taking measures to involve young people as participants and advocates in the movement for the protection of war-affected children.

It is, however, important to engage regional organisations and networks beyond norm-setting, which is an important first step in regional child protection drives. There is a need to find more effective ways to translate these norms into concrete action for the protection of war-affected children on the ground. Ensuring that these principles are translated into policies that are harmonised throughout the sub-region will be a major challenge. The Plan of Action's call for the establishment, within the ECOWAS secretariat, of a focal point dedicated to the protection of war-affected children in West Africa could prove to be an important tool for harmonising child protection policies in the sub-region. The ECOWAS Child Protection Unit, which is supposed to be responsible for the situation of war-affected children and to promote preventive mechanisms, became operational in 2002.[15] However, this unit has become increasingly obscure and it has made no prominent contribution to regional debates and initiatives since 2003.

The ECOWAS Child Protection Unit will do well to explore innovative ideas for regional initiatives, which can be championed by ECOWAS. One proposal that is worth exploring is that of a regional youth service scheme that targets older children and implements a structured programme that equips them with a variety of skills that will be useful upon their return to their various communities. Youth service programmes will provide an opportunity to keep these young people engaged in community and other development work, away from the lure of armed groups.

A regional youth policy, which ECOWAS recently developed, can help outline a comprehensive implementation framework for dealing with cross-cutting issues from child recruitment to child trafficking and labour.[16] Through such an approach, a degree of mutual inter-dependence can be achieved in which national processes are strengthened by regional ones and vice versa. It is conceivable, for example, that gaps in demobilisation and reintegration of war-affected children can be filled by regional youth programmes, when children who fall through the cracks appear in neighbouring countries.

Regional organisations also have some potential for generating additional resources to support the child protection agenda. Strategies for leveraging regional resources have not been adequately explored in part because it is often assumed that these regions affected by armed conflict are too poor to provide human and material resources for child protection. Engaging regional and locals actors to contribute to child protection will ultimately tune their attention to their responsibility and provide avenues for sustaining any gains made in the area of child protection.

## Conclusions

Much remains to be done in the effort to find more effective responses to the needs of children affected by armed conflict. The challenge for child protection actors is to think creatively and engage a strategic framework for addressing these problems. At a minimum, this requires engagement with multiple actors and institutions across borders and regions. And of necessity, some of these actors are not those with whom the child protection community has traditionally interacted. It will require a great deal of cross-learning in addition to a sea change in mind-set as well as a measure of flexibility in approach.

It is, however, important to understand context and recognise that contexts vary. Local conditions in the affected countries will dictate the relevance of the approaches proposed in this chapter. There is no point, for example, placing young people in ill conceived and poorly structured security reform programmes, where they are again likely to fall prey to unprofessional and unaccountable security personnel. It is therefore important that any approach that seeks to integrate child protection into security sector reform programmes be adapted to the specific needs of the target environments and adequately monitored to ensure that such programmes will improve the lot of children.

The tendency for top-down approaches to child protection work means that local knowledge is lost and local examples of child protection can be lost in the process. It is a difficult balancing act that those seeking the protection of children have to undertake. It is difficult to accept that the same communities that condone the abuse of children in such grave proportions during war time can have solutions that enhance the protection of children in the aftermath of war. Concerted efforts should be made, however, to explore good local ideas and scale up effective initiatives taking place at the local level.

Ultimately, financing sustainable child protection initiatives is an expensive endeavour. It requires long-term commitment. Agencies traditionally responsible for the protection of children, particularly in war-affected terrains, are often overstretched and understaffed. However, proposals for new initiatives to advance the cause of children affected by armed conflict require corresponding ideas and strategies for resource mobilisation, particularly from regional sources.

## Endnotes

1 United Nations, *Impact of Armed Conflict on Children*, Report of Graça Machel, Expert of the Secretary-General of the United Nations, UN doc. A/51/306 (New York: August 1996).

2 Funmi Olonisakin, 'Lessons Learned Study: The Impact of Child Protection Advisers in UN Peacekeeping Operations, Peacekeeping Best Practices Sections' (May 2007), http://pbpu.unlb.org/pbps/Library/LL_CPA_PBPS_May07_Final.pdf (accessed October 2008).

3 As part of this process, I hosted at King's College London, the first meeting of United Nations Child Protection Advisers and UNICEF Child Protection specialists based in New York and various field locations. The discussion at this meeting also provided invaluable

insight to the challenges confronting those responding to the needs of children affected by armed conflict.

4 See for example, Funmi Olonisakin, 'Children and Armed Conflict' in *West Africa's Security Challenges: Building Peace in a Troubled Region*, eds. Adekeye Adebajo and Ismail Rashid (Boulder, London: Lynne Rienner, 2004), 245-261.

5 Ibid.

6 The Ten Recommendations outlined in the Machel Study cover the following areas: (1) Peace and Security, (2) Monitoring and reporting violations of child rights, (3) Health, psychosocial well-being and education, (4) Adolescents, (5) Gender-based violence, (6) Internally displaced children, (7) Child soldiers, (8) Land-mines, (9) Prevention, (10) Special Representative.

7 Olara Otunnu's term as SRSG ended in 2005 and, following an interim period in which Karen Shampoo was in charge of the Office, the Secretary-General appointed Radikha Coomaraswamy, previously Special Rapporteur on Violence against Women, as SRSG for Children and Armed Conflict in April 2006.

8 United Nations Mission in Sierra Leone (UNAMSIL) and United Nations Mission in Angola (UNMA) have since closed.

9 Not all of the existing 60 posts are filled at the moment. The breakdown of the provision of CPAs consisting of both international and national staff is as follows: Democratic Republic of Congo (DRC), 34; Burundi, 1; Haiti, 3; Liberia, 1; Cote d'Ivoire, 4; and Sudan, 17. Please note that these numbers were correct as at October 2006.

10 Olonisakin, 'Lessons Learned Study'.

11 I was the Focal Point in the office of the SRSG for Children and Armed Conflict for Sierra Leone and worked with the Ministry for Social Welfare, Women and Children's Affairs in Sierra Leone and the Office of Canada's Minister for Foreign Affairs (Lloyd Axworthy) in 1999 and 2000, to develop the Commission's Terms of Reference. The Commission was established in 2001 by an Act of Parliament.

12 Olonisakin, 'Children and Armed Conflict'.

13 Ibid.

14 The Accra Plan of Action, adopted by the Economic Community of West African States (ECOWAS) Ministers at the Conference on War-Affected Children in West Africa, in Accra, Ghana, 28-30 April 2000.

15 Like the National Commission for War-Affected Children in Sierra Leone, I worked with the Canadian Foreign Ministry to facilitate the establishment of the CPU as part of my brief in the office of the SRSG. From the development of its Terms of Reference in August 2000, the office became operational in early 2002.

16 ECOWAS also adopted, in December 2007, a Conflict Prevention Framework, which has among other things a clear agenda for youth development in West Africa. There is scope within this framework for advancing the agenda of older children in situations of armed conflict.

# Chapter 11

# Engaging Armed Non-state Actors on the Issue of Child Recruitment and Use[1]

*Philippe Gazagne*

Armed Non-state Actors (NSAs) play a central role in contemporary armed conflicts, in which egregious violations against children are perpetuated, including the recruitment or use of children within their ranks.

This chapter explores the work of Geneva Call with NSAs in mine action, drawing lessons that can guide approaches aimed at encouraging NSAs to stop the recruitment and the use of child soldiers. Geneva Call has been exploring possible commonalities over the past three years, and this chapter draws on those experiences.

Key elements that will be developed here include the importance of entering into inclusive, pragmatic discussion; listening to the concerns of NSAs; ensuring that local communities, as well as the NSAs themselves, are engaged; ensuring that initiatives are based on local ownership; acknowledging that long-term strategies may be necessary to realise change; and that robust monitoring needs to be put in place.

Engaging NSAs specifically on the issue of child soldiers should be considered as part of a broader engagement to bring attention to human rights standards and international humanitarian law in general. It can be counter-productive to simply engage NSAs on the issue of recruitment and use of child soldiers, and therefore broader discussions about how conflict impacts on children, not just those involved with fighting forces, should be encouraged. This wider view can assist in promoting better understanding and respect for child rights, and encourage the development of child protection activities, such as ensuring that children are allowed secure access to education and health facilities.

Geneva Call has actively promoted an inclusive approach to NSAs, seeking to promote dialogue and co-operation (as opposed to measures such as denunciation). Through negotiations with approximately 60 NSAs, Geneva Call has gained a recognised expertise and practice in obtaining formal commitments towards the prohibition of the use of anti-personnel mines. Thirty-four have subscribed to the norms embodied in the 1997 Mine Ban Treaty (MBT), through their signature of a declaration called the 'Deed of Commitment for Adherence to a Total Ban on Anti-Personnel Mines and for Co-operation in Mine Action' (hereafter the Deed of Commitment), a mechanism provided by Geneva Call.

Based on three case studies (Colombia, the Philippines and Somalia), section one of this chapter explores lessons learned on the anti-personnel mines issue that have relevance to the issue of the recruitment and use of children. Section two considers the similarities and differences between anti-personnel mines and the recruitment and use of children by armed groups. Using this heuristic methodology, an appreciation of where lessons learned can be drawn, and where they cannot, will be developed. This will lead to recommendations on how to encourage NSAs to end the recruitment and use of children.

## The Geneva Call Experience in Mine Action

Through an overview of Geneva Call's activities in Colombia, the Philippines and Somalia, this section looks at the facets and specificities of Geneva Call's approach that influenced the outcomes of negotiations in securing commitments from NSAs towards the prohibition of the use of anti-personnel mines. The three case studies reflect very different contexts that have required specific approaches adapted to each situation. Geneva Call's experience in Colombia reveals the potential of a step-by-step approach in building confidence and eliciting better respect to humanitarian norms. Two other case studies in the Philippines and in Somalia will look at the challenges of supporting implementation of the Deed of Commitment, where recurring and long-term efforts are similarly required.

### *The National Liberation Army in Colombia*

In Colombia, the contact between the ELN (Ejército de Liberación Nacional/National Liberation Army) and Geneva Call was first established in 2003. At that time, the ELN declared that it was not prepared to ban anti-personnel mines and adhere to Geneva Call's Deed of Commitment, considering this method of warfare as vital in an imbalanced/asymmetric military situation against a government equipped with heavy weapons.

In cases where the NSA is not ready to abandon the use of anti-personnel mines[2] is it preferable to opt for an 'all-or-nothing' approach, therefore postponing or ending dialogue until the NSA concurs to a total ban on anti-personnel mines? Or is it better to maintain the dialogue and explore alternative means to reduce progressively the impact of anti-personnel mine use on civilians? The choice made in Colombia by Geneva Call attests the potential of a step-by-step approach.[3]

*a) Maintaining Dialogue, an Opportunity for Prevention*

Bearing in mind its ultimate objective – adherence to the Deed of Commitment and full compliance to its terms – Geneva Call has adopted a gradual approach, which entails a flexible strategy, continuous dialogue and negotiation. Even though a total ban cannot be reached yet, this progressive approach has opened the door for civilian-friendly provisional measures, among them local mine-clearance agreements.

As a result of the ongoing dialogue with the ELN, the group publicly announced a new mine-use policy in December 2005, which would respect international humanitarian standards. The ELN claimed that it would lay mines in such a manner as to target only security personnel, instruct its commanders to map mined areas, warn the local communities about the locations of mines, and remove mines that served no purpose. The ELN has indeed initiated mine-clearance operations in the seriously landmine-affected village of Micoahumado (in 2005) and has announced its willingness to further clear mines in several hamlets in Samaniego (in October 2006). These initiatives are part of a humanitarian agreement between the ELN and the local communities, facilitated by Geneva Call. As a result of this process, the risks associated with anti-personnel mines faced by the local populations have been reduced. The ELN has since shown a willingness to collaborate with Geneva Call in mine-action activities in other regions and localities. Although not yet sufficient, the measures taken, beyond saving life in the interim, have generated a constructive process of confidence-building and better understanding between involved actors, which enhances the prospect of a total ban of anti-personnel mines. Today, Geneva Call continues to meet with the ELN, constantly educating them on the international norms in operation, with the prospect of them formulating a broader policy regarding the use of landmines, for instance by means of an internal code of conduct, which hopefully will lead to a total ban.

One decisive lesson learned by Geneva Call during seven years of practice in different parts of the world is that the process of negotiation, and the building of a relationship, is just as important as the signing of a Deed of

Commitment. The essence is the relationship itself, a relationship that is built little by little throughout many meetings and problem-solving sessions. Progress is evaluated in terms of changes that occur on the ground.

*b) Developing a Sense of Ownership*

In Colombia, the initiation of a pilot zone for mine action in Micoahumado in 2005 helped to build confidence, not only with the ELN, but also with the local communities and authorities. The mine clearance project in Micoahumado, together with awareness and prevention workshops within mine-affected communities, has contributed to the empowerment of the local population. Understanding their needs and their capacity, the Micoahumado community initiated a dialogue commission (Assemblea constituente de Micoahumado para la justicia, la paz y la vida), allowing itself to voice and negotiate humanitarian and human rights obligations with the ELN and other NSAs. While collecting data on how anti-personnel mines affect people, Geneva Call and its local partner the Colombian Campaign against Landmines have, together with local communities, looked at the best strategies for engaging the ELN towards the mine ban. Such action has cultivated an environment where civil society organisations and local communities truly and openly give support towards this issue. Geneva Call's experience has proved the benefit of engaging not only the NSAs but also the local populations. This is a crucial development, bearing in mind that, in some cases, NSAs have indeed initiated mine action under the pressure of local communities.

It is instructive to look at how negotiations on mine clearance of sectors in Micoahumado have helped to strengthen and broaden relationships with the ELN. The case in Colombia demonstrates how time is necessary to gain the confidence of armed groups and understand their concerns. This requires a careful analysis of the situation, taking into account local sensitivities and perspectives. Through the discussions on mine clearance in the area of Micoahumado, Geneva Call raised awareness with local commanders in the Magdalena Medio region, in association with local community and religious leaders and the Colombian Campaign against Landmines. In this way, the local commanders developed a sense of ownership of the actions they were required to implement rather than being compelled by external actors. Often, NSA command structures are fragmented, with physical distance separating the political leadership from military commanders. In such situations, the decisions of the political leaders may not necessarily bind the commanders and combatants who are actually engaged in combat on the ground. Through constant dialogue with multiple horizontal and vertical levels of the chain of command, Geneva Call has succeeded in dealing with these internal dynamics. Of particular importance is identifying and conversing with individuals who express not only the determination but also a pragmatic perspective of how the NSAs can move forward in terms of mine action. The pace of achievement, between periods of fast accomplishments and flat phases, relies to a great extent on relationships with such negotiating interlocutors. Flexibility and constant negotiations with, and information provision to, all concerned actors are key components for negotiations.

In Colombia, even if no formal Deed of Commitment has been signed yet, the steps already taken are encouraging to future prospects concerning mine eradication and a formal commitment on a mine ban. Potential interim options could consist of a moratorium on the use, production and transfer of anti-personnel mines, limitations on the use of anti-personnel mines, marking initiatives, mine clearance operations, destruction of cleared mines, etc. In a comparable context and phase in Burma, Geneva Call is currently exploring a similar approach and is considering interim mechanisms with several NSAs since a total ban is not immediately conceivable for these groups. While maintaining a dialogue with the NSAs, the approach enables Geneva Call to examine the potential for the armed groups to make a formal commitment.

Yet, even when the Deed of Commitment has been signed, regular efforts in conjunction with gradual measures are necessary. The signature has to be considered more as part of a long-term process than the end in itself. Getting NSAs committed is a synchronised matter of obtaining their trust and will to act, while building their capacity, involving local communities and finding resources for implementation. The two following cases, involving the Moro Islamic Liberation Front (MILF) in the Philippines and 17 factions in Somalia, illustrate these challenges.

*The MILF in the Philippines*

The MILF committed to banning anti-personnel mines by signing Geneva Call's Deed of Commitment in March 2000. It has committed to never using anti-personnel mines, to co-operate in mine action and to allow for monitoring, as well as to take the necessary measures to enforce its commitment – the core obligations under the Deed of Commitment. The engagement of MILF was a great achievement, considering it is one of the largest groups in terms of number of members in the Philippines, and because it was using and even producing anti-personnel mines and victim-activated improvised explosive devicess before signing the Deed of Commitment.

Nevertheless, the signature of a Deed of Commitment has to be considered as a long-term process rather than an end in itself. Crucial to any formal engagement mechanism is the question of supervision and monitoring.

*a) Supporting Implementation and Monitoring Commitments*

In 2000 and 2001, the MILF was accused by the Armed Forces of the Philippines to have used improvised victim-activated mines around their camps in Mindanao. Following these allegations and after a long exchange of regular written and verbal communications with the MILF leadership, as well as with Philippine officials, Geneva Call was able to organise a verification mission in April 2002.[4] At this occasion, the process of dialogue entailed some elements of verification as well as of clarification of the requirements of the Deed of Commitment.

The mission indeed revealed that the MILF had misconceptions regarding the types of mines covered by the ban. Remote-controlled devices are not inconsistent with the Deed of Commitment because of their discriminate nature. Yet, the string-pulled devices used by the MILF, when left behind by its fighters upon withdrawal, effectively functioned as victim-activated (i.e. trip-wire) mines, and were as such prohibited under the Deed of Commitment. The mission was able to secure a clear and definitive commitment from the MILF at a very high level to an unconditional ban on anti-personnel mines, understood to be victim-activated. Rather than condemning, solutions were found by making an effort to address the matter with the group. By enabling the process to move along, Geneva Call was able to keep building confidence with the MILF. By receiving and responding to the mission regarding alleged violations, the MILF has shown accountability on its side. The establishment of the International Monitoring Team within the framework of the peace process in March 2004, at the request of the MILF, has brought better supervision capacity. No further accusations have been registered against the MILF since then. In June 2005, Geneva Call organised training on mine/unexploded ordnance (UXO) safety for over 100 monitors of the Bantay Ceasefire, a civil society-led group who is also monitoring the truce in the Philippines. This training has improved local capacity to supervise compliance with the Deed of Commitment.

*b) The Importance of Building Capacities*

In addition, the mission was able to get a fair idea of the extent of technical assistance needed by the MILF to implement its commitments. The case of MILF reveals the complexity inherent in implementing the Deed of Commitment, but also the challenges faced by NSAs in enforcing the ban. The responsibility for ensuring compliance lies with each signatory group. Nevertheless, they may face a number of difficulties in order to do so. The lack of capacity and equipment of these actors is a major challenge to implementation. In such cases, failure to comply may be less a matter of will than a lack of capacity or resources. For this reason, Geneva Call is committed to assisting signatory groups in complying with their obligations. Support from Geneva Call can take the form of training, facilitation of technical assistance from specialised mine-action organisations, and promotion of mine-action activities in areas controlled by signatory groups. As a result of the verification mission organised in 2002, a set of measures were agreed upon, including implementing guidelines, a verification mechanism, mine clearance and a range of trainings.

Armed groups may face fragmented links between commanders and soldiers as well as lack of proper discipline and training, which might make it difficult for them to convince their ranks to renounce the use of anti-personnel mines or to control their behaviour. Concerned with possible cases of non-compliance within their ranks, the MILF expressed its will to conduct dissemination efforts with Geneva Call. In November 2005, Geneva Call, in collaboration with the International Committee of the Red Cross, the Institute of Bangsamoro Studies and the Coalition to Stop the Use of Child Soldiers, conducted a weeklong ‘training of trainers’ workshop on the mine ban, International Humanitarian Law (IHL) and human rights for MILF commanders. In addition, trainings for women and youth involved in this group were given in 2006.

Supporting the implementation of the Deed of Commitment is a long-term process. Time is necessary to simultaneously build confidence and capacities, provide appropriate training and find support for implementation. For instance, significant progress was made in 2006 with the view to launch a joint Government of the Philippines-MILF UXO clearance project designed as a measure for confidence-building, for which the MILF had been requesting assistance in launching since 2002. Armed groups' compliance is certainly related to getting their trust and will to act, but it is not least a matter of capacity and resources. Hence sustainable efforts do not stop with the signature of the Deed of Commitment.

The following section looks into the process engaged by Geneva Call in assisting signatory Somali factions in implementing their commitment. Their reasons for signing the Deed of Commitment, the challenges of supporting its implementation and the importance of engaging local authorities, leaders and communities are emphasised.

*Factions in Somalia*

Geneva Call has been engaging the main Somali factions in the mine ban since 2002, in the background of the Somali National Reconciliation Conference and the cessation of hostilities. In reality, continued fighting has been ongoing since. Nevertheless, 17 leaders have signed the Deed of Commitment.

Even if many Somali factions used to rely more on anti-vehicle mines than on anti-personnel mines, their commitments are significant because these groups had anti-personnel mines in their stocks at the time of the signing. Somalia is entrenched in a conflict and emergency situation that has existed for the past three decades, leaving the country with a serious landmine/UXO problem. As a result of this situation, no international humanitarian mine action is being conducted outside the northern areas (Somaliland and Puntland). In a country where there has been no effective central government since 1991, large stocks of landmines are believed to be in the hands of factions and private individuals.[5]

Further to the establishment of the Transitional Federal Government in October 2004, many signatory faction leaders have become members of the government, including its President, Abdullahi Yusuf. Most Somali signatory groups have a dual status: they are members of the Transitional Federal Institutions (Government and Parliament) while still controlling their militia forces and territory. The signing of the Deed of Commitment by most of the ministers as faction leaders has somehow prepared the ground for the Transitional Federal Government's adherence to the MBT in continuity with their commitment with Geneva Call's mechanism.[6] Today, Geneva Call continues to build on the relationships and confidence that have been developed with them to secure full implementation of the Deed of Commitment.

*a) Raising Awareness at Multiple Levels, Key to Successful Implementation*

Partly because of the volatile security environment, Geneva Call was only able to go to the field for the first time two years after the signing. In September 2004, Geneva Call sent a field mission to signatory areas of northeast Somalia/Puntland, Hiran and Bakol. The objectives of the mission were to conduct a general assessment of the landmine situation, to monitor the progress made by signatory factions in implementing the Deed of Commitment and to evaluate the possibilities for launching humanitarian mine action. A high degree of co-operation from the signatory factions has been observed, some of whom gave access to their stockpiles, which they had never previously done. In a second phase in May and June 2005, Geneva Call visited regions not covered by the 2004 mission (Gedo, Bay and Juba). In October 2005, after repeated calls for assistance to the international community, the signatory faction United Somali Congress/Somali National Alliance granted Geneva Call unprecedented access to the stockpiles under its control in Mogadishu. In 2006 and 2007 Geneva Call returned to the Gedo region with the Danish Demining Group to survey mine stocks held by the Somali National Front and to assess opportunities for stockpile destruction.

These recurring field visits in seldom inspected areas have brought much knowledge from the grass-roots level. Regular dialogue is needed to fully implement the Deed of Commitment. Gaps can be found in NSAs' practices and understanding. In Somalia, Geneva Call found that group members and their constituency at grass-roots level have limited awareness of the obligations that are intrinsic to the Deed of Commitment. There is definitely a need to give additional information to the groups about their duties and responsibilities with respect to IHL – not least challenging the behaviour and raising the awareness of the local population.

*b) The Importance of Engaging Local Communities*

Geneva Call has discovered that many local people consider the possession and use of landmines as legitimate in many circumstances, such as for self-defence or for economic purposes. For example, explosives extracted from AP mines might be used for stone extraction, digging rainwater catchments, or be recycled for military purposes. Therefore, besides the need for capacity-building and training of NSAs, it is crucial to build trust, and to seek the involvement of the local authorities and local communities. Current anti-personnel mine users, such as sub-clans, business persons or 'freelance' militia, are not necessarily allied to or under the control of the faction leaders. Some of them hold stockpiles. There is thus a need to engage them and denounce mine use via educational campaigns. Three Somali signatory groups have reportedly co-operated with local non-governmental organisations in mine and UXO awareness workshops. The workshops were aimed at educating the local population living in areas under their control (Gedo, Hiran and Bay/Bakol regions respectively) on the dangers associated with landmines. This is a crucial issue, especially because there are currently no international NGOs carrying out mine risk education in central and southern Somalia.

Conducting regional mine-ban education workshops, targeting not only military factions, but also local authorities (including governors and district commissioners) and civic leaders (among them elders, traditional and religious leaders, heads of local non-governmental organisations and community-based organisations), should assist them in disseminating this knowledge to their constituencies. These constituencies have a critical role to play in advocacy, public awareness and monitoring, and they should be provided with opportunities to build their capacity. Involving local communities could help to foster local ownership of the mine ban, build a broad base of support for it and improve compliance by signatory factions. This will certainly enhance greater awareness among the population of its role in supporting and monitoring the implementation process. Beyond the case of Somalia, it is important to mention the importance of collaborating openly with the concerned state. In that manner, it will indeed facilitate, or at least not obstruct, the implementation and monitoring phase.

Building from this experience in the anti-personnel mine environment, the next section looks at the challenges of translating lessons learned to child recruitment and use.

## From Mines to Addressing Child Recruitment and Use

Comparing similarities and differences between the fight against anti-personnel mines and the issue of child recruitment and use will provide a better appreciation of where lessons learned may be applicable and where they are not.

There are certain similarities between the two environments that global initiatives against both anti-personnel mines and the recruitment and use of child soldiers have acknowledged. One of the most important of these is the central role of NSAs, and therefore the need to include them in dialogue as key actors in addressing the issues. The majority of anti-personnel mines are laid in the context of armed conflict where both state and non-state armed forces may be laying mines, while 70 percent of child soldiers worldwide are estimated to be found in the ranks of NSAs. What is clear is that both practices have a negative impact on children.

Also, in both cases, NSAs are not part of, or consulted in, the setting of international norms and standards, and it has largely been the efforts of non-governmental organisations that have succeeded in placing the issues on the agenda of states and the international community.

However, it is the differences between the two areas that are the most telling when it comes to policy considerations and approaches to be adopted. Regarding Geneva Call's own experience with landmines, and recently stated commitment to expand its engagement to the issue of child soldiers, perhaps the most striking has been the way in which the child soldiers issue has taken on a character far beyond the humanitarian discourse that surrounds landmines. This is reflected most notably in the UN Security Council's 'naming and shaming' approach, including the recent introduction of a monitoring and reporting mechanism, and the fact that those responsible for the recruitment or use child soldiers can be brought before the International Criminal Court.

Fundamentally however, it is clear that an inanimate object such as a landmine cannot possibly be considered or handled in the same way as a child who has feelings, opinions, expectations and rights, and who is likely to require specialised support to help facilitate reintegration into a 'normal' way of life.

Further differences in the ways that the respective normative frameworks have evolved and developed are explored in the next section.

*Comparing the Legal Frameworks*

Banning landmines is not about disarmament, it is a humanitarian issue with implications for the human rights (civil and political as well as economic, social and cultural) and the human security of affected communities. At the moment, the use of anti-personnel mines has not been defined as an international crime, although this could change in the future. The MBT goes beyond prohibiting the use, production, manufacturing and transfer of anti-personnel mines by requiring that States Parties also destroy stockpiles and co-operate in mine clearance and other mine-action activities. These obligations give concrete expression to the prohibition by indicating positive measures to be taken in peacetime as well as in times of armed conflict.

As parties to armed conflicts, NSAs are prohibited from carrying out indiscriminate attacks by, for instance, using weapons that are incapable of distinguishing between combatants and civilians. This is the normative basis for inviting NSAs to join the mine ban. When they sign the Deed of

Commitment, NSAs undertake obligations that by and large replicate the obligations of states under the MBT.

The precision, certainty and transparency of the MBT and the Deed of Commitment have facilitated their endorsement by NSAs.

Regarding efforts to address the recruitment and use of children by armed forces and groups, a series of significant but relatively more complex developments have taken place in norm-setting both internationally and regionally in recent years. Key elements of the legal framework are to be found in both humanitarian and human rights law.

International humanitarian law provides broad protection for children and plays a key role in the prohibition against the recruitment and use of children as soldiers. In the event of armed conflict, either international or non-international, children benefit from the general protection provided for civilians (Geneva Conventions of 1949 and their Additional Protocols of 1977). In terms of humanitarian negotiations, engagement with NSAs on the anti-personnel mine issue incorporates both 'negative' obligations (abstaining from using anti-personnel mines) and 'positive' obligations (mine action activities and other measures undertaken by NSAs to protect the population). Likewise, the humanitarian engagement of NSAs on child recruitment and use should most likely focus both on the negative responsibility (refraining from recruiting and using children) and on positive actions by NSAs to protect children in armed conflict. The notion of a Deed of Commitment on child soldiers may therefore include provisions for non-recruitment of children in the future and for release of those within ranks, as well as requirements in respect of other relevant aspects of child protection in times of conflict.

The 1989 Convention on the Rights of the Child and its recent Optional Protocol also set limits on children's participation in hostilities. Whereas the Deed of Commitment mostly replicates the obligations of states under the MBT, Article 4 of the Optional Protocol establishes a stricter standard for NSAs than the one that is applicable to states. NSAs are likely to consider that it sets a precedent of unequal treatment. By and large, with respect to applicable definitions and approaches to those who recruit children, this set of international legal tools leaves room for interpretation and debate. The ambiguity of distinguishing between voluntary and forced recruitment, between direct and indirect participation in hostilities, and the differentiation of treatment granted to states and NSAs (mainly on the question of age limit for involvement in hostilities and voluntary recruitment) have notably been subject to controversy.[7]

Children are not only used by armed groups for combat roles, but also in other military activities and support functions. Due to this multiplicity of roles, some commentators no longer refer to child soldiers, but to 'children associated with fighting forces'. The Paris Principles, designed to foster greater programmatic coherence, define 'a child associated with an armed force or armed group' as 'any person below 18 years of age who is or who has been recruited or used by an armed force in any capacity, including but not limited to children, boys and girls, used as fighters, cooks, porters, messengers, spies or for sexual purposes. It does not only refer to a child who is taking or has taken a direct part in hostilities'.

The issue of child recruitment by NSAs is multi-faceted and challenging in ways that the anti-personnel mine issue is not. The fact that children are active agents makes the issue more complex with respect to its causes and the actions to be taken in response to it.

*Rights and Agency*

Whereas an anti-personnel mine is a mere object that can be destroyed, a child has rights and a will of her/his own and needs to be considered as such. Responses to be undertaken can obviously not be as simple as when one destroys anti-personnel mines.

The use of anti-personnel mines is strictly a military decision, which can be taken by one individual. On the other hand, the recruitment of children by NSAs is by and large the result of a more complex process. The responsibility for their use may be in the hands of military commanders, but a range of other factors related to the rationale of the children and their families come into play. In trying to understand the complex dynamics associated with addressing the recruitment and use of child soldiers, a small number of commentators have tried to offer insights into NSAs' perspectives on the issue, providing the recruiters' point of view.[8] Others have sought to capture the views and motivations of children themselves.[9] Most of the young ex-soldiers who were interviewed in their samples defined themselves as 'volunteers'. They most likely make that decision because there is a perceived gain to be had in joining an armed group rather than in staying away. And there may be a variety of contributory reasons such as, among them, poverty, hunger[10], socio-economic reasons, lack of other alternatives, need of protection, revenge or payback, kin or peer pressure, the presence of relatives in the NSA, ideology, etc. In the short-term, they may feel better off with the income, occupation, status, respect and sense of belonging, education and/or protection that NSAs may offer.

There is indeed a multitude of factors and structural reasons without which a child would probably not volunteer to join. This should be considered by any approach that seeks to prevent children from becoming involved in armed conflict. It is important to target the recruiters, the children themselves, as well as those who influence their choice such as family and community. Considering the complex array of factors that contribute to child recruitment, a pragmatic approach must take specific realities into account. This is the *sine qua non* in developing strategies for prevention or release of child soldiers that are relevant and appropriate to the local situation. The treatment of children by NSAs differs greatly with location and typology of the conflict environment, and it is important to bear this in mind when strategising for solutions to the problem of child recruitment by NSAs. It is also important to acknowledge their different roles and activities.

## Applying Geneva Call's Approach to Child Recruitment and Use

Geneva Call's Deed of Commitment has proven its efficacy as regards anti-personnel mines. The challenge, to convert it to a valuable mechanism to address the issue of child recruitment and use, is vast. Assessing the feasibility of extending Geneva Call's approach to this issue raises a number of questions. In this section, key characteristics of Geneva Call's step-by-step approach and the question of incentives are discussed in the context of child recruitment and use.

As with anti-personnel mines, NSAs might not be willing to adhere to a Deed of Commitment as an initial step. There are obvious and significant obstacles to overcome. The issue of confidence (re)building, for example through an 'inclusive approach', is crucial. From a humanitarian perspective, a strict 'all-or-nothing' standpoint appears to be insufficient as it risks maintaining a status quo that would not be in the best interests of the children affected.

### *The Step-by-Step Approach*

Geneva Call's experience has exposed the complexity and challenges of securing commitments from NSAs, be that through obtaining the signature of the Deed of Commitment or its subsequent enforcement. In Colombia, the Philippines and Somalia, a flexible strategy has been implemented in order to understand and adapt to a specific political and conflict situation.

Whatever their initial attitudes, dialogue has been maintained with the NSAs concerned. In all cases, maintaining dialogue and progressively establishing a relationship has been critical for obtaining co-operation in the introduction of international humanitarian norms.

Thirteen signatory groups have taken intermediary steps prior to signing the Deed of Commitment, through various means, to ban, suspend or limit the use of anti-personnel mines.[11] A total of eight NSAs engaged worldwide by Geneva Call have actually committed to limiting the use of anti-personnel mines or have begun mine-action activities without having yet signed the Deed of Commitment.[12] As a result of this approach, some positive debates have taken place within many groups. NSAs have been sensitised on related humanitarian issues and have frequently recognised the harm caused by anti-personnel mines and the need to reconsider their mine policy. In many cases, interim measures have reduced the risks and impact faced by local populations due to anti-personnel mines. It is suggested here that addressing the recruitment and use of children in armed groups could also benefit from progressive interim measures.

*Progressive Interim Measures*[13]

Engaging NSAs should start with sensitisation campaigns focussed on the importance of respecting IHL standards, directed principally at their leaders, but also, importantly, at potentially receptive constituencies such as women or youth. The entry point for negotiation could be a commitment on 'no new recruitment'.

*1) Cessation of under-age recruitment*

Negotiate a cessation of further under-age recruitment based on and in accordance with a minimum recruitment age of 18. This could form the basis of a specific Deed of Commitment, as it represents a step towards compliance with the most stringent international standards.

*2) Better protection for those who are already engaged*

Negotiate and reach agreements with the NSA concerning children already engaged into the ranks, e.g. agree on guarantees that they do not participate in direct hostilities. Many of the children concerned in this case may be former combatants who could be transferred into support roles. The special needs of girls and the particular vulnerability of young children would also be priority for discussion.

*3) Release of children able to return/reintegrate unassisted*

Negotiate the voluntary release of children associated with the armed group who are able to return unassisted to their families/communities of origin. This would, as above, represent a step towards compliance with international standards, and could be an element of a Deed of Commitment. Such a group of children may well have been involved in peripheral or support functions, for example as couriers or spies rather than as front-line combatants. They may have been unable or reluctant to leave earlier due to peer pressure or restrictions imposed by the hierarchy but, with security guaranties and explicit agreement of their commanders, they may be happy to be released.

*4) Negotiate the release of all children under the age of 15*

A next step in negotiation, and one based on international humanitarian law, could be the release of all children under the age of 15. This will obviously require specialised intervention including careful and sensitive assessment on a case-by-case basis of any special needs these young children may have, as well as best-interest determination to decide on return and reintegration options. Geneva Call does not have the capacity to be directly involved in the complexities of reintegration, but is well placed to act as an interlocutor to negotiate access for specialised agencies such as the United Nations Children's Fund.

*5) Negotiate the release of particularly vulnerable or at-risk children*

Beyond the various stages of release suggested above, it may be that the NSA would agree to a broader release that would include children who had suffered traumatic experiences, perhaps front-line combat or rape, and who again would require specialised, individual assistance to support their rehabilitation and reintegration.

*6) Negotiate a comprehensive release*

Ultimately the aim would be for the dialogue to develop to an agreed comprehensive release. Again, this would require specialised assistance to identify the specific needs of individual children, to ensure security guaranties, and to undertake rehabilitation and reintegration activities.

## Towards a Better Understanding of the Concerns of NSAs

Fundamental to any effort to encourage attitudes to change and co-operation to develop is the need to identify arguments that will be relevant and meaningful to an NSA as well as being adaptable to the local context. As a community of practice, we must work to develop a more profound insight into their perspectives, ideas and concerns if we are to realise the aims of our work against child recruitment and use.

Benefiting from its relationship with NSAs, Geneva Call has begun seeking their perspectives on this issue and has observed an openness to share their policies and approaches.[14] Dialogue is a two-way process, informing NSAs on the international norms in operation while exploring their views and identifying potential opportunities for mechanisms and commitments that are relevant and applicable to them. Sensitising groups on their obligations and responsibilities with respect to IHL, more specifically on the humanitarian impact of the involvement of children in their ranks, is part of a systematic effort aimed at raising recruiters' awareness.

In the light of preliminary consultations with a number of groups, recurrent concerns have been noted, among them the fear of re-recruitment of children by other security forces and the apprehension that children might be recaptured and forced by others to divulge information about the group.[15] Other concerns raised include the lack of occupational alternatives for children, the desire to have children educated in their own tradition and culture, the poor results of past release and reintegration programmes and the fact that NSAs are not, by and large, involved in this phase. What is manifest about many of these concerns is that they focus on threats and dangers that children might face whilst outside the group or once released.

## And What Could Convince Them?

Appreciating the concerns and motives articulated by NSAs is fundamental. What would encourage NSAs to make commitments towards child non-use and protection? In other words, what could be, for them, the benefits of not counting children within their ranks?

One important benefit of the inclusive approach is that it provides NSAs with an opportunity to appropriate and internalise humanitarian norms that they might otherwise consider inapplicable to them or biased in favour of states.[16] In fact, this constitutes a key incentive toward greater compliance. In the context of child recruitment and use, like with other humanitarian issues, NSAs may see some value in avoiding the use of children, but incentives may lack. In order to successfully engage NSAs on this issue, there is a need to think strategically about incentives. One of the challenges in dealing with recruiters or potential recruiters of children is therefore to identify compelling mechanisms to inhibit child recruitment and use that are adapted to the reality of the children in question.

There are various explanations as to why NSAs have become involved in mine action. Recurring motives include humanitarian and development concerns, such as the impact on the civilian population, requests by the community or self-interest, such as maintenance of their international reputation and respectability, expected reciprocal respect by state actors, facilitation of aid and assistance to conflict-affected areas.[17] As in Somalia, one important motive in signing the Deed of Commitment has been the expectation that this would create momentum, foster international interest in mine action and therefore facilitate provision of the technical and material support that the NSAs needed to address the issue. A signature brings the prospect of mine action and humanitarian assistance that might not otherwise be forthcoming. Such assistance benefits the NSAs directly, but also indirectly in terms of the political capital gained by NSAs when they are able to tell their constituency that with their commitment they have opened the doors to international assistance.

The prospect of humanitarian assistance and of viable alternatives for the children of communities where NSAs are active has emerged as a major incentive for NSAs. As such, it could be beneficial to consider practical incentives for NSAs related to children, such as rehabilitation of schools, access to vocational training, job creation initiatives, access to vaccination campaigns, water and sanitation supply, etc. This should be developed on a case-by-case basis, according to the context, and may well be made dependent on verifiable measures taken by the NSA, or the signing of a Deed of Commitment. Such incentives could be made progressively as a way of generating progress towards further steps.

## Conclusions

The question of child recruitment by NSAs encompasses a wide range of issues that are, without any doubt, beyond the capacity and expertise of Geneva Call. Yet, in view of current shortcomings of programmes working to end child use within NSAs, lessons learned by Geneva Call might be relevant in several ways. The above brief contrast between the question of anti-personnel mines and child recruitment reveals why the latter is more complex than the former. There are many compound variables to the equation, among them the causes of the phenomenon, the number of influential actors – NSAs, local communities, families and of course the children themselves – and the scale of efforts necessary to create a truly protective environment for children in conflict. Yet this complexity seems not to be fully acknowledged. It is even questionable as to whether it is appropriate to separate the child soldier issue from the broader framework of child protection. Developing strategies to engage NSAs on the issue of child recruitment and use requires responses that are relevant and adaptable to local realities. It is therefore essential to create relationships at multiple levels and to raise awareness of every constituent of the society.

Considering the cost and complexity of release and reintegration programmes, action should not only be reactive but also preventative. Prevention and community involvement are two inter-related activities. Local civil society in particular has an important role to play in establishing ownership of the process. This means encouraging pro-active engagement and dialogue, not only with NSAs, but also with youth and local communities, who might represent a strong support-base of the engaged NSA. Better informed, they could themselves generate practical ideas and be a great source of help in building strategies for engaging armed groups. They might become actors of prevention, thereby conveying constructive inputs and improving prospects for compliance by NSAs. Sensitisation of each element of the society – local authorities, communities, traditional and religious leaders, elders, community-based organisations, families, children, etc. – is essential for changing behaviours and practices little by little. This, in turn, can be best achieved by promoting local ownership, enhancing responsiveness among all the local actors in its role of backing child protection and sensitising the international community on the benefit of an inclusive approach.

## Endnotes

1 The author wishes to thank Elisabeth Reusse-Decrey, President of Geneva Call, for providing the opportunity to work on this fascinating project, and for her invaluable input. He would also like to give special thanks to David Nosworthy, of DCAF, for his important contributions. Key contributions were also made by Mehmet Balci, Pascal Bongard, Gemma Huckerby, Katherine Kramer and Anki Sjöberg, of Geneva Call.

2 There have also been groups which were willing to sign the Deed of Commitment but did not because of lack of capacity to implement it or lack of monitoring possibilities.

3 Elizabeth Reusse-Decrey, 'The struggle against landmines: an opening for peace talks in Colombia' in *Choosing to engage: Armed groups and peace processes*, ed. Robert Ricigliano, Accord, Issue 16 (2005), 48-51, http://www.c-r.org/our-work/accord/engaging-groups/ colombia.php (accessed October 2008).

4 Geneva Call, Report of the Geneva Call mission to the Moro Islamic Liberation Front in Central Mindanao Philippines (Geneva, Manila: 30 April 2002).

5 Anki Sjöberg, Armed Non-State Actors and Landmines. Volume I: A Global Report Profiling NSAs and their Use, Acquisition, Production, Transfer and Stockpiling of Landmines (Geneva: Geneva Call and the Program for the Studies of International Organizations, 2005), 53-58. For more information, see Landmine Monitor 2004 and the report of the Geneva Call follow-up mission to Somalia, September 2004.

6 In December 2004, the Prime Minister of the Transitional Federal Government declared his government's intention to accede to the MBT in continuity with the signing of the Deed of Commitment by faction leaders.

7 For more detailed accounts of these debates and analyses of the United Nations Convention on the Rights of the Child and the Optional Protocol on the involvement of children in armed conflict, see: Kristina Anne Bentley, 'Can there be any universal children's rights?' *The International Journal of Human Rights* 9, Issue 1 (March 2005): 107–123; Alexandra Boivin, *Study on Child Soldiers* (Geneva: Geneva Call Internal Document, 2006); Andy Dawes and Ed Cairns, 'The Machel Study: Dilemmas of Cultural Sensitivity and Universal Rights of Children' *Peace and Conflict: Journal of Peace Psychology* 4, no. 4 (2001): 335-348.

8 Susan Shepler, 'The Social and Cultural Context of Child Soldiering in Sierra Leone', Paper for the PRIO sponsored workshop on Techniques of Violence in Civil War (Oslo: 20-21 August, 2004).

9 Rachel Brett and Irma Specht, *Young Soldiers: Why they choose to fight* (Boulder: Lynne Rienner, 2004); Krijn Peters, *Re-examining Voluntarism: Youth Combatants in Sierra Leone* (Pretoria: Institute for Security Studies Monograph no. 100, 2004).

10 UN Human Rights Council, Implementation of General Assembly Resolution 251, establishing the Human Rights Council, UN doc. 60/251 (March 2006); Report of the Special Rapporteur on the Right to Food (2007), 14-16.

11 Pascal Bongard, Engaging Armed Non-State Actors in a Landmine Ban: An Assessment of Geneva Call's Performance (2000-2007) (Geneva: Geneva Call internal document, 2007), 24-25.

12 Bongard, *Engaging Armed Non-State Actors*, 33; Anki Sjöberg, *Armed Non-State Actors and Landmines. Volume II: A Global Report of NSA Mine Action* (Geneva: Geneva Call and the Program for the Studies of International Organisations, 2006).

13 This section contains views on strategies currently in development by Geneva Call, alongside ideas provided by David Nosworthy (see *Food for Thought Paper* developed by David Nosworthy, 2007, internal, copy with Geneva Call).

14 Boivin, Study on Child Soldiers.

15 Ibid.

16 Ibid.

17 For more information about reasons for the National Security Agency involvement in mine action, see Sjöberg, *Armed Non-State Actors and Landmines. Volume II*, 11-15.

# Chapter 12

# Children and Young People in Post-conflict Peacebuilding

*Claire O'Kane, Clare Feinstein and Annette Giertsen*

> Whoever wins the war children are always the losers and their lost childhood never comes back.[1]

## Overview[2]

Armed conflict affects the lives of children and young people, as well as their families, their communities and their nations.[3] The actions – and inactions – of a range of security actors have a different impact on girls, boys, men and women given the distinct roles they play during war, peacebuilding and post-conflict reconstruction. Research suggests that around half of all armed conflicts that have ended will re-emerge within ten years.[4] Many post-conflict states are left in a state of fragile peace with no real closure of the issues. Understanding how children experience conflict, post-conflict and peacebuilding – and through this how they view and experience both insecurity and security – is vital in interpreting short-term and long-term consequences on their development. What happens to children in their early years significantly determines the way they grow and develop and, in turn, their cost or contribution to society.[5] Children and young people have a crucial role to play in either taking forward peace or conflict.

> I can help bring peace in Northern Uganda if only my views are heard and acted upon. I don't hold a gun anymore; I hold the power of my voice. When visitors come to see us in the centers they normally ask us about our experiences and how we managed to escape… But, they should also be asking us how we can participate in the peace process ourselves because we also fought in the war.
> (Formerly abducted girl associated with rebel group, Northern Uganda).[6]

This chapter reflects on the importance of finding out and listening to the perspectives of children and young people who have lived through and experienced the insecurities of conflict and post-conflict situations. It emphasises the importance of children's participation. That is, of creating the space for girls and boys of different ages and abilities to express their views and experiences, so that these can be heard, listened to and acted upon by a range of adults to further the realisation of children's rights. In particular, it highlights the contributions of children to peacebuilding efforts such as reconciliation, reconstruction and rehabilitation, which bring with them the hope of a more secure world. It supports arguments that security sector issues affecting children can be more effectively addressed through strengthening the existing security governance framework, in particular through reinforcing the human rights perspective of security.[7]

By sharing children's perspectives on insecurity and practical examples of children's participation, the authors hope that more actors – governments, civil society, the UN system and security actors – will:

- Recognise the importance and value of listening to children's perspectives.
- Recognise the practical ways in which children participate, including examples of how children are – and can be – engaged in efforts to enhance their own protection and their community's security at local and national levels.
- Respond to the roles and responsibilities of children and support and help to strengthen their peacebuilding initiatives, promote the inclusion of children's voices in peace processes and make commitments to comprehensive plans of action to fulfil children's rights in peace agreements.

Abuse of children contravenes human rights and international humanitarian law that entitle children to special protection in armed conflicts. The United Nations Convention on the Rights of the Child (the 'Convention') requires the state and concerned agencies to '... take all feasible measures to ensure protection and care of children who are affected by an armed conflict'.[8] In the mid-1990s, the Report of Graça Machel, Expert of the Secretary-General stated: 'Senior officers and soldiers alike must learn more about codes of behaviour, humanitarian law and, especially, about the fundamental rights of children'.[9]

The Convention is the most ratified convention in the world.[10] It outlines the responsibility of the state and other duty-bearers, including a wide range of security sector actors, to ensure the protection of children's rights to survival, protection, development and participation. Children's rights are human rights and apply to all children regardless of age, gender, race, colour, country of origin, religion, physical or mental dis/ability, or socio-economic background. Children's rights are part of a complete package and cannot be 'cherry-picked' according to what is convenient, palatable or preferred. Each of the rights set out in the Convention interrelate to each other. Participation goes hand-in-hand with protection, development and survival. The full set of children's rights is equally applicable whether during times of violent conflict or peace. Key principles that guide implementation of the Convention include: children's right to life, non-discrimination, children's participation in decisions affecting them (with respect to their evolving capacity), and decision-making in children's best interests.

In accordance with the Convention framework, in this chapter the term children refers to all children and young people under the age of 18 years. However, 'children' are not a homogeneous group and girls and boys of different ages will have different perspectives and experiences relating to their priority security concerns, which may also vary according to their socio-cultural-political context. Children's 'evolving capacity' is linked both to children's development – to age and dis/ability – as well as to opportunities, and to exposure to opportunities, in their local context. As will be elaborated in this chapter, it is crucial to recognise the diversity of children's experiences and to create opportunities for the views and opinions of children of all age groups to be heard.

A range of security sector actors, directly involved in conflict, post-conflict and peacebuilding, all have roles and responsibilities to respect and protect children's rights. In their efforts to secure protection for all civilians and to meet security governance benchmarks, it is crucial that these actors give increased recognition to children and young people. To understand how children and young people are affected by conflict, which of their rights are being violated, what roles they take on, what they learn and how they feel they can be supported – it is crucial that their views and experiences are heard. Listening to the views of girls and boys can lead to their better protection. Their perspectives should therefore inform security sector activities and reforms. And, as children in Afghanistan remind us, children's role as agents of peace can be best fostered when the younger generation is engaged with a focus on their potential and their priorities.

> If you are involved in bringing security to Afghanistan, talk to us to hear why we feel afraid or why we feel safe in a place ... If you are involved in community development, make sure you listen to what we think our communities need. We look forward to contributing to a greater society, where adults and children work together and are respected by one another.
> (Extract from Children's Declaration, Northern Gathering of Children's Group Representatives, Afghanistan, August 2004).

## Understanding and Responding to Children's Perspectives and Priorities

In situations of armed conflict and insecurity children may have been identified and acknowledged as victims, but they are rarely engaged as social actors with their own views, beliefs and contributions, either by their communities, governments, wider civil society, the UN system or security actors.[11] Girls' and boys' roles and contributions to their families, communities and nation are generally unrecognised, and often undermined.[12] In efforts to protect children and families, or to make communities safe, security actors have neglected to take into account the different perspectives that children and young people have of what constitute priority issues. However, in recent years the importance of engaging with children as social actors, and the need to understand and respond to the political and social reality of children's lives, has been highlighted by a number of practitioners and academics.[13]

It is increasingly recognised that children have their own very valuable perspectives and priorities – which are often very different to those of adults.[14] For example, during Save the Children's rapid assessment of child protection concerns in Northern Uganda in 2006, children living in camps for internally displaced persons (IDPs) expressed more fear of abuse and harassment faced at the hands of the government army who were meant to protect them than they did of the Lords Resistance Army rebel forces.[15] In post-Taliban Afghanistan, in exploring dangers and risks faced and ideas to create a safe environment in Kabul in 2002-2003, children prioritised concerns of road safety and were supported in child-led initiatives to train traffic police and raise awareness of road safety amongst children.[16] In Sri Lanka and Zambia groups of children have prioritised concerns relating to insecurity and domestic violence caused as a result of their parents' (mostly fathers') excessive use of alcohol, and have lobbied for restricted opening times of the bars.[17] Children's priorities often reflect concerns and challenges grounded in their day-to-day reality rather than more distant fears or worries.

The need to recognise children and young people as social and political beings is also evident. For example, while some children are forced into their association with armed forces through violence, threats and abduction, or are compelled due to poverty, Drummond-Mundal and Cave stress how it must not be assumed that all children involved in armed conflict are manipulated by adults. Western concepts of childhood as a time of innocence, dependency and powerlessness need to be challenged if we are to find ways to divert children and young people from violent action to non-violent action for positive social change.[18]

In situations of violent conflict, faced by threats to their survival and development – from which adults may not be able to protect them – children may resort to a range of strategies, including engagement in political-military action.[19] For example, Hart describes how children in the Occupied Palestine Territories are 'often willing participants in the national struggle. Their political consciousness is developed to an extent and from an age that commonly takes outsiders by surprise. They also display great awareness of their role, as children, in the effort to influence public opinion through the media'.[20] Reynolds makes a similar observation in relation to children in South Africa choosing to take part in the struggle against apartheid – she stresses that they took 'profoundly serious political and moral decisions in relation to their own safety and ambitions, as well as the safety and interests of their families'.[21]

Children may also engage in a variety of other actions to protect themselves, their families, peers and communities, examples of which from Guatemala, Nepal and Uganda will be presented later in this chapter.

### *Capturing the Perspectives of Children*

Listening to children, taking their views seriously and recognising the various roles and responsibilities taken on by girls and boys (within their families, communities and in broader society) requires a change in the way that most adults perceive children and engage with them. Adults, including security sector actors, need to recognise the capacities and contributions that girls and boys (of different ages, abilities and backgrounds) can make and be prepared to share information and engage with them in more constructive ways.

In their daily lives children often take on a variety of roles and responsibilities outside of the house. During situations of violent conflict children may face increased risks while undertaking these responsibilities – for example, the risk of sexual harassment, abduction into armed forces and/or the danger of landmines. Others may be obliged to take on additional roles and responsibilities as a result of violent conflict because, for example, the adult (usually male) head of the household is absent. In addition, as has been highlighted above, children may choose to be directly involved in various socio-political-armed activities in their communities and broader society.

Genuine children's participation generally requires a commitment of time to a process in which girls and boys are given space to express their views on matters that concern them. Children's participation in practice means, for example, supporting children to form groups in their local communities, within their schools or in other settings so that they can come together and talk about real issues that affect them. Support from local adults is crucial, especially in initial efforts to create space for children to express their views within their communities and to build local ownership of their participation initiatives. Local child focussed non-government organisations (NGOs) often take on the role of facilitators to prepare adults (for example, parents, community and religious leaders, teachers) to take children and their views seriously. Adult support and guidance is also important to help children assert their rights. Children can be supported to build their capacity to speak out (to lose their 'fear' of participating), to analyse issues of importance to them and to take appropriate action.

Examples of children's participation are many and varied and include, among others: action in support of the right to education for out of school children and the development of a Code of Conduct for teachers and students (Nepal); preventing violence in school through the establishment of school councils (Zambia); action around protection issues including reporting on violations of their rights (Angola); action against violence and sexual abuse (Cambodia) and against corporal punishment and early marriages (Nepal); and support to and care for children affected by HIV/AIDS (Zimbabwe). Through their own and adult-supported media initiatives children have undertaken awareness-raising on discrimination and punishment (Afghanistan), have influenced local and national policy-making by presenting their concerns on their rights to presidential candidates (Nicaragua) and their proposals to the interim constitution (Nepal), including on issues such as the right to education, protection and health, name and nationality.

### *Children's Role in 'Keeping Safe'*

As will be illustrated by this chapter, providing children with a regular space to organise their own groups and initiatives can enhance children's confidence and skills to identify, analyse and initiate action and advocacy initiatives around concerns affecting their security and protection. Through their collective initiatives children are also in a stronger position to negotiate with adults with regard to any roles that are inappropriate or damaging to their age and development.[22]

For example, girls in Nepal have identified unsafe places and sought support and protection from community leaders to create safer places in their neighbourhood and schools. This project was conceived of by a group of girls from various ethnic backgrounds, with the support of adult facilitators from NGOs.[23] Initially the girls were supported to undertake surveys to map the places in their community that they felt were unsafe for them. The school, the road, the public transport system, the cinema and the public tap where they collected water on a daily basis were all found to be unsafe. The girls collected evidence of harassment and the impacts on them. The girls also received some training in facilitation, communication and leadership skills from the NGO adult facilitators. The girls developed recommendations to make these places safer and then used them to negotiate with key persons – such as the cinema manager – to make the spaces safer for girls. The girls also provided support to other girls who have suffered abuse or harassment to make sure that they were not made to feel guilty or isolated. Such peer support was crucial in helping to rebuild self-esteem, confidence and morale. Building upon the success of this initial project, it has now been implemented through schools in other districts with the involvement of both boys and girls. Adult support groups, including guardians, teachers, locally elected officials, and representatives of governmental and non-governmental organisations, have been formed in the project areas or in the schools to respond to children's concerns.[24]

In many different contexts creative participatory tools, such as risk-mapping to understand where girls and boys feel safe and unsafe, and body-mapping to explore children's experiences of conflict or post-conflict, can also be used to help children's perspectives to be shared and acted upon.[25] For example, risk-mapping undertaken by a girl's representative from conflict-affected Northern Uganda highlighted the dangers of walking to the well to collect water due to fears of abduction or landmines.[26] In contrast the girls felt safest in schools, as many children are present in school and they were able to share their experiences and support each other.

The situation of children can be a sensitive indicator of change and should be of direct interest to security sector actors at all levels. For example, if children and their parents feel it is too unsafe to travel to school and/or to remain in school this may be an early warning of other problems.

## Ethical Issues and Challenges

In any participation process, but perhaps especially when working in insecure environments, there are many ethical issues and challenges involved in working with children in participatory ways. Hart and Tyrer note how the 'environment of armed conflict poses particular challenges for safe, ethically responsible research involving children'.[27] They emphasise the need for good preparation and the need to be aware of and anticipate possible risks beforehand and have strategies to deal with them. Ethical issues can be better understood and better addressed by listening and responding to local people's ideas (children and adults) that build upon their understanding of the local socio-cultural, political context.

**Diagram 12.1 Children Map Places of Insecurity**

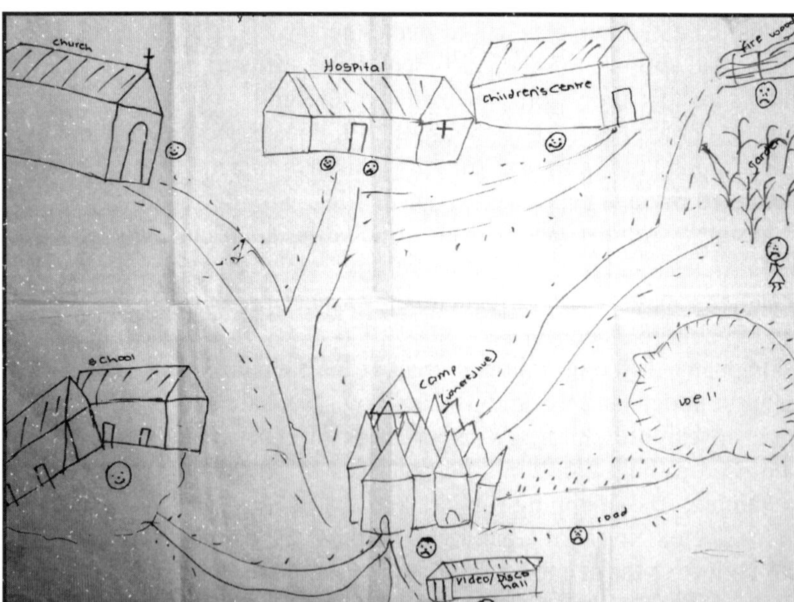

In this way, strengthening local ownership of participatory initiatives contributes to ethical practice. At the beginning of any process, a framework to ensure ethical, meaningful and inclusive participation practice with and for girls and boys should be established. This may mean, among other issues:

- Ensuring that practice standards on children's participation are used and implemented.[28]
- Developing child-friendly information and participatory tools, including use of local forms of cultural expression such as poetry, drama, and songs.
- Ensuring that the full diversity and range of children's experiences are captured.
- Ensuring that issues that reflect or reinforce child-adult power relations are dealt with, such as making sure that children have the space to express their own views and ensuring that adults do not dominate, dictate or manipulate these views.
- Exploring discrimination and ensuring that non-discrimination is practiced.
- Ensuring that child protection issues are dealt with appropriately and sensitively.
- Exploring possible risks faced when working with children in conflict situations and ensuring that children face no harm as a result of their participation.
- Ensuring that there is a process of continuous reflection and action planning resulting in quality, ethical and inclusive child participation practice.
- Ensuring that children's perspectives inform action planning both at local levels (where impact may be more immediate for some children), and at national policy and practice levels.
- Ensuring wider accountability – preparing adults to acknowledge the capacities of children, and to respond and act upon them.

Children's experiences of childhood are diverse and are affected by gender, dis/ability, level of family income, ethnicity, culture, geography, socio-political context and other factors. In addition, children's evolving capacities mean that the level and nature of participation of a five-year-old will be very different to that of a 17-year-old, although the Convention's reference to 'due-weight' in accordance with the age and maturity of the child, means that the views of a five-year-old in relation to what makes them feel safe and unsafe are equally important and can equally be elicited and acted upon.[29] The diversity of children's experiences of armed conflict and post-conflict needs to be adequately explored and reflected so that:

- There is a better understanding of the experiences, reflections, views and aspirations of both boys and girls in different contexts.
- Some of the most marginalised groups of children are supported to share their experiences and views.

Additional efforts may be required to encourage groups of children who typically suffer discrimination – non-school-going children, refugee and internally displaced children, children with different abilities/disabilities, children formerly associated with armed or military groups – to have equal opportunities to be involved. Children themselves should be encouraged to reflect on who is included in, and excluded from, their participatory and peace initiatives.

Save the Children has developed practice standards[30] through years of experience supporting children's participation at local, national and global levels (see Box 12.2). The primary purpose of these practice standards is to ensure consistent, high-quality child participation practice. They aim to provide a framework that gives guidance and direction first and foremost to field staff and partners in continuously improving their participatory practice.

Child protection goes hand-in-hand with and is integral to good child-participation practice. The use of codes of conduct, particularly when developed in consultation with girls and boys as well as their parents and guardians within community settings, can be useful as they help to identify behaviour and good practice to make sure that children's participation takes place within safe and respectful environments.[31] Such codes of conduct should include procedures to both protect children from risks and potential exploitation and abuse, as well as sensitive procedures to deal appropriately and effectively with possible disclosures of harm or abuse. This includes the need to identify in advance local organisations and/or individuals who have skills to provide psycho-social support to children who have faced traumatic experiences – particularly when working with children who live in insecure environments caused by armed conflict. In all situations the principle of 'the best interests of the child' should guide decisions with regard to what are and are not appropriate activities for children of different ages and abilities to engage in.

**Box 12.2 Practice Standards in Children's Participation**

**Standard 1:** An Ethical Approach: Transparency, Honesty and Accountability – Adult organisations and workers are committed to ethical participatory practice and to the primacy of children's best interests.

**Standard 2:** Children's Participation is Relevant and Voluntary – Children participate in processes and address issues that affect them – either directly or indirectly – and have the choice as to whether to participate or not.

**Standard 3:** A Child Friendly, Enabling Environment – Children experience a safe, welcoming and encouraging environment for their participation.

**Standard 4:** Equality of Opportunity – Child participation work challenges and does not reinforce existing patterns of discrimination and exclusion. It encourages those groups of children who typically suffer discrimination and who are often excluded from activities to be involved in participatory processes.

**Standard 5:** Staff are Effective and Confident – Adult staff and managers involved in supporting/facilitating children's participation are trained and supported to do their jobs to a high standard.

**Standard 6:** Participation Promotes the Safety and Protection of Children – Child protection policies and procedures form an essential part of participatory work with children.

**Standard 7:** Ensuring Follow-up and Evaluation – Respect for children's involvement is indicated by a commitment to provide feedback and/or follow-up and to evaluate the quality and impact of children's participation.

Source: International Save the Children Alliance, 2005.

Local NGOs and community groups are therefore often in the best position to regularly engage with children and young people, and to support them in raising their issues to the local authorities or to other security sector actors. Local and international NGOs and the United Nations can also support opportunities for children's voices to be heard in peace processes and efforts to develop comprehensive plans of action to fulfil children's rights in peace agreements. This will require the establishment of child-friendly structures and processes for communication and dialogue between children and adult actors.

## Security Actors Responding to Children's Perspectives and Experiences

Awareness-raising, training and capacity-building initiatives with different security actors are critical, as paradoxically the rights of the most marginalised groups of children living in insecure contexts, including internally displaced and refugee children, street and working children and trafficked children, are often most violated by security actors who have state powers to protect them – such as the military, police and border security guards.

In government camps, squatter areas and relocation areas in Khartoum, Sudan, for IDPs – the lives of children and their families are characterised by insecurity and marginalisation, with gross violation and denial of their rights by state security actors. During an inter-agency situation assessment[32] in which focus group discussions and mind map drawings with children were used to elicit children's views, girls and boys highlighted the manner in which their IDP families were subjected to regular raids, harassment, demolition and forced relocation by the law enforcing agencies. Some older children, women and men were also arbitrarily arrested and unlawfully detained during the demolitions.

**Box 12.3 Children's Mind Map Drawings, Khartoum**

The children see guns and people with guns as potential threats and they feel insecure in the IDP camps and in the squatter areas, especially after the riot of 1 August 2005. Some children want to carry guns in order to take revenge on the people and law enforcing agencies who have killed, harassed or detained their family members. Some children want to become police.

The implications that today's security actions can have on tomorrow's security situation need to be more clearly understood and given careful consideration, especially in terms of their impact on children. Demolition of their shelter and forced relocations have had a detrimental impact on livelihoods, family integrity, children's education and general well-being interfering with their rights to life, dignity, liberty and security. The agencies involved in undertaking the assessment are involved in advocacy efforts with relevant government ministries to try to address children's concerns.

Strengthening the role of the local police to protect and fulfil children's rights and creating positive linkages between the police and child-focussed community-level initiatives are required to improve security sector interventions – particularly in terms of harnessing children's perspectives on security and developing responses that are appropriate. Initiatives to establish Child Protection Units (CPU) within local police stations in Ethiopia and Kenya with strong linkages (and referral mechanisms) to local community-based structures, local NGOs, international NGOs and to the relevant ministries[33] have been effective in ensuring more appropriate responses to children's care and protection needs, particularly when working with children who have come into conflict with the law. In Kenya, better relationships between children and the police were reported: 'In the four CPUs, police officers treat children more humanely, pay more respect to their rights and opinions and provide better separate facilities for boys and girls. CPU officers wear civilian clothes, use friendly language, are more child-focussed and do not assume children are criminals'.[34] Understanding and responding to the diversity of children's perspectives and experiences is a step towards addressing their specific needs and rights. Children living in situations of armed conflict and post-conflict will have their own priorities. For example, during a global evaluation of children affected by armed conflict, displacement or disaster, the priorities identified by children included protection from abduction and from being used as soldiers and sex slaves; protection from other forms of abuse, from hunger and disease; the importance of access to education and health services at all times (even in the midst of conflict); peace and reconciliation; projects that build on children's self-esteem, provide hope and which reduce stigma; support to families to relieve poverty and conflict; fair distribution of aid; and opportunities to participate and be heard.[35]

International military peacekeeping forces, UN observers and UN civilian police have an important mandate and presence to monitor, prevent, report and respond to abuse and exploitation faced by girls and boys during conflict. Protecting civilians is one of the most important tasks of peacekeeping forces. However, protection issues affecting children are often neglected. To address such neglect, training opportunities for armed peacekeepers, observers and civilian police on issues relating to children's rights have grown in recent years.[36] For example, training of military and peacekeeping forces on child rights and protection has been undertaken by Save the Children in Sweden and East and West Africa.

> Before we took part in the Save the Children Sweden's training programme we always referred to civilians as a single entity, without seeing children as a group in need of special protection.
> (Soldier, southern Sudan).[37]

In Uganda, Save the Children has signed a Memorandum of Understanding with the Ministry of Defence that spells out their respective roles. This includes a role as a 'watch dog' to monitor the military vis-à-vis their role in protecting and respecting children's rights, and in supporting the training of the Ugandan military (the Uganda People's Defence Force, or UPDF).[38] Save the Children has undertaken training on child rights, including the Optional Protocol to the Convention on the involvement of children in armed conflict, and child protection, with hundreds of senior army officers and with more than 10,000 soldiers from the Local Defence Units. The overall aim of the co-operation with the military has been to strengthen UPDF's capacity to protect children and respect children's rights and to mainstream child rights into the policies and structures of the UPDF.

The main achievements have included the establishment of a human rights desk within the UPDF structure at a national level and the establishment of CPUs at local levels to respond in practical ways to child protection issues, including to children abducted by the rebel forces.

In terms of the 'watch dog' role, Save the Children and their NGO partner staff have been involved in monitoring cases of child rights violations by UPDF forces, especially at local levels. There have been practical cases in which underage children have identified, employed as child soldiers within UPDF. In such cases Save the Children, in collaboration with the United Nations Children's Fund (UNICEF), have taken action to ensure that the young person is removed from the army. However, in general, the task of monitoring and reporting is very sensitive as local staff may be intimidated by UPDF soldiers. To ensure anonymity in reporting, and responses from high-level management, reports by local staff are shared directly with the Save the Children Head Office in Kampala, which reports directly to senior staff within the government. However, a lack of effective documentation of cases and fears of intimidation remain a challenge. In addition, accountability mechanisms in terms of how the government responds to and follows up on the reports need to be substantially strengthened.

At a global level, the Security Council has followed up advocacy recommendations to appoint Child Protection Advisers (CPAs) in peacekeeping missions. CPAs currently operate in some of Africa's most war-affected countries including Sierra Leone, Democratic Republic of the Congo and Angola. The role of CPAs includes the provision of training for all mission personnel on child rights and protection, as explicitly requested by the Security Council, as well as systematic reporting on children's concerns in all country-specific reports to the Security Council. The child protection adviser serves also as a contact-point and interlocutor on issues related to children between peacekeeping operations and United Nations country teams, NGOs working to protect children, national governments and civil society groups, supporting and complementing work, in particular the work of UNICEF, on the ground.

In understanding situations of armed conflict and insecurity from children's perspectives, the significance of gang and gun cultures has been highlighted by children and young people in different parts of the world, particularly in South, Central and North America. A cycle of violence and insecurity is perpetuated by gang and gun culture, as children have to be tough in order to survive.[39] In Honduras a community-based model for the prevention of violence has been developed to support gang members' reintegration and rehabilitation in the city of San Pedro Sula.[40] Together with its partner organisations, Save the Children UK has set out to address the lack of understanding and mechanisms to promote a positive community response to the gang phenomenon and to support gang members who want to withdraw from their gangs. Awareness-raising is being undertaken with key actors – including the government, the police, the judiciary and the public – to support reintegration efforts and to stop the killing of young people by police and security forces. Generation X, a youth-led organisation, has been developed enabling peer support and giving ex-gang members access to education, vocational training, employment opportunities and psychosocial support programmes. Training has also been provided for community police, who are a relatively new department of the Honduran Preventive Police.

## The Role of Children as Agents of Peace and of Their Own Protection

This section of the chapter focusses on the contributions that children and young people can make to peacebuilding and the creation of a protective environment for girls and boys. When working towards a vision of peace, conflict transformation and peacebuilding efforts are important strategies to minimise and address violent conflict and insecurity, which negatively affect the lives of children and their families.

> Peace is life and survival. It is to live in our houses and sleep without being displaced. It is reflected in how we treat each other and how we work and live. It is to respect each others silence and listen to each others song; to respect and realise that every single human being has a worth. It is having social order and freedom of opinion; and having a government.
> (A child's description of peace).[41]

There are many examples that illustrate how living through violent times has strengthened girls and boys' aspirations for peace.[42] In many contexts children condemn violence and urge that it be replaced by peaceful and caring ways of resolving conflict. Some practitioners[43] have suggested that children and youth may have unique contributions to make to peacebuilding by virtue of their stage of development: '(The) transitional state (of youth) is regarded as valuable for initiating change at the grassroots level, which can, in turn, affect peace processes on higher levels'.[44]

Also, as articulated by Drummond-Mundal and Cave: 'Social and political inclusion of children, in particular youth, in conflict transformation and peace building makes pragmatic and constructive sense. These young people may have experience and capacities that can either work for or against new social and political constructions. For peace to be sustainable, the adults of tomorrow need to feel a sense of ownership and responsibility for the creation and maintenance of a climate of peace'.[45]

Children are participating in peacebuilding initiatives and contributing to peace across the world, even in some of the most insecure – or formerly insecure – contexts. Children's participation can help children to build upon their own resilience and make changes in their lives. 'It makes you feel useful, you can help others, you can be an actor'.[46] Meaningful participation and space to come together with their peers, to share their experiences and express their views can give children strength and increase their life skills and self-confidence. Participation and association are part of a process that helps children to promote their rights and fight for social justice.[47]

> I stayed alone, with no parents. I used to think about the past. It was difficult to forget what happened to me in the bush. I felt alone. No-one wanted to stay with me, to share with me. I then joined an association and began to find peace within myself. My family came back to me. I have friends and I have learned from others. These days I am fine. I know what to do at the right time and right place.
> (Formerly abducted child soldier, Northern Uganda).[48]

Children can actively contribute to peace in a myriad of ways: through rebuilding social relationships, contributing to a culture of peace and rebuilding social structures. Their contributions play a role in enhancing security, in reconciliation, in the search for truth and justice, and in rebuilding education, the economy and livelihoods. For example, in Sierra Leone, Guatemala and South Africa, children have participated in truth commissions, contributing to justice restoration. Children in Angola, Nepal,

Sierra Leone, Sri Lanka and Uganda participate in demobilisation, rehabilitation and reintegration processes.[49]

In the northern conflict-affected region of Uganda children's peace clubs and associations within schools and communities are using song, traditional dance, debates and radio programmes to create messages and action for peace. The associations (which include formerly abducted children) also support reintegration activities by helping to prepare families and communities to receive their sons/daughters/community members who were formerly abducted children. The children's representatives are also advocating for space to include children in the formal peace talks[50] so that the views and experiences of girls and boys, including formerly abducted children, many of them with experiences as soldiers, may be heard and acted upon. This is seen as an important step to increase action towards the fulfilment of children's rights.

In Guatemala the indigenous Mayan communities were first and foremost the ones who suffered death, displacement, disappearances and torture during the 36 years of internal armed conflict. Children suffered the same treatment as adults since they were viewed as future guerrilla members. Despite the fact that peace accords were signed by the government in 1996, the current generation is still affected by the experiences of conflict. However, children and young people acting as youth promoters in their communities are contributing to building peace by providing training on conflict resolution to other children and young people. Children are also taking part in the process of piecing together the history of the violent conflict to ensure that the memory of it does not get lost.

In Nepal the conflict between the Government and Maoist rebels since 1995 has negatively impacted children and adults in communities, particularly in the period between 2001 and 2006. In October 2006 a peace agreement was reached and processes are underway to establish a federal government. During the conflict period children, together with adult partners including government officials, have implemented the concept of children as zones of peace (CZOP). Children as zones of peace has led to various initiatives including the formation of a national Coalition for CZOP; a public commitment by five major political parties to respect children as zones of peace; the issuance of child protection guidelines for security forces by the Prime Minister's Office; and, the announcement by the government that schools are also zones of peace.[51] Such initiatives have been initiated as the Maoist rebels have been targeting schools and Child Clubs to organise Maoist propaganda programmes and to lure students and teachers to their cause. At the community level children and child clubs have successfully negotiated with both warring parties not to involve children, not to use or involve schools in the conflict, and not to interfere in the work of Children's Clubs. The CZOP initiative in Nepal also contributes towards efforts by the government to establish comprehensive child protection systems (from community to district to national levels). Village child protection committees have been formed to identify and address child care and protection issues at the local level. Children's representatives from the Child Clubs are part of such committees. In addition, district-level Child Club Forums have been established to share information, undertake joint advocacy and elect representatives for district-level structures, including the District Child Welfare Boards. At the national level, concerned Ministries are currently developing a Child Protection Policy and have made commitments to ensure space for children to inform policy developments. In addition, processes are underway to support space for children's voices and children's rights to be heard and reflected in the constitutional assembly.

## Adults Supporting Children's Peace Initiatives

Adult support to children's contributions to peacebuilding and to the development and strengthening of their own initiatives is crucial. Children will benefit from encouragement and practical support from their parents, teachers, community elders, non-governmental organisations and government actors, including security actors. For example, as outlined above, adults can support the establishment and strengthening of structures such as children's peace clubs, child protection committees and children as zones of peace. This support may take place at different levels. At the local level, adults (from local NGOs, local government, schools or community leaders) may facilitate children's groups and networks to meet together and develop peace initiatives. Non-governmental organisations may provide children with practical resources (for example, a basic fund for materials and transport), with relevant information (for example, a child-friendly version of relevant government policies or legislation) and skill training (for example, training on children's rights, life skills, conflict-resolution). Links to existing media organisations such as radio stations or news journalists may support the development and integration of child-led media initiatives (for example, radio programmes, newsletters, children's articles in mainstream newspapers) to increase dissemination of children's views and advocacy messages. One such initiative – the Children's Radio Manifesto[52] – builds on the understanding that radio can help transform conflict and can support children's and young people's efforts as peacebuilders within their communities.

For children and young people the issues and concerns affecting them are most clearly manifested at the local level. Many of the case examples shared above illustrate how children's more direct contributions to peace and to their own protection have mostly taken place in projects at the local level that are rarely scaled up to the national level. This limits the impact of children's contributions in terms of political process, and should be seen as a missed opportunity in terms of contributing to sustainable peace, which has to build on the social relationships of mutual trust and respect at all levels – in families and communities, in schools and working places, at district and regional levels. Children's contributions and impact at local and community levels are therefore very important, especially in terms of protection responses and reconciliation processes. Nosworthy suggests:

> Civil society and local authorities will be the prime actors in recognising and responding to (young people's) protection needs. The notion of 'local ownership', central to security sector governance, means encouraging pro-active engagement and dialogue, including with youth, in the identification and resolution of local security problems … This engagement in local security agendas between young people, civil society and the local authorities can subsequently be directed and used in informing and influencing national security agendas in a meaningful way.[53]

The challenge remains to ensure government policy-makers and the range of security actors respond to a commonly expressed priority of children who have lived through violence, insecurity and efforts to build peace: to be able to influence peace processes at every level including the national level.

Adult civil society organisations can co-operate in identifying and providing the arrangements and conditions needed to support children and young people to speak with decision-makers at various levels. They can find ways to build and strengthen children's and young people's groups at local, sub-national and national levels so that regular or permanent cross-generational dialogue forums can be established between government and groups of young people's representatives that, in turn, can create national ongoing inter-generational dialogue. Such representative structures imply structural changes and more long-term processes. They can play a role in committing adults in terms of their accountability to children and open up space for more sustainable peace initiatives. Through such representative structures, children's views can begin to more systematically influence the development of peace agreements, comprehensive peace plans and/or efforts to monitor and report back on progress made towards the implementation of such agreements or plans.

## Moving Forward through Strengthening Accountability

In child-rights terms, accountability to children and young people means that adult decision-makers take action that responds to children's concerns, priorities and recommendations about violence, security and peace, and which ensure the fulfilment of children's rights to protection, participation, development and survival. Adult duty-bearers (including parents, teachers, civil society organisations, government officials, police, military, private security actors, the United Nations, etc.) have responsibilities to protect children's rights. Increasing the available opportunities for listening to children, sharing information with them in accessible ways, and providing feedback to children about how their views and recommendations have (or have not been) addressed are mechanisms that reflect accountability to children.

Such mechanisms need to be specifically identified and developed within the process of security sector reform to engage security sector actors and strengthen their accountability towards children and young people. Adherence to international human rights treaties, including the Convention, must be integral to such efforts, as experience shows that children's needs and rights are not adequately considered. The importance of developing clear management and reporting mechanisms is essential to ensure systems of accountability that may hold to account any security actor (private or state) that violates human rights or child rights standards. The increasing privatisation of security services by government agencies could further complicate the process of ensuring accountability.

As was illustrated earlier in this chapter, the training of security sector actors including the police, judiciary, border control officers, military groups and private security actors on children's rights, children's protection, gender awareness and children's participation is very important. It helps to ensure recognition of children, to enhance security sector actors' knowledge, skills and values towards the fulfilment of children's rights and the importance of taking into consideration children's views. Child-focussed NGOs, local or international, can play an important role in providing such training and monitoring its impact. Advocacy to institutionalise children's rights training within the training curricula for all military, police, border control and security guard personnel should continue so that such efforts are mainstreamed. Existing good-practice mechanisms could be scaled up and expanded, including the appointment of CPAs in peacekeeping missions and the training of key security sector actors.

In addition to training of security sector actors and the appointment of CPAs, the establishment of child-friendly complaints procedures would contribute to accountability mechanisms – allowing child or adult civilians to report any complaints with regards to any violations of their rights by security actors, which should be systematically and sensitively followed up. In addition, the Child Protection Advisers should undertake pro-active efforts to ensure that the views and experiences of girls and boys are incorporated in reports of the United Nations Special Representative of the Secretary-General for Children and Armed Conflict (SRSG) and Special Rapporteurs, to be heard in the UN Security Council.

The development of comprehensive child protection systems, including the formation of child protection committees in communities and at district and national levels, would also enhance holistic, sustainable efforts towards children's care, protection and participation. At each level children and young people should be supported to form their own groups and initiatives (including peace initiatives) so that girls and boys (of different ages, and backgrounds) can identify and address key security and protection issues affecting them, and elect their own representatives to be part of the protection committees at each level. In particular, children and young people can identify and ensure a response to protection, security and peace issues that affect them at the local level. A review of national legislation, policies and practice should be undertaken in order to build a more effective child protection system that incorporates children's suggestions to better protect girls and boys and to hold perpetrators of violence against children accountable.

Capacity-building initiatives with children on life skills, conflict-resolution, organisational development and peacebuilding could also be scaled up to support the strengthening of child-led organisations and initiatives. Child-led media initiatives and partnerships with mainstream media institutions (including radio, newspaper and television) can also be pro-actively supported to increase awareness-raising with and by children and young people around their concerns and messages. Media can be a practical and powerful way to raise and amplify the voices of children and to help adults to recognise children's capacities and potential as change agents.

Linkages and partnerships between children's groups and other civil society groups that engage in security, protection and peace initiatives (at local, sub-national and national levels) should also be encouraged to exchange knowledge and strategies to promote and support children and young people's role as agents of peace. As highlighted in this chapter, local civil society organisations are often best placed to support practical responses to children's priority concerns, especially when partnerships with local authorities have been established.

In addition, entry points for dialogue with both government and security providers should be explored and key interlocutors identified and engaged. Inter-generational dialogue fora between the government and groups of children's representatives could be established at local, district, national levels to support children and young people to influence the development, implementation and monitoring of government policies and practices that affect their security, including peacebuilding activities and national action plans.

## Conclusions

Children are longing for peace. This message can be clearly heard from children living in violent situations and insecurity. To respond to this message, children should be protected and empowered as agents of peace. In addition, mechanisms must be found and implemented to ensure that children's rights are respected even, and especially, in situations of armed and violent conflict, as well as in efforts towards comprehensive peacebuilding. When talking about and acting upon security issues, it is crucial that all actors understand and respond to the different ways in which girls and boys of different ages and abilities are affected by violent conflict and insecurity. Continual efforts are needed to ensure that the actions of security actors have a positive impact on the lives of girls, boys, women and men through the promotion and protection of children's rights as an integral part of efforts to fulfil human rights in war, peacebuilding and post-conflict reconstruction. Ongoing efforts are also needed to ensure that children and young people play a role in taking forward peace rather than conflict. As expressed in the quote from a formerly abducted girl associated with the rebel group in Northern Uganda, shared at the outset of this chapter – we should listen and act upon children's views. We should support the power of children's voices, and not the power of the gun.

Children, while being bearers of rights and representing a significant proportion of any society, have little or no access to political process. It is therefore incumbent on those in positions of authority to both acknowledge and respond to the concerns of children and to begin to transform relationships between adults and children so that children and children's groups can be recognised and engaged as important actors in civil society processes. When children are recognised as civil society actors, when they feel that their views are being listened to and taken into account, when they feel their concerns and aspirations are being addressed, only then will their rights be realised, and their full potential as active agents within society be recognised.

In instances where community-based child protection systems have been established, children have been able to send their own representatives to report on violations affecting their rights. Collaboration between children and adult representatives, including representatives from local authorities, allow more systematic and appropriate response to children's concerns.

At district and national levels, children's perspectives should also be heard and acknowledged. Opportunities for the meaningful engagement of different civil society organisations in decision-making should be supported at all levels. This includes creating genuine opportunities for children to inform, influence and monitor all peace-related initiatives and actions at local, national and global levels, including formal peacebuilding processes.

This chapter is intended as one contribution to these efforts by bringing children and young people's perspectives and actions on transforming conflicts and working towards reconciliation and peace to the attention of a wider audience and sensitising 'all concerned to stop war and bring peace for the sake of … children as captured in the song from children in Nepal above.'

> We tell everyone time and again we are children, let us live in peace.
> This is the time for us to grow, learn and get an education.
> Please do not involve us in playing with bombs, firearms and explosive things.
> Education is our right.
> The whole village, all places are shaken by bombs
> What is the future for us?
> We are without proper clothes, are lost, displaced and orphaned
> Why is this happening to us?
> We tell everybody concerned to stop it.
> We want to hold books and pens in our hands, not guns.

Peace talks are going on. It is said there will be peace, killing will be stopped
Let us try our best, let's bring our peace rallies,
And sensitise all concerned to stop war and bring peace for the sake of us children
We are the children of Nepal.
(Song by Children in Nepal).[54]

## Endnotes

1 Participant from Nepal quoted in Save the Children Norway, *Building peace out of war: Children and Young People as Agents of Peace, The Young Generation's Challenge* (Oslo: Workshop Report 2005).

2 We would like to acknowledge contributions from Save the Children's Practice Exchange Network on children's participation and child protection in emergencies; as well as country teams who are participating in Save the Children Norway's Thematic Evaluation on Children's Participation in Armed Conflict, Post-conflict and Peacebuilding, Guatemala, Uganda, Bosnia-Herzegovina and Nepal. We also appreciated information from Elizabeth Jareg and useful feedback from Jo de Berry and from David Nosworthy.

3 The term 'children' refers to all persons below the age of 18, including children and young people.

4 Karen Brounéus, *Reconciliation: Theory and Practice for Development Co-operation* (Stockholm: Swedish International Development Co-operation Agency, 2003), http://www. sida.se/?d=118&a=2891&language=en_US (accessed October 2008).

5 Elizabeth Jareg, Keynote One 'Children in war and peace' in *Building peace out of war*.

6 Jessica Lenz, *Armed with Resilience: A study addressing the issues of reintegration and resiliency of formerly abducted girl child soldiers in Northern Uganda and their potential role as peace builders*, Dissertation for the Masters of Science Degree in Humanitarian Relief and Development at the Center for Development and Emergency Practice (Oxford Brookes University, 2004).

7 David Nosworthy, *Children's Security in Post-Conflict Peacebuilding* (Geneva: DCAF, 2007).

8 United Nations Convention on the Rights of the Children (1989), Article 38

9 Birgit Arrelano, *Training Peacekeepers and Military Forces in Child Rights and Protection* (Stockholm: Save the Children Sweden, 2004).

10 The UN Convention on the Rights of the Children has been ratified by all countries in the world except two, USA and Somalia.

11 Organisation for Economic Co-operation and Development (OECD), *The DAC Guidelines: Helping Prevent Violent Conflict* (Paris: OECD, 2001).

12 Gerison Lansdown, 'Innocenti Insight: The Evolving Capacities of the Child' (Florence: UNICEF, 2005); Claire O' Kane, *Children and Young People as Citizens: Partners for Social Change* (Kathmandu: Save the Children South and Central Asia, 2003).

13 Lori Drummond-Mundal and Guy Cave, 'Children as the seeds of peace: Exploring children's potential contribution to conflict transformation and peacebuilding', Draft submitted to the *Journal of Peacebuilding and Development* (unpublished manuscript, 2006); Jason Hart and Bex Tyrer, *Research with Children Living in Conflict Situations:*

*Concept, Ethics and Method*, Working Paper no. 30, (University of Oxford: Refugee Studies Centre, 2006); Jo Boyden, 'Childhood and the Policy Makers: A comparative perspective on the globalisation of childhood' in *Constructing and Reconstructing Childhood: Contemporary Issues in the Sociological Study of Childhood*, eds. Alison James & Alan Prout (Norfolk: The Falmer Press, 1997), 190-229 ; Gerison Lansdown, *Can You Hear Me?*, Working Papers in Early Childhood Development no. 36 (May 2005); Cairo Arafat and Neil Boothby, 'A Psychological Assessment of Palestinian Children' (July 2003); Yvonne Kemper, *Youth in War-to-Peace Transitions: Approaches of International Organizations*, Berghof Report no. 10 (Berlin: Berghof Research Centre, 2005); Claire O'Kane, 'Supporting the development of children's groups and networks in Afghanistan: Reflections on practice and possibilities' *Children, Youth and Environments* 17, no. 1 (2007): 222-237; Julie Guyot, 'Suffer the Children: The Psychological Rehabilitation of Child Soldiers as a Function of Peace-Building' (2007).

14 O'Kane, *Children and Young People as Citizens*; Lansdown, *Can You Hear Me?*

15 Informal discussion between Save the Children assessment team members and one of the authors, Autumn 2006.

16 Save the Children USA and UNICEF, *The Children of Kabul: Discussions with Afghan Families* (Kabul: Save the Children Federation, 2003).

17 Maggie Brown, *Global Evaluation: Children Affected by Armed Conflict, Displacement or Disaster* (Save the Children Norway, 2005). Zambia case example shared by a Children's Christian Fund adviser to one of the authors March 2007.

18 Drummond-Mundal and Cave, 'Children as the seeds of peace'.

19 Hart and Tyrer, *Research with Children Living in Conflict Situations*.

20 Jason Hart, *The Participation of Conflict Affected Children in Humanitarian Action: Learning from Zones of Armed Conflict*, Refugee Studies Centre Working Paper no. 30 (Oxford, 2004), http://www.rsc.ox.ac.uk/PDFs/workingpaper30.pdf (accessed October 2008).

21 Pamela Reynolds, 'Activism, politics and the punishment of children' in *Childhood abused*, eds. Geraldine Van Bueren (Hampshire: Ashgate, 1998), 45.

22 Herman Ketel, *Proud to Work and Happy to be Organised: Working Children in West Africa and their Participation in their Own Movement* (Stockholm: Save the Children Sweden, 2002); O'Kane, Children and Young People as Citizens; O'Kane, 'Supporting the development of children's groups'.

23 Save the Children Norway, 'Thematic Evaluation on Children's Participation in Armed Conflict, Post Conflict and Peace Building' (2007), http://www.reddbarna.no/chp (accessed October 2008).

24 International Save the Children Alliance, *Ten Essential Learning Points: Listen and Speak out against Sexual Abuse of Girls and Boys*, Global Submission to the UN Study on Violence against Children (Oslo: Save the Children, 2005).

25 Save the Children Norway, 'Thematic Evaluation on Children's Participation in Armed Conflict'.

26 Ibid. – with permission given for the reproduction of this risk map by the young person participating in the thematic evaluation.

27 Hart and Tyrer, Research with Children Living in Conflict Situations, 18.

28 International Save the Children Alliance have developed practice standards in children's participation which cut across all work with children. The practice standards can be downloaded at www.savethechildren.net (accessed November 2008).

29 Judy Miller, *Never Too Young: How Children Can Take Responsibility and Make Decisions* (London: Save the Children, 1997); Alison Clark, *Spaces to Play: gathering the perspectives of young children* (London: Thomas Coram Research Unit, Institute of Education, 2006); Gerison Lansdown, 'The Evolving Capacities of the Child'.
30 Save the Children, 'Practice Standards in Children's Participation' (2005), http://www.savethechildren.net (accessed November 2008).
31 Save the Children, 'Code of Conduct for Save the Children Staff' (2005).
32 Save the Children UK, Sudan, Interagency Situation Analysis of Child Protection and Education in Jabal-Awlia IDP Camp, Fateh-el Moubin 3, Soba Arradi and Shigla Haj Yusuf Squatter Areas (24th October to 6th December 2005).
33 Florence Martin and John Parry-Williams, *The Right Not To Lose Hope. Children in Conflict with the Law: a policy analysis and examples of good practice* (London: International Save the Children Alliance, 2005).
34 Martin and Parry-Williams, *The Right Not To Lose Hope*, 82.
35 Brown, Global Evaluation.
36 Birgit Arellano, 'Training Peacekeepers and Military Forces in Child Rights and Protection'.
37 Ibid.
38 Information received by email from a Save the Children Denmark colleague Lene Steffen in May 2007.
39 Martin and Parry-Williams, *The Right Not To Lose Hope*.
40 Ibid.
41 Save the Children Norway, *Building Peace out of War*.
42 Ibid.
43 Drummond-Mundal and Cave, 'Children as the seeds of peace'; Kemper, *Youth in War-to-Peace Transitions*; Arafat, 'A Psychosocial Assessment'.
44 Kemper, Youth in War-to-Peace Transitions, 43.
45 Drummond-Mundal and Cave, 'Children as the seeds of peace', 3.
46 Save the Children Norway, 'Thematic Evaluation of Children's Participation in Armed Conflict'.
47 Brown, Global Evaluation; O'Kane, Children and Young People as Citizens; Hart, The Participation of Conflict Affected Children in Humanitarian Action; Hart and Tyrer, Research with Children Living in Conflict Situations.
48 Drummond-Mundal and Cave, 'Children as the seeds of peace', 3.
49 Brown, Global Evaluation.
50 Formal peace talks have taken place between the Government of Uganda and the Lords Resistance Army rebel forces in Juba, Southern Sudan since September 2006.
51 Save the Children Norway, *Building Peace out of War*.
52 Copies of the Radio Manifesto can be downloaded in French, English or Portuguese from the World Radio Forum website www.worldradioforum.org (accessed November 2008).
53 Nosworthy, *Children's Security in Post-Conflict Peacebuilding*.
54 Save the Children Norway, 'Thematic Evaluation on Children's Participation in Armed Conflict, Post Conflict and Peace Building'.

# Part V

# Conclusion

Chapter 13

# Moving Forward – Conclusions and Recommendations

*David Nosworthy*

## Children, Youth and Security

The last few chapters have been focussed very much on issues concerning children recruited or used by armed forces or groups (often referred to as 'child soldiers'). These children will have experienced first-hand some of the worst atrocities of war, not only as observers but in many cases as perpetrators. While the issue of 'child soldiers' has been well researched and extensively documented, the challenges associated with achieving their successful reintegration into society once the conflict is over remain largely unresolved.

The term 'children affected by armed conflict' is also widely used to refer to this specific group of children. In reality though, children whose lives have been 'affected by armed conflict' also include, among others: those who have directly experienced the loss of family members or friends; those whose lives have been up-rooted by displacement, internally or as refugees; or those who have been denied access to food and shelter, or other basic services such as security, health and education. While the best estimates of the number of child soldiers globally indicate a figure of around 250,000[1], the numbers of children affected by armed conflict mount into the millions – just by way of example, in the last decade an estimated 20 million children have been forced to flee their homes, and more than 1 million have been orphaned or separated from their families.[2]

The post-conflict vacuum can lead many young people into adopting negative coping strategies, often exacerbated or exploited by the presence of peace-spoilers (both political and criminal). Such spoilers are generally intent on using and maintaining the prevailing instability for their own means and ends. A frequently observed modus operandi of these peace-spoilers is to use youth either in creating political tension through staged violent protest or, similarly, in propagating violent crime. It is clear that in a fragile post-conflict environment the presence of large numbers of disengaged and disaffected youth, with limited outlook or prospects for the future, could potentially impact on efforts to re-establish stability and break the cycle of violence.

Post-conflict transition brings many challenges, not least the need to address these issues of violence and criminality. A feature of public debate on public security, however, is the tendency for children and youth to be presented as the demons of the piece – an apparently easy enough target for generating political capital. Public perceptions of youth violence are easily manipulated, and generally inflated in the negative, youth violence often being equated to social breakdown.

As has been acknowledged from the outset of this publication, children and youth do come into contact with the law as offenders. However, statistics suggest that most tend to be involved in one-off offences that they do not repeat. This is not to say that there are no repeat or habitual offenders, some do become involved in a life of crime, but often their experiences as younger children have pre-disposed them into adopting the negative coping strategies that bring them into contact with violence and criminal activity. It is often argued that discernable characteristics of such outcomes may already appear among primary age pupils.

What is important is to not push those one-off offenders into a life of crime through short-term, 'sticking-plaster' policies that expose them to hard-core criminal elements, by placing them directly into the criminal justice system. Alternatives exist, and what is clear is that the child's close environment, particularly the influence of the family and community, have a huge bearing on the likely outcomes for any particular child, and therefore represent a significant opportunity for developing preventive strategies.

While parents, families and communities are responsible for ensuring the immediate well-being of children, the state in the form of its national and local authorities is responsible for ensuring that children's rights are respected. Of all the statutory security providers it is the police who have the closest contact with communities and the security issues they are facing. However, one of the biggest obstacles to introducing preventive measures is that the very communities experiencing the highest levels of insecurity also tend to be those that have the least trust and confidence in the police.

Such a dynamic can be characteristic of urban areas with elevated crime figures, but equally of communities emerging from conflict, where they often have no choice but to assume responsibility for providing their own security. Such situations can risk perpetuating a cycle of violence with individuals or groups descending to summary justice with reprisals and vigilante action.

Law enforcement agencies across the world face the dilemma of how to go about breaking such a cycle and a wide variety of approaches have emerged that attempt to breakdown the 'us and them' attitude that is so often prevalent. The notion of non-co-operation with the police riddles many of the communities were insecurity is at its most pernicious – the idea of someone co-operating with the authorities being seen as enough to brand them as a 'traitor'.

In addition to responsibilities as key duty-bearers in protecting and promoting the rights of children, there are also operational implications for the security sector related to the obligation of 'duty of care' for the children and youth that they come into contact with.

This publication has aimed to address what is for many the not-so-obvious link between security and children. One of the challenges has been to engage security actors in thinking beyond the immediate image of the child soldier, to focus their attention on the wider responsibility of the security sector, and its vital contribution to the protection of children and securing the protective environment so essential for social development.

The following section revisits some of the key findings that call for a better understanding of children's lives and security realities, and the policy implications involved in providing for their security and the security of those around them.

## Looking Forward: Children and Youth, Seen and Listened To

The title of the book, *Seen, but not Heard*, alludes to the images of children that are used to convey the trauma and human suffering associated with emergencies and disasters, whether due to armed conflict or natural disaster. These visual assaults of the senses are used for the very reason that threats to our children encapsulate the worst of threats to us all. However, not all of the violence and abuse aimed at children happens in front of the world's cameras. Much of it happens behind closed doors, including within the family home.

Significantly, children's perceptions of how they experience security and their priority concerns are not factored in to security policy. When we consider the priorities that guide security provision, children become all but invisible, and they are certainly not consulted on their security aspirations. Not withstanding the notion of due weight, which should be applied to the views and opinions of the developing child, children have valuable insights into social behaviour and trends at the local level that can have direct significance for the security sector, but which for the main part are either not considered or are hidden from view. Particularly in situations of post-conflict peacebuilding, children and youth have an enormous contribution to make, but traditionally little investment has been made in harnessing their positive energies and engaging them as active agents in their own security.

## Underlying Causes of Children's Insecurity

This publication has very consciously considered both day-to-day threats to children's security, as well as the additional burden that armed conflict brings with it, as many of the underlying causes, and the principles for addressing them, apply before, during and after conflict. Many of the arguments developed here are not exclusively related to war-affected children, or those migrating or seeking refuge from armed conflict, but apply equally to children in developing and industrialised countries. The reason for highlighting this point is that Security Sector Reform (SSR) should not just be considered as a band-aid to be applied to fragile states, but should be seen as a tool of good governance for promoting and improving human security everywhere. Many of the issues affecting children are universal, and while each situation may be different and require distinct approaches, they are generally marked by similar characteristics, such as injustice and exclusion.

One of the biggest factors leading to negative outcomes for children is exclusion. Exclusion can be marked by disaffection that can emerge in violence, and in a potential vulnerability to the attentions of 'violence entrepreneurs' or 'peace-spoilers'. While poverty is often cited as the key factor, in reality it is more of a potent symptom. Exclusion is related to injustice, which will likely manifest itself in poverty. Injustice provides a far clearer motive to explain the potential vulnerability to a range of related threats, be they organised crime or the radicalisation that has been linked to a number of recent high-profile terrorist acts. Mental health issues are also often closely linked, whether in relation to the children coming into conflict with the law, or with reluctance on the part of child soldiers to demobilise or reintegrate because of concerns about the need for support.

Particularly in relation to children who endure unimaginable hardship in the shape of abuse or violence, it is also important to remember the innate resilience that characterises children and youth, and therefore to focus policy approaches on supporting individuals to achieve positive outcomes.

**Why Children's Security Matters**

Unpacking why children's security matters to the security sector, children can be seen to be of importance in the guise of victims, witnesses and perpetrators. Establishing children on the security agenda should be based on pragmatic argument, rather than the often emotive language that generally accompanies the debate. The characterisation of 'children and youth' in the public domain tends to be polarised between those who present children as helpless innocent victims, and those who demonise youth as 'yobs' and trouble-makers.

The most important message, however, should be that children are active agents in their own lives and in their own development, with positive contributions to make, whether to post-conflict peacebuilding or tackling street violence. Their energy, enthusiasm and creativity needs to be harnessed and tapped for the positive contribution that they can make to society. Building a protective environment for children, a key United Nations Children's Fund (UNICEF) policy approach, means also providing a secure environment.

Other important elements of why children's security matters include:

1) Human Rights Obligations – human rights, and child rights in particular, provide a framework of standards for governing the delivery of security services for children (the security sector has an obligation to protect those rights, and to avoid violating them)
2) The Need to Protect Social Capital – a security system that respects human security and good governance principles needs to be established – a system that will be inherited by today's children and should encourage their meaningful participation in security matters from the outset
3) Population Demographics – the sheer numbers of children make them a significant portion of the population anywhere

The responsibility of all actors should be to help guide young people through the difficult transition that is 'adolescence', towards finding active and positive roles in society. The vast majority of children do this on their own – it is called growing-up – but for some it is not so straight forward.

Having demonstrated why children's security matters, it then becomes necessary to identify the mechanisms that are required to produce a pro-active engagement on the part of security actors in the identification and delivery of security services adapted to the needs and aspirations of children and youth.

## Good Security Governance

A key premise of this publication is that good security governance provides the framework through which security provision can be made more relevant to the protection needs of children. The very notion of good governance is based on respect for human rights. Human rights represent the standards by which security provision should be judged, and provide a guide for the development of security sector reform activities.

Security governance obliges consideration of the security of the individual, as well as the security of the state. It also acknowledges the wide spectrum of actors that need to be factored into the debate, and the various levels of interaction that need to be considered – a key issue here being the need to expand the constituency of actors involved in child protection. A holistic security governance approach is necessary to ensure the protection of children, requiring consideration of all levels of interaction in post-conflict security governance from the local to the sub-state, state, regional and global.

The post-conflict setting is important as it provides perhaps the most challenging environment for security sector reform activities, but at the same time provides a window of opportunity for open and frank discussion of broader security issues – an otherwise extremely sensitive area to influence.

## Human Rights Include Child Rights

The governance approach enables security discussion under the commonly adopted thread of human rights, which reflect states' legal obligations under international law. This framework provides a set of standards for governing the delivery of security services, and establishes the security sector as a key duty-bearer in assuring security to all, including children.

By signing and ratifying the Convention on the Rights of the Child (the 'Convention'), states have taken on a commitment to implement the provisions laid out in its various articles. One of the stated principles is that children are given just consideration in all matters concerning them. A core indicator of 'good governance' therefore becomes the extent to which children and their needs are integrated into multi-sector decision-making, at all levels.

One of the issues that often seems to get in the way of positive discussion about children, an entirely unintended effect of the Convention, is the perception that the end of childhood is somehow defined as an event that happens on reaching 18 years of age. The Convention's definition of a child being someone under the age of 18 years is actually a legal construct. It should not to be interpreted as a line defining the end of a development process at which point a child somehow suddenly becomes an adult. Indeed, for many children childhood is already a distant memory by the age of 18, as they take on responsibility for themselves in the labour market, or in taking care of siblings, or even raising their own families. However, and whatever their circumstances, children are still entitled to the special protection that the Convention offers until they are 18. In effect they are able to claim the benefits of majority where necessary, while benefiting from the protection that the Convention offers them.

## Security Sector Reform and Child Protection

SSR has gained an increasing profile in recent years and has become a topical issue of debate appearing on the agendas of a variety of international fora. Significantly, the United Nations Security Council initiated debate on SSR in February 2007, calling for a report on the issue to be prepared by the UN Secretary-General. The report, *Securing peace and development: the role of the United Nations in supporting security sector reform,* was presented to the Security Council in May 2008, with the resulting President's Statement affirming that:[3]

> Member States are the primary providers of security, which contributes to the protection of human rights and sustainable development. The task of the United Nations is to support national actors in achieving their security, peace and development goals. To that end, the development of effective and accountable security institutions on the basis of non-discrimination, full respect for human rights and the rule of law is essential.
> (Statement by the President of the Security Council).[4]

These recent high-level discussions on SSR have included gender aspects within their deliberations, but apart from oblique references to vulnerable groups do not reflect the security needs of children. A major rallying point for the discussion on gender has been Security Council Resolution 1325. There is a compelling argument to suggest that a similar framework is required in order to better promote the state obligation to the special protection of children and youth within the security debate.

While the security sector may be failing to take account of the special security needs of children, the child advocacy community are largely failing to establish the link between child protection and the role and activities of the security sector.

Early last year a 10-year strategic review of the ground breaking 'Machel Study' was launched. The original report on the Impact of Armed Conflict on Children, presented by the UN Secretary-General to the General Assembly in 1996, identified the peace and security agenda as central to promoting the protection of children affected by armed conflict.[5] In the intervening ten years, the security debate has advanced considerably, but despite the sector having a crucial role to play in protecting children's human rights, their security needs have remained largely invisible. Similarly, the preparatory work for the review hardly made mention of children's security. However, the Special Representative's report presented to the General Assembly in October 2007 did include a paragraph making reference to the importance that the SSR agenda has for children. This acknowledgement of the link between SSR and children is highly significant in that it provides a mandate for UN agencies to engage in a wider debate of children's security. The paragraph noted that:

> The issue of security sector reform is an important emerging area of engagement that carries significant implications for children. There are considerable security challenges in post-conflict situations, including the reconstitution or reform of the military and police.
> (Report of the SRSG for Children and Armed Conflict).[6]

Reflecting on the Security Council's SSR debate and the Machel Review, the two processes apparently share common goals, but it is hard not to sense a certain disconnect in the process of their implementation. Both aim to provide a secure environment for societies emerging from conflict, but there seems to be a real challenge in how to bring the two together into creating a common cause.

In the post-conflict setting, there is an often heated debate about the nature of the humanitarian space with, perhaps justifiably, many arguing that maintaining a disconnect between the military and police components of peacekeeping missions and humanitarian concerns such as child protection are essential. This, however, misses the point that by their very presence the international community has become a player in a security environment that directly impacts on the well-being of children. It is therefore essential that, even if not directly implicated in humanitarian affairs, the potential impact of all security actors on children is assessed and mitigated. As mentioned earlier in this publication, a security governance framework provides us with the opportunity to analyse and anticipate the dynamics of any given security environment and encourages, even obliges, that children and youth be factored into this analysis.

A key element to bear in mind in considering the above argument is the near customary acceptance of the shift in security provision from the security of the state and its institutions to an obligation to provide for the security of all. Although still hotly debated, and open to interpretation as to its scope, human security has marked a move from the traditional notion of state security, to a responsibility for security of the individual. What is particularly important about the human security concept is its underlying message of the linkages between security, development and human rights.

## Defining the Security Sector

While discussions on security governance may reflect children's security needs, by the time we reach SSR, children are likely to have disappeared from the agenda. From here the discussion is likely to be focussed on the technical aspects of institutional reform including structures, procedures and resources. Even the Organisation for Economic Co-operation and Development – Development Assistance Committee (OECD DAC) Security System Reform Handbook reflects this dilemma – while stressing the importance of local ownership, when it comes to the definition of stakeholders, the analysis shifts to the traditional notion of those institutions or individuals directly tasked or mandated with security provision.

In broad terms, the security sector comprises all those responsible for protecting the state and communities within it.[7] In defining the security sector in the introduction of this publication, five categories of security 'stakeholders' were presented, stressing the particularly important role of civil society. This cannot be under-estimated in terms of guaranteeing children's safety and security.

When developing security policy it is essential that we engage all those who have a stake in security. Without their long-term commitment to supporting plans, process and initiatives the chances of success will be limited. It is important that any distinction presented between mandated security providers and 'stakeholders' does not cloud the crucial role that both have to play in terms of the ultimate effectiveness of security provision. Both human security and child protection 'happen' (or not) at community level. As such, engaging civil society in the security dialogue is essential for advancing both agendas, requiring mobilisation and empowerment of civil society.

For children and youth, the issues and concerns affecting them are most clearly manifested in their local surroundings. Civil society and local authorities will as such be the prime actors in recognising and responding to issues and concerns. In terms of statutory or formal security actors, it will be the police who will have the most important and direct day-to-day contact in relation to promoting children's security.

Recognising young people as stakeholders obviously means that their views and opinions need to be consulted in defining policy. This is particularly evident if we are considering children not just as victims but also as potential perpetrators if left to the influences of peace-spoilers.

## 'Especially Girls' and 'Especially Boys'

Numerous references, including within many United Nations documents, draw special attention to, and call for action, on behalf of 'especially girls'. References to 'especially boys' are far less common and tend to be focussed on drawing attention to negative behaviours associated with being young and male.

The last 30 years have seen special emphasis being paid to girls' education, but in various industrialised countries a decline in boys' attainment at school is now being reported. Studies show that boys are underperforming in literacy, are less engaged with school, more girls than boys are completing their schooling, and in some schools boys account for eight out of every ten suspensions and exclusions.[8] In addition, figures in the United Kingdom have indicated that boys under ten are almost twice as likely to suffer mental illness, but are far less likely to seek help.[9] An approach that is too focussed on the girl child, with a presumption of the coping abilities of boys, risks skewing from the outset the very assessment mechanisms that should be detecting child protection concerns for all children.

As referred to earlier in this publication, women, girls and boys are all generally less often heard, and as such do not have their needs and aspirations reflected in policy formulation and decision-making.[10] Ultimately, a more egalitarian message for all, and one that would be more consistent with what equality strives for, is that both the girl child and the boy child receive our special attention. If all individuals are born equal, then all deserve to be given equal opportunity to develop to the fullest of their potential. Focussing disproportionately on the girl child distorts what is otherwise an important message, and risks making the boy child feel like a second-rate citizen.

In addition, it is widely acknowledged that boys have an active and constructive role to play in tackling many of the forms of gender-based violence that exist today. Addressing gender issues requires that both boys and girls are engaged. And, in the same way that girls should not be made to feel that they are victims of their gender, neither should boys.

Gender is about power relations and social structures, and security sector reform activities need to be cognisant of the implications that social inequalities can have on the security of individuals and groups within the population, and ensure that its own structures and procedures promote equity throughout.

**Participation**

It is at the community level that the participation of children and youth is most relevant. Children's participation is often talked about and promoted, but too often the reality is that it is something that is parachuted into communities by outsiders, facilitated by outsiders, and based on the purpose or agenda of the outsiders. Participation is only truly meaningful when local communities engage with and address real issues. The key role that external actors can play is to act as catalysts and maybe facilitators. Their interventions to raise issues, such as reproductive health or HIV/AIDS, are often essential to bringing about positive social change in areas that local populations may otherwise have been reluctant to address because of the sensitive nature of the discussion.

A key principle of security governance is the notion of 'local ownership', which means encouraging dialogue and pro-active engagement, including with children and youth, in the identification and resolution of local security problems. Public debate needs to be influenced in such a way as to ensure that there is an open discussion on what public expectations are of security and its delivery, so that all parts of society are able to make their concerns and expectations heard. Ensuring that this debate is well informed will require capacity-building with both local authorities and civil society actors.

## Policy Driven Approaches and Programme Realities

The protection issues that affect children tend to be categorised into separate thematic areas and, as such, approached as separate areas of technical expertise. There are, however, some dangers associated with this. A generalist, for example, may feel overwhelmed or under-qualified by the complexity and technical nature of the subject matter, and therefore be unwilling to get involved. Equally, labelling experts or focal points to address thematic issues can lead to abdication of responsibility on the part of others, claiming it is not their role. Perhaps the most significant dynamic, however, is at the level of donors who allocate funding against thematic projects, meaning that many broader, purely protection-based initiatives go unsupported.

There are other tensions though. Child soldiers are a specific and high-profile concern, and interventions require specialist assistance and considerable resources. Significant commitments have been made by the international community regarding the release and reintegration of all children associated with armed forces or groups – but, it remains to be seen whether funding levels will be provided to realise these commitments in practice. In addition though, child soldiers represent only a small percentage of the children whose lives are impacted by armed conflict and many others will be equally in need of support. All children affected by conflict should warrant due attention, and each should be given the possibility to actively engage in the peacebuilding process. Once again, however, recognition of this fact needs to be supported by adequately resourced programmes in the field.

A specific area requiring more attention is that of research. Many of the social trends and impacts of armed conflict, and their potential long-term impact on security, remain unclear. Improved empirical data would enable better policy-and decision-making in this area. One thing that is for sure is that children are an important barometer of social patterns.

Adopting a 'holistic approach' is a phrase that is often used but yet rarely unpacked to explain what it really means. Certainly the promotion and implementation of protection strategies on behalf of children, most notably in relation to prevention, require a systemic approach that recognises the need for multiple actors to work collaboratively at multiple levels.

## Recommendations

These recommendations are not exhaustive and do not claim to be original. However, based on DCAF's work in this area, it is the first time that they come together in an analysis aimed at advancing children on the security agenda – a policy area that is so vitally important, but so conspicuously overlooked. The recommendations aim to highlight initial steps that will assist security policy-makers in responding to the security needs of children and youth, beginning by bringing together key stakeholders. Advancing this agenda will require increased understanding of the dynamics that are at play between children's security and social development, and call for the voices and perspectives of children to be sought and listened to. In particular, the importance of bottom-up initiatives to promote democratic governance of the security sector is stressed.

Acknowledging that the effective delivery of security to children and young people requires multiple actors working together at multiple levels, a range of recommendations are put forward specifically targeting civil society organisations, security providers and democratic institutions. The international community is also included because of their specific moral obligation to protect and promote human rights and democratic governance, but also the significant role that they have to play in transition and peacebuilding processes.

Civil society organisations (CSOs) are emphasised in particular as they have a crucial role to play in the oversight of the security sector from the national to the local level. Their involvement is also vital to promoting children's security as a key element of social development. By engaging with and listening to children and youth, CSOs can represent the views and opinions of young people in national and local debate with the aim of advancing their rights and security claims simultaneously. They also play a double role in not only working with the security sector and democratic institutions to promote respect for human rights, but equally in monitoring the security sector's performance against these human rights standards.

Having highlighted the important role that CSOs can play, it is also important to highlight that they each tend to have their own agenda, and that they are not a homogenous group of philanthropic organisations that represent all of society. In dealing with the representation of children, the selection of appropriate organisations becomes particularly important and highly sensitive. Organisations working for and with children have a responsibility to make sure that their operations do not put children at risk, which at a minimum should require that they have a coherent child protection policy.[11]

At the local level, CSOs are closest to and most acutely aware of the security realities of children. They are also in a position to establish pro-active mechanisms for enabling children and young people to express themselves in terms of their concerns and aspirations – an essential element of this being the provision of confidential referral points where child victims can turn for support. CSOs have a responsibility to accord due weight to the opinions of the children in their representations to the relevant authorities in a neutral and unbiased way. At the local level, CSOs will be largely responsible for facilitating contact and dialogue with local government structures and law enforcement agencies.

At the national level, CSOs can provide vital testimony, information and analysis to parliament and other democratic institutions about the way in which national security policies and activities are affecting children and society as a whole. CSOs concerned with freedom of speech, human rights, policing or access to justice issues all tend to be in the forefront of discussions on security sector issues, and all should have a vested interest in promoting respect for children's rights.

Democratic institutions have a pivotal role to play as interlocutors and facilitators between civil society and security providers at national, district or local levels. In relation to security providers, the security governance approach obliges consideration of all security actors including private security companies and/or armed non-state actors. Child protection concerns can provide an entry point for discussion on a range of related human rights and security matters.

Bearing the foregoing considerations in mind, the following broad recommendations are proposed.

*For Civil Society Organisations (CSOs)*

1) Work with national and local authorities to develop strategies aimed at tackling social exclusion and in particular support disadvantaged children and youth.
2) Establish outreach mechanisms with communities, families and schools to provide avenues for children to express themselves on issues affecting them, including security.

3) Establish links at the local level with their local parliamentarian, local media, and the local representatives of government departments and democratic institutions.
4) Establish mechanisms for dialogue with local law enforcement agencies on child protection concerns including complaints mechanisms.
5) Work with local authorities in ensuring the early identification of child victims and children at risk, and ensure availability and access to adequate support services and assistance.
6) Develop monitoring and analytical capacities in order to document and report on security issues affecting children, young people and society as a whole.
7) Develop lobbying strategies at the national level with parliament, national media, government departments and democratic institutions.
8) Support security sector and democratic institutions in developing and delivering awareness-raising and training capacities.
9) Establish networks of CSOs engaged in promoting prevention, protection and empowerment strategies for children.
10) Use established networks to create and share campaign platforms with other CSOs working on security sector oversight issues.
11) Participate in legislative consultation and the formation of regulatory networks.
12) CSOs must ensure accountability and transparency in their own activities in order to remain credible.

*For Security Providers*

1) Ensure that all activities are guided by human rights principles.
2) Monitor and analyse critical threats to children and young people at both the national and local levels.
3) Engage in active research to identify and promote good practices in relation to remedial and preventive actions on behalf of children.
4) Establish dialogue with civil society organisations that are involved in security and child protection activities.
5) Promote internally and externally an understanding of the notion of human security, going beyond state security to encompass the civil and political rights of the population.
6) Reinforce the principle of the responsibility to protect, and not to abuse, in clear and transparent operating procedures for all security institutions (including duty of care).

7) Establish mechanisms and procedures for dealing humanely with children in conflict with the law and respecting their human dignity, including a juvenile justice system that is established in accordance with international human rights norms and standards.
8) Ensure the independence of the judiciary to oversee court cases against security actors, including access for law-enforcement investigators.
9) Identify levels of interaction in respect to child protection and develop institutional strategies including assessments, operating procedures, accountability mechanisms, resource allocation and targeted capacity-building.
10) Provide specialised and qualified personnel where necessary for dealing with sensitive child protection matters, including consideration of dedicated units.
11) Develop Codes of Conduct for servicemen and law enforcement officials that cover their obligations towards children whether as victims, witnesses or perpetrators.
12) Work to create trust, mutual confidence and understanding between communities and the security sector, particularly through engaging civil society organisations.

*For Democratic Institutions*

1) Place special emphasis on listening to, and addressing, the concerns of children – the fact that children are politically invisible places a special moral obligation on democratic institutions to act on their behalf.
2) Develop a national development plan that places children and young people centre stage, identifying strategies to harness their positive contribution to society.
3) Lobby for predictable funding to be provided to preventive strategies involving children, promoting a move away from the predominant project mentality.
4) Review the national legislative framework to ensure that it is in compliance with international legal norms and standards.
5) Ensure that the general public is informed about national human rights obligations, and security and child protection policies, including through the use of the media.
6) Ensure that parliament has the statutory power to hold inquiries and hearings into matters involving the security sector that impact child

protection issues.

7) Provide ombuds institutions with statutory powers to monitor, investigate and report on security actors in relation to children.
8) Develop where necessary policy and guidance documents for security sector actors detailing their role and responsibilities towards children, based on democratic governance principles of oversight, transparency and accountability.
9) Ensure that parliamentary committees monitor the status of child rights within their deliberations on different components of the security sector, and establish a dedicated parliamentary committee to report on implementation of child rights obligations.
10) Ensure that children's security is an integral part of any policy-level consideration of security-related matters and that this is done from the outset of discussions.
11) Establish formal and informal co-ordination bodies at the national, district and local levels, including government officials, law enforcement agencies and local non-governmental organisation representatives.
12) Ensure the independence of the judiciary and ombuds institutions, including robust legal instruments, access to enforcement mechanisms, and availability of adequate resources to ensure the transparency, stability and accountability of the security sector.

*For the International Community*

1) Call for the ratification of all international instruments addressing children and democratic security provision.
2) Reiterate the central role of human rights to security provision and respect for rule of law, acknowledging that security sector governance is a dynamic process.
3) Promote security sector reform initiatives, informed by good governance principles, as a vital step in the process towards sustainable peace, security and human development.
4) Address child protection considerations in all technical assistance agreements, whether with ministries of defence or interior.
5) Ensure that the focus of security sector reform activities is not limited to simply the executive and formal security providers, but also encompasses democratic institutions, civil society organisations and non-statutory security forces.

6) Promote the notion of human security as an alternative vision to the state-centric security agenda.
7) Stress the importance of engaging civil society in consultative processes to create local and national ownership of security matters and in seeking ways to affect change.
8) Develop civil expertise in security issues related to children and among democratic institutions, supporting capacity-building activities where appropriate.
9) Promote cross-government approaches with national governments to children's security, with special attention to adolescents and youth.
10) Collect and disseminate good practices to illustrate the expected roles of specific security sector institutions in democratic governance and under the rule of law.
11) Support research to obtain a better understanding of the dynamics between children's security and long-term outcomes, including national development.
12) Adapt assistance programmes that promote youth as active participants in peacebuilding and democratic oversight of the security sector.

## Concluding Observations

The security of children and youth does matter, and the best way of advancing this important element of the security agenda is through strengthening the existing security governance framework, in particular with a focus on local ownership and through reinforcing the human rights aspect of security.

Further analysis is required to develop approaches within the security sector that enable systematic approaches to be developed to the protection of children. Issues of co-ordination and co-operation need to be revisited if meaningful accountability is to be established. Communication across such a wide range of potential stakeholders represents a key challenge. Each actor, at each level, has a significantly different role that requires reflection and engagement on their part to develop their role in the provision of a secure environment for children. This must include the institutional implications of capacity, training, procedure, financing and personnel. A commitment is required from a full range of actors to engage where appropriate across a range of activities including prevention, detection, protection, solutions, monitoring and justice.

And finally:

1) The broader security governance agenda, and what this implies for human security, should be used to define the objectives, priorities and outcomes of SSR.
2) Research is required into the linkages between the security environment and children's protection status. Lessons learned and best practices need to be captured in order to better guide future policy-making, particularly in relation to security and social trends and work in the area of prevention.
3) Thirdly, we need to develop approaches to generating public debate on what is expected of security – this should be part of a capacity-building process with civil society.

The aim has been to provide a catalyst that will encourage a range of security sector actors to reflect on their role, and the responsibilities that this carries in terms of realising children's rights and integrating child protection principles into their work.

It is hoped that this publication will succeed in generating discussion around the linkages between security provision and children, and that this will be taken forward in developing secure environments for children that assist young people in realising positive outcomes and have a real and positive impact on their lives.

***

## Endnotes

1 UNICEF, 'Child Protection Information Sheet: Children Associated with Armed Groups', http://www.unicef.org/protection/files/Armed_Groups.pdf (accessed October 2008).

2 UNICEF, 'UNICEF's role in emergencies', http://www.unicef.org/emerg/index_33296.html (accessed October 2008).

3 United Nations Security Council, *Securing peace and development: the role of the United Nations in supporting security sector reform*, Report of the Secretary-General, UN doc. A/62/659–S/2008/39 (New York: January 2008).

4 UN Security Council, Statement by the President of the Security Council on the occasion of the 5890th meeting of the Security Council, UN doc. S/PRST/2008/14 (New York: May 2008).

5 United Nations, *Impact of Armed Conflict on Children*, Report of Graça Machel, Expert of the Secretary-General of the United Nations, UN doc. A/51/306 (New York: August 1996).

6 Part Two of the Report of the SRSG for Children and Armed Conflict (UN doc. A/62/228) presents the findings of a strategic review of the Report by Graça Machel.

7 UK Department for International Development (DFID), 'Understanding and Supporting Security Sector Reform' (2002), http://www.dfid.gov.uk/pubs/files/supportingsecurity.pdf (accessed November 2008).

8 Autralian Government, Department of Education, Science and Training, 'Educating Boys: Issues and Information' (2003),

9 Economical and Social Research Council, 'Mental Health and Mental Illness in the UK' (July 2007), http://www.esrcsocietytoday.ac.uk/ESRCInfoCentre/facts/UK/index56.aspx?ComponentId=12917&SourcePageId=18133 (accessed November 2008).

10 Claudia Hasanbegovic, *Children and Gender-based Violence: An overview of existing conceptual frameworks* (Stockholm: International Save the Children Alliance, 2003).

11 Keeping Children Safe Coalition, 'Keeping Children Safe, Tool 1: Standards for child protection' (Second edition revised, September 2007).

Annex 1

# List of Key Legal Instruments

## International Human Rights Treaties

*Universal Declaration of Human Rights, 1948.*
Adopted and proclaimed by General Assembly resolution 217 A (III).

There are nine core international human rights treaties. Each of these treaties has established a committee of experts to monitor implementation of the treaty provisions by its States parties. Some of the treaties are supplemented by optional protocols dealing with specific concerns – in the case of the Convention on the Rights of the Child the two optional protocols are included below (a full list of the instruments is available from the website of the Office of the High Commissioner for Human Rights at, http://www2.ohchr.org/english/law/index.htm):

*Convention on the Elimination of All Forms of Racial Discrimination, 1966.*
Entry into force: 4 January 1969.
Status: Signatories: 85, Parties: 173. (As of April 2008).
(N.B. 5 countries are signatories to the Convention but have not ratified).

*International Covenant on Civil and Political Rights New York, 1966.*
Entry into force: 23 March 1979.
Status: Signatories: 70, Parties: 161. (As of April 2008).

*International Covenant on Economic, Social and Cultural Rights, 1966.*
Entry into force: 3 January 1976.
Status: Signatories: 67, Parties: 158. (As of April 2008).

*Convention on the Elimination of All Forms of Discrimination against Women, 1979.*
Entry into force: 3 September 1981.
Status: Signatories: 98, Parties: 185. (As of February 2008).

*Convention against Torture and Other Cruel, Inhuman or Degrading Treatment or Punishment, 1984.*
Entry into force: 26 June 1987.
Status: Signatories: 75, Parties: 145. (As of April 2008).

*Convention on the Rights of the Child, 1989.*
Entry into force: 2 September 1990.
Status: Signatories: 140, Parties: 193. (As of February 2008).

*Optional Protocol on the involvement of children in armed conflict, 2000.*
Entry into force: 12 February 2002.
Signatories: 123, Parties: 121. (As of July 2008).

*Optional Protocol on the sale of children, child prostitution and child pornography, 2000.*
Entry into force: 18 January 2002.
Status: Signatories: 115, Parties: 127. (As of July 2008).

*International Convention on the Protection of the Rights of All Migrant Workers and Members of their Families, 1990.*
Entry into force: 1 July 2003.
Status: Signatories: 28, Parties: 37. (As of July 2007).

*Convention on the Rights of Persons with Disabilities, 2006.*
Entry into force: 3 May 2008.
Status: Signatories: 129, Parties: 29. (As of July 2008).

*International Convention for the Protection of All Persons from Enforced Disappearance, 2006.*
Not yet in force.
Status: Signatories: 73, Parties: 4.

**Other Relevant International Treaties**

*Supplementary Convention on the Abolition of Slavery, the Slave Trade, and Institutions and Practices Similar to Slavery, 1956.*
Entry into force: 30 April 1957.
Status: Signatories: 35, Parties: 119.

*Convention on Protection of Children and Co-operation in respect of Intercountry Adoption, 1993.*
Entry into force: 1 May 1995.
Number of Contracting States to this Convention: 76.

*ILO Convention C138, concerning Minimum Age for Admission to Employment, 1973.*
Date of coming into force: 19 June 1976.
Ratified: 150.

*ILO Convention 182, concerning the Prohibition and Immediate Action for the Elimination of the Worst Forms of Child Labour, 1999.*
Date of coming into force: 19 November 2000.
Ratified: 168.

*Rome Statute of the International Criminal Court Rome, 1998.*
Entry into force: 1 July 2002.
Status: Signatories: 139, Parties: 105.

*United Nations Convention against Transnational Organised Crime, 2000.*
Entry into Force: 29 September 2003.
Status: Signatories: 147, Parties: 144.

*Protocol to Prevent, Suppress and Punish Trafficking in Persons, Especially Women and Children, 2000.*
Entry into force: 25 December 2003
Status: Signatories: 117, Parties: 119.

*Protocol against the Smuggling of Migrants by Land, Sea and Air, 2000.*
Entry into force: 28 January 2004.
Status: Signatories: 112, Parties: 112.

*Protocol against the Illicit Manufacturing of and Trafficking in Firearms, Their Parts and Components and Ammunition, 2001.*
Entry into force: 3 July 2005.
Status: Signatories: 52, Parties 74.

## Other International Instruments

*United Nations Standard Minimum Rules for the Administration of Juvenile Justice ('The Beijing Rules').*
Adopted by General Assembly Resolution 40/33 of 29 November 1985.

*United Nations Rules for the Protection of Juveniles Deprived of their Liberty.*
Adopted by General Assembly Resolution 45/113of 14 December 1990.

*United Nations Guidelines for the Prevention of Juvenile Delinquency (The Riyadh Guidelines).*
Adopted and proclaimed by General Assembly Resolution 45/112 of 14 December 1990.

*United Nations Guidelines on Justice for Child Victims and Witnesses of Crime.*
Adopted by the UN Economic and Social Council, 47th plenary meeting, 21 July 2004, Resolution 2004/27.

## Selected Regional Instruments

*African Charter on the Rights and Welfare of the Child.*
OAU Doc. CAB/LEG/24.9/49 (1990), entered into force Nov. 29, 1999.

*European Convention on Recognition and Enforcement of Decisions Concerning Custody of Children and on Restoration of Custody of Children.*
Luxembourg, ETS 105, 20 May 1980.

*European Convention on the Exercise of Children's Rights.*
Strasbourg, ETS 160, January 1996.

*Declaration on the Commitments for Children in ASEAN.*
Association of South East Asian Nations (ASEAN), Singapore, 2001.

*SAARC Convention on Preventing and Combating Trafficking in Women and Children for Prostitution.*
South Asian Association for Regional Co-operation, Kathmandu, 2002.

*Inter-American Convention on Conflict of Laws Concerning the Adoption of Minors.*
Adopted: La Paz, Bolivia, May 1984.

**International Humanitarian Law**

The first Geneva Convention of 1864 dealt exclusively with care for wounded soldiers; the law was later adapted to cover warfare at sea and prisoners of war. In 1949 the Conventions were revised and expanded (Geneva, August 1949):

*Convention (I) for the Amelioration of the Condition of the Wounded and Sick in Armed Forces in the Field.*
*Convention (II) for the Amelioration of the Condition of Wounded, Sick and Shipwrecked Members of Armed Forces at Sea.*
*Convention (III) relative to the Treatment of Prisoners of War.*
*Convention (IV) relative to the Protection of Civilian Persons in Time of War.*

In addition, there are three additional protocols to the Geneva Convention:

*Protocol I (1977) relating to the Protection of Victims of International Armed Conflicts.*
Ratified by 167 countries (January 2007).

*Protocol II (1977) relating to the Protection of Victims of Non-International Armed Conflicts.*
Ratified by 163 countries (January 2007).
*Protocol III (2005) relating to the Adoption of an Additional Distinctive Emblem.*
Ratified by 17 countries (June 2007).

**Refugee Law**

The legal framework for protecting refugees is composed of the 1951 Convention Relating to the Status of Refugees and its 1967 Protocol, and regional refugee instruments, as well as UNHCR EXCOM conclusions, policies and guidelines.

*Convention relating to the Status of Refugees, Geneva, 1951.*
Entry into force: 22 April 1954.
Status: Signatories: 19 ,Parties: 140.

*Protocol relating to the Status of Refugees, New York , 1967.*
Entry into force: 4 October 1967.
Status: Parties: 138.

# Annex 2

# List of Contributors

**Bernard BOËTON,** lic. philosophy, is Head of Child Rights Department, Terre des hommes Foundation, working on juvenile justice (advocacy and training), prevention of violence and sexual abuse in institutions, and against child trafficking.

**Eden COLE** is the Deputy Head of Operations for New Independent States at DCAF. He currently works on security sector oversight capacity-development projects with democratic institutions, civil society organisations, the media and the security sector in the former Soviet states, South East Europe, Turkey, Afghanistan, Nepal and Indonesia.

**Aleya El BINDARI HAMMAD** is a Founding Member and Member of the Board of the Suzanne Mubarak Women's International Peace Movement, and a Co-chair of the United Nations Global Initiative to Fight Human Trafficking. She is also a member of the Board of François-Xavier Bagnoud Centre for Health and Human Rights at Harvard University. She served for more than 30 years as staff member of the World Health Organization, where she was appointed Executive Director/Assistant Director General.

**Clare FEINSTEIN** is currently working as a freelance advisor on children's participation for various organizations, including Save the Children. She has 16 years of experience in the field of child rights with a specialization in children's participation.

**Philippe GAZAGNE** is a doctoral researcher at the Graduate Institute of International and Development Studies, Geneva, with a focus on youth strategies in post-conflict peacebuilding. The contribution was written while he worked at Geneva Call as a Research Officer and Africa Programme Officer.

**Annette GIERTSEN** is Senior Adviser on children's participation in Save the Children Norway. Since 2005 she has been working on children and young people's participation in peacebuilding.

**Claire O'KANE** is currently Child Protection in Emergencies Adviser with Save the Children in Myanmar. She has more than a decade of experience of children's participation and protection work in diverse settings.

**'Funmi OLONISAKIN** is director of the Conflict, Security and Development Group at King's College, University of London, an active member of the African Security Sector Network, and a member of DCAF's International Advisory Board.

**Margaret MCCALLIN** is an independent consultant working on child protection issues, children's rights and resilience. She has conducted assessments of the psychosocial impact of armed conflict and violent displacement on children and families in a number of countries, and developed community-based programmes to address these issues. She was a researcher on child soldiers for the Machel Study on the Impact of Armed Conflict on Children, and co-author of Children: The Invisible Soldiers.

**Brent PARFITT** is a member of the UN Committee on the Rights of the Child and an international consultant. He was formerly Deputy Ombudsman for the Province of British Columbia and lawyer for the Ministry of Attorney General.

**Irma SPECHT** is the director of the consultancy firm Transition International. She is an anthropologist with 15 years of experience in the socio-economic reintegration of former combatants and other war-affected groups. She is a trainer, practitioner and researcher in the field of disarmament, demobilisation and reintegration. Recent publications include: Young Soldiers, why they choose to fight (with Rachel Brett) and Red Shoes, Experiences of girl-combatants in Liberia.